D0341063

A MIGHTY LONG WAY

ONE WORLD

BALLANTINE BOOKS / NEW YORK

A MIGHTY LONG WAY

*My Journey to Justice
at Little Rock Central High School*

Carlotta Walls LaNier

with Lisa Frazier Page

Copyright © 2009 by Carlotta Walls LaNier

Published in the United States by One World Books, an imprint
of The Random House Publishing Group, a division
of Random House, Inc., New York.

ONE WORLD is a registered trademark and the One World colophon
is a registered trademark of Random House, Inc.

Title page photograph: Will Counts Collection,
Indiana University Archives

ISBN 978-0-345-51100-3

Printed in the United States of America

www.oneworldbooks.net

2 4 6 8 9 7 5 3 1

First Edition

Book design by Victoria Wong

This book is dedicated to my parents, Juanita and Cartelyou Walls,
who taught me determination, commitment, and perseverance
so I could take the journey with confidence.

To my sisters, Loujuana and Tina, who learned the same lessons and
took them to another level. My love for you is immeasurable.
You share in every bit of recognition I receive.

To my comrades, who shared the journey with strength and courage:

Ernest Green
Minnijean Brown
Elizabeth Eckford
Thelma Mothershed
Melba Pattillo
Gloria Ray
Terrence Roberts
Jefferson Thomas

To my loving husband, Ira (Ike), whose support, patience, and
wisdom have encouraged me to stay on track.

To my son and daughter, Whitney and Brooke, who continue to bring
me joy. I am glad I completed the journey so that you could
explore your own paths freely and with conviction. Carry on
knowing that you have my unconditional love.

And to generations yet unborn who will adopt the spirit and carry
on the Walls-Cullins-LaNier legacies.

FOREWORD

by President Bill Clinton

I was eleven years old on September 25, 1957, when Carlotta Walls, Minnijean Brown, Thelma Mothershed, Melba Pattillo, Elizabeth Eckford, Ernest Green, Gloria Ray, Terrence Roberts, and Jefferson Thomas, supported by their mentors Daisy and L. C. Bates, bravely walked into the halls of Central High School, and into the pages of American history.

I lived fifty miles away in Hot Springs, Arkansas, and although I had never attended school with black children, I supported integration and was pulling for those kids. So were my mother and grandparents. In his small grocery store, in Hope, Arkansas, my grandfather served both black and white working people. He treated them equally, including giving them food on credit when times were tough and they were doing their best.

Seeing the Little Rock Nine face down the angry mob fascinated me, and inspired an emotional bond that has lasted a lifetime. In the 1970s, I became friends with Ernie Green, the only senior in the group. Our friendship has grown stronger with the years.

In 1987, on the 30th anniversary of Central High's integration, I invited the nine to the Arkansas Governor's Mansion, where Governor Faubus had laid his plans to keep them out of school and use the turmoil to win himself a third term. Hillary and I had a great time with them, a group of survivors and achievers who enjoyed one another's company and seemed able to relive their historic moment without being imprisoned by it. I was very impressed by the youngest of the nine, Carlotta Walls LaNier—by her intelligence, her controlled energy, and the kind, wise look in her eyes.

I met Carlotta again, in 1997, when the Little Rock Nine celebrated their 40th anniversary at Central High School's campus. Governor Huckabee and I held open the school's doors for them as they walked in, doors that once led to hostility and harassment, now open wide in welcome, respect, and gratitude.

We had come a long way, but not all the way. Just a few months earlier, I had established the President's Initiative on Race to engage millions of Americans in assessing the current state of race relations, and offer specific proposals on how to close our remaining racial divides. My final meeting with the Little Rock Nine as president was in 1999, when they came to the White House to receive the Congressional Gold Medal.

I was thrilled when Carlotta and the rest of the Little Rock Nine asked me to serve as Honorary Chair for the 50th anniversary celebration on September 25, 2007. After a wonderful banquet the night before, there was a celebration on the steps of Central High. All nine spoke, each in their own way, about what that long ago event meant to them, and in the process, revealing the people they had become in the five decades since. Carlotta spoke with the clarity and force that have made her the de facto "mother hen" of the nine.

As she and the others went their separate ways after high school, they never forgot their historic bond. They established the Little Rock Nine Foundation, with Carlotta as president. By the fifth anniversary, the Foundation had raised $800,000 to fund a scholarship program to help underserved students overcome their educational obstacles. In return for the scholarships, each group of recipients is required to mentor the next year's scholarship winners. This process will help to preserve the history of the Little Rock Nine, deepen their legacy, and produce students who understand the importance of giving back while moving forward.

This wonderful book is Carlotta's story. She reminds us that the Civil Rights Movement was led, in no small measure, by people she calls "unlikely candidates." This book shares how the Little Rock Nine, in a simple quest for a good education, opened new horizons for themselves and for future generations, but only after they paid a very high price. And it is the personal testament of Carlotta Walls LaNier who, of them all, spent the most days at Central, enduring day after day of being kicked, pushed, spit upon, and verbally abused.

A Mighty Long Way will make you ashamed and proud, angry and hopeful, heartsick and happy. Carlotta tells it as it was, a story we all need to know.

PROLOGUE

Remembering Central High — Fifty Years Later

All week, I managed to keep my composure.

Through the touching anniversary speeches by politicians and civil rights leaders. Through the lunches, dinners, and a reception at the Arkansas Governor's Mansion. Through a provocative musical drama that told the story of the Little Rock Nine. Even through a preview of the new visitors' center for the high school where the real-life drama took place fifty years ago. Through it all, I hardly shed a tear.

I walked around the multimedia exhibits inside the center and watched the black-and-white television footage captured on that day—September 25, 1957. But something wouldn't let me linger. I didn't want to see the fourteen-year-old black girl, climbing those steps in her new, store-bought dress, surrounded by armed military men under presidential orders to keep the spitting, clawing white mob at bay. I didn't want to know her fear again.

Then, on the last day of city-sponsored events celebrating the golden anniversary of the Little Rock Nine, President Bill Clinton cracked my armor. As I sat on a makeshift stage at the foot of the steps that I had climbed the same day five decades earlier, the former president's words took me back. He was talking about courage, gratitude, and the responsibility that each of us has to contribute to the world, to do something more than talk, even when stepping up comes at a cost. He turned slightly away from the podium and looked sideways at us, the gray-haired men and women seated behind him.

"These nine people didn't just have an opinion," he said. "They didn't just say, 'Wouldn't it be nice if someone did something to change things.' These nine people and their families stepped up and said, 'Here am I, Lord, send me.'"

My lips started to quiver. Instinctively, my hands went up to cover them, as though they were a shield, as though they could keep back all of the memories and pain. I thought about Mother, sitting out there in the audience, still beautiful and elegant at eighty-two. And I remembered watching her soft, jet black hair turn gray during that tumultuous and uncertain school year. I thought about Daddy, a devoted family man and World War II veteran who didn't live long enough to see this day. And I remembered the chilling fear that crept into my soul when the FBI took him away late one night for questioning and held him for at least two days after our home was mysteriously bombed during my senior year. I thought, too, about Herbert, my childhood friend and neighbor, who was convicted by an all-white jury for the bombing and served nearly two years in a maximum-security prison, next to death row inmates, for a crime that I believe to my core he did not commit. I looked to my left and right on the stage and caught glimpses of my eight comrades, my dear friends, some of whom are now grandparents. We'd come a mighty long way, and all nine of us were still here. By now, nothing could keep back the tears.

Here am I, Lord, send me.

I hadn't intended anything heroic when I signed up to attend Little Rock Central High School, which was less than a mile from my home and, at the time, all white. The school system had come up with a plan to phase in the desegregation order issued by the U.S. Supreme Court in its 1954 *Brown v. Board of Education* decision. So when the homeroom teacher in my ninth-grade class at the all-black Dunbar Junior High School passed around a sheet of paper in spring 1957 and instructed those of us who lived within the boundaries to sign if we would be interested in attending Central the following fall, I did so without hesitation. I didn't ask my parents' permission or even mention it to them right away. It was just a given that I would pursue the top-quality education that Mother and Daddy had always preached about at home. But that simple declaration changed the course of my life, my family's, and that of countless black students for generations to come.

The change would have to be forced, though. Arkansas governor Orval Faubus and staunch segregationists throughout Little Rock resisted with all their might. In a show of federal force, President Dwight D. Eisenhower ultimately sent the U.S. military to escort the nine of us, who came to be known around the world as the Little Rock Nine, to integrate Central High School for the first time. White students ostracized and harassed us daily, and many teachers looked the other way. My father lost jobs and had to travel cross-country, sometimes for weeks, to find work.

Eight of us survived that turbulent first year. But for me, the story did not end there. After Faubus shut down all three of Little Rock's high schools for the entire school year to avoid integration, just two of the original nine of us returned to Central. I was one of them, and that was my senior year. Then, just three months before my graduation, my home was mysteriously bombed, and my father and childhood friend were targeted as suspects by an unjust legal system. But I persevered through it all and became the first black girl ever to walk across the stage to receive a diploma from Little Rock Central High School.

The morning after my graduation, I took the first train out of Little Rock and promised never to look back. Shaken by the bombing and its traumatic aftermath, the rest of my family soon followed. We eventually settled in the Denver, Colorado, area, about as far away from home as we could get in both distance and character. There, I met my husband, Ira, and raised two children: a son, Whitney, born in 1971; and a daughter, Brooke, who came along three years later.

For thirty years, I didn't utter a public word about what had happened to me and my comrades at the place once known as "America's Most Beautiful School." I rarely even talked about it at home. To this day, Mother and I still have never sat down and held a serious conversation about that time. Part of it, I suspect, is just our nature. We're not prone to dwell in the past, examine our feelings publicly, or show much emotion. The wounds opened in Little Rock—I've come to realize—are deep and, in some cases, still raw. For Mother, a kindhearted soul who was ushered through adulthood idolizing the glitz and glamour of black life portrayed in the *Ebony* and *Sepia* magazines of the 1950s and 1960s, it's easier just to paint on her characteristic pink smile and never look back.

Not so, though, for me.

I've pushed myself to remember, even at times when my natural tendencies have tugged in the opposite direction. It's a commitment I made to myself in 1987, the first time the nine of us returned as a group to Little Rock Central High School. Former president Bill Clinton was the state's governor then, and we had been invited back as guests of the National Association for the Advancement of Colored People (NAACP). The stalwart civil rights organization was holding its annual meeting in Little Rock to commemorate the thirtieth anniversary of the city's school desegregation battle. It was the first time I had seen most of my comrades since we'd left Central, and it was my first trip back to the school since my graduation. As I walked through those halls, it was almost as if I could hear those vile words bouncing off the walls again: *nigger . . . nigger . . . nigger.* I could see the contorted faces of my classmates and their snickers and jeers again. I could feel the slimy wet spit. For a moment, it felt as though sadness might suffocate me. I realized then that even though I had built a new life clear across the country, I hadn't moved an inch from Little Rock.

Late that night, after the NAACP event, Governor Clinton on a whim invited the nine of us to join him at his home in the Governor's Mansion. His wife, Hillary, hadn't been feeling well enough to join him at the NAACP dinner, but when we arrived at the mansion, she rose from her sickbed, greeted us warmly, and escorted us to her kitchen table. We sat there for hours, until about three a.m., chatting like old friends. Governor Clinton told us that as a sixth grader growing up not far away in Hope, Arkansas, in 1957, he had rooted for us. He said that we inspired him and significantly impacted how he viewed race. I was touched by the couple's genuine curiosity and concern for how our Central journey had shaped the rest of our lives. That conversation helped me to open up and talk about my experience freely for the first time. The reunion also reconnected the nine of us, some of whom had been strangers to one another when our fates first intertwined at Central. We pledged to stay in touch—a promise that has enabled us to build deep and enduring friendships over the past two decades. The experience also set me on a quest for healing and a greater understanding of what we had been through.

This book is the result of that journey.

It is as much a story about the dedication of family, perseverance, and sacrifice as it is about history. It is a salute to my parents, Cartelyou and Juanita Walls, who stayed silently in the background and swallowed great risk and suffering. They were the ones who had ingrained in me the quiet confidence that, Jim Crow be damned, I was not a second-class citizen. It was that confidence that told me I deserved the quality education the Supreme Court said I was due, the confidence that steadied my feet to defy the racists with my mere presence at school every single day. My parents bequeathed to me the confidence of their fathers, both hardworking black entrepreneurs in control of their own economic lives. My family may have seemed unlikely candidates for involvement in a movement that would spark nationwide change. But then again, that is the point of this book: to show that determination, fortitude, and the ability to move the world aren't reserved for the "special" people.

My forever role as a member of the Little Rock Nine has defined much of the latter part of my life, and I've come to some peace with that. These days, the former baby of the group has become the mother hen—or at least, that's what the other eight say. It's true that I'm the one usually pushing to make sure we get to speaking engagements on time and that our events flow without a glitch. And I'm probably the most likely among us to send out an email beforehand, reminding everybody to bring their medicines. I'm a classic busybody and a stickler for detail, which is why my comrades say they chose me to head the nonprofit foundation we created. The foundation means a great deal to me because it gives us a vehicle to continue making a difference in education. By the fiftieth anniversary, we had raised more than $800,000, far exceeding our goal of half a million. We created a scholarship program to help send deserving young people to college. Each of us has taken on the responsibility of mentoring the first group of scholarship winners. The plan is for our first group of scholars to mentor our next group, and so on. In this way, we will touch the lives of children for generations to come and leave behind a legacy that extends far beyond Little Rock Central High School.

Few people our age still have more than one good friend from high school. I'm grateful to have at least eight: Ernie, Melba, Minnijean, Elizabeth, Gloria, Terry, Jefferson, and Thelma. In the public mind, we are one, the Little Rock Nine. But we are, in essence, nine distinct personalities with nine different stories.

This book shares mine.

A MIGHTY LONG WAY

CHAPTER 1

A Different World

For the longest time, I wanted nothing more to do with Little Rock. After leaving in 1960, I returned only when necessary, usually for funerals. But my work as president of the Little Rock Nine Foundation brings me home often these days, and I inevitably wend my way down Interstate 630 to my old neighborhood. Most often, I go there to see Uncle Teet, who still lives in my great-great-grandfather Hiram Holloway's old house, five houses down from the one where I grew up. But every now and then, I pull up alongside the redbrick bungalow at 15th and Valentine streets, park the car, and get out.

This was the center of my world as a child. The place looks abandoned with its boarded-up windows and weeds where lush green grass used to grow. There is no sign of the big gardenia bush that once graced the front yard. Mother would pick a fresh flower from that bush and place it in her hair just so, like Billie Holiday. But the gardenias are long gone. So, too, is the tree in the backyard that used to grow the plumpest, sweetest figs around. The pecan tree still stands, and as I picked up a few dried nuts one scorching summer day, I was reminded of the lean Christmas in junior high school when that tree provided perfect homemade gifts for most of my family and friends. Money was tight that year, so I made date-nut cakes from the bounty in our backyard to give away as presents. There were three of those huge trees, perfectly aligned in a row from our yard to the Davises' yard next door to the other Davis property down the street. So, of course, someone in the neighborhood was always making homemade pecan ice cream or baking pecan pies or some kind of nut cookies or cake.

I'm amazed at how small it all seems now—our house, the yard, and even those pecan trees, which to a little girl staring up seemed just a few steps from heaven. I still call the place "our house," as if it remains in my family. But Mother finally sold it several years ago when the upkeep became too much and I convinced her that none of her three girls would ever return. She was reluctant at first to let go. The memories, I guess. And our family roots—they run pretty deep through there.

I was three years old when Daddy bought the house at 1500 S. Valentine Street, just blocks away from the all-white Central High School. Even then, the school was known throughout the country for its Greek-inspired architecture, beauty, and high academic achievement. Daddy had just returned from the Philippines, where he served in World War II until December 1945. Mother was weary of having moved with me at least four times, mostly among relatives, while he was away. My parents paid $3,000 for the house, sold to them by my mother's grandfather, Aaron Holloway, who had raised her practically all of her life after his daughter moved away to St. Louis.

Papa Holloway, as I knew my great-grandfather, looked like a Spaniard with his tan skin, dark eyes, thick, wavy black hair, and mustache. I'm told that in his younger days, his hair would sprout into a nest of thick black curls—and thus the source of his nickname among some of our neighbors: Curly. He stood about six feet tall, and family members say that I—tall and slender as a child—inherited his height and thin build. I probably inherited some of his other characteristics, too, like my hair, which is naturally pretty wavy. When I was a child, it grew like weeds, so long and thick that I had trouble grooming it, and Mother had to plait it into neat braids or pull it into ponytails until I was well into junior high school. I wasn't allowed to get my first haircut until eighth grade, and I've mostly kept it short ever since.

The Spanish roots in my family tree can be traced back to Papa Holloway's father, Hiram. I never knew him, but in recent years I've read interviews he granted to federal workers in the 1930s for a collection of ex-slave narratives as part of the Federal Writers' Project. Hiram was described in the report as a "tri-racial free person of color," born in 1848, about thirteen years before the Civil War. He said in a transcript of the interview that his mother was a "full-blooded Cherokee" and his father a "dark Spaniard." He used the N-word liberally as he talked about the Africans who were enslaved. That word still stings when I see or hear it, but I've tried to refrain from harsh judgment of my great-great-grandfather, even as he set himself apart from the slaves. As difficult as some parts of his story were to digest, the interview reminded me just how much my ancestors endured in their pursuit of education, generations before I ever stepped foot onto Central.

"In slave times, they didn't have any schools for niggers," said Hiram, who managed to learn to read and write. "Niggers better not be caught with a book. If he were caught with a book, they beat him to death nearly. Niggers used to get hold of this Webster's Blue Back Book and the white folks would catch them and take them away. They didn't allow no free niggers to go to school either in slave times."

Hiram's story gave me fresh insight into how much my family valued education even then. He expressed disappointment that the younger generation of blacks—those born after the Civil War—didn't seem as persistent as their forefathers in the quest for education. His words are still relevant; they capture some of my concerns today:

"One thing, they don't read enough," he said. "They don't

know history. I can't understand them. Looks like they had a mighty good chance; but it looks like the more they get the worse they are. Looks like to me their parents didn't teach them right— or somethin'."

Although Hiram referred repeatedly in the interview to his wife and children, little is known about most of them in our family. I once asked Papa Holloway about his brothers and sisters. He told me he had several siblings but that he knew the whereabouts of only one, a sister, Maude, who lived in Cleveland. He said that he suspected his other brothers and sisters were scattered throughout the country and passed as white. But Papa Holloway identified himself as "colored" and was proud of the status he achieved as one of the first colored building contractors in Arkansas. He helped to build houses throughout Arkansas, including many of the higher-end homes in the wealthy white Pulaski Heights neighborhood in Little Rock. He also built White Memorial Methodist Church, just up the street from my house. Much of my family worshipped there. Papa was on the board of trustees, a real mover and shaker who was there practically every time the doors of the church opened. Most Sundays, I sat beside him on the front pew.

Papa's wife, Mary, died in 1922 at age thirty-four while giving birth to their sixteenth child. The baby girl died, too, as did a set of twins who had been born earlier. Papa raised the remaining children and never married again. His oldest son, Hugh, would become one of only two black men who worked as skilled laborers on Central High School when it was built. Papa's longtime girlfriend, Dora Holmes, was a widow who lived down the street and owned the house at 1500 S. Valentine Street. Mother and I stayed with her briefly while my father was away at war. How much of my memory of Mrs. Holmes is influenced by family stories, I don't know. But I remember being terrified of her. She dressed like a witch or a woman on the frontier, in long black cotton dresses and black high-top boots. I didn't realize then that she may have been trying to cover a prosthetic leg.

On some Sunday mornings, my paternal grandfather, Big Daddy, would drop me off at Mrs. Holmes's house after I had spent the weekend with him. As soon as we approached the house, I'd start screaming and hollering that I didn't want to go. I'd fall out, kicking and wailing, on the front porch. But when the front door opened silently, I saw from the corner of my eyes those high-top boots and the hem of her long black dress moving toward me. I immediately turned off the tears, rose to my feet, and followed Mrs. Holmes inside as though I had some sense.

When Dora Holmes died, she left her estate in the care of Papa Holloway, who offered the house to my father. None of us could have imagined then how much that address would dictate the course of our lives in the years ahead. The house was located just west of downtown Little Rock, a few miles beyond 9th Street, which was then a bustling strip of black-owned businesses and nightspots. The community surrounding 9th Street was all black. My end of town was more racially mixed—black families lived on one block, whites on the other. In some cases, black and white families lived across the street from one another. But our white neighbors may as well have been living on Mars for all we knew of their lives. When my family moved there, the neighborhood was still new. Most of the houses were box-shaped with wooden frames, built along a grid of narrow dirt roads after World War II. They were modest but well kept. A few had porches, and most had small yards, though they didn't seem small then. Our house stood out because Daddy, who earned a living as a brick mason, meticulously covered it from top to bottom with the same red bricks that remain on the house today. The only other brick house in the neighborhood belonged to Papa Holloway.

Daddy had learned the brick masonry trade from his father-in-law, Med Cullins, a master contractor who did brick masonry work on Central High in the 1940s. Grandpa Cullins, my mother's father, was a real character. He was a big, imposing man who stood over six feet tall with a heavyset frame, a gravelly voice, and a gruff disposition that matched his size. His beige skin and straight hair gave him the appearance of a slightly tanned white man. He walked with his shoulders squared and head high and carried a half-pint of liquor stuffed in his back pocket. He also couldn't finish a sentence without at least one "goddamn." Grandpa was his own man. He had one suit and wore mismatched socks, but he considered those kinds of things trivial. When I met Thurgood Marshall in later years, his aura reminded me in an odd way of Grandpa Cullins. Neither man kowtowed to anyone. Confidence seemed to radiate from them both, but the likeness ended there.

Grandpa Cullins had an intimidating—and sometimes crude—presence, which worked to his advantage when it came time to collect from someone who had hired him to do a job. He could be less than forgiving on money matters, even if the delinquent client was a house of worship.

"Your father just embarrassed the heck out of me," I heard my father tell Mother one Sunday afternoon when I was in junior high school after the two men returned from a church service in a nearby town.

Grandpa Cullins had asked Daddy to drive him to the church. But as the service wound to a close, the pastor made the mistake of recognizing my grandfather to say a few words. Grandpa Cullins strolled to the front, told the congregants what a pretty goddamn church they had, but he reminded them that he was still waiting for his money.

Grandpa was not a patient man. He called every man "son" and every woman "daughter," including his own children and grandchildren, who say he did so because he didn't want to bother remembering any names.

"Daughter, let me speak to daughter," he commanded one day when I answered the phone at home.

I looked at Mother and her sister and responded: "Which one?"

"Goddammit," Grandpa barked. "The one who lives there!"

Grandpa Cullins had dropped out of Philander Smith College in Little Rock to start his contracting business, but he was a highly intelligent man who stayed abreast of current events. He'd insisted that his four children—Mother, her younger brother, and two older sisters—go to college. The schools of choice were Philander Smith or Talledega College in Alabama. Grandpa loved politics, particularly presidential history. Many times, I heard him start with Truman and work his way back, reciting the years each president served, the president's party, and something significant about each man's time in office. But when Grandpa got to Taylor, he always said, "And next is that goddamn Zachariah Taylor. . . ."

At first, I didn't understand what he meant, so I asked: "What's wrong with Zachary Taylor?"

"That's Sam Mumford's grandfather," Grandpa Cullins responded, referring to his good friend and fellow contractor.

"Oh, Grandpa, you know a president wouldn't marry a colored woman," I shot back.

He looked at me with a sly grin. "Whoever said anything about getting married?"

Grandpa Cullins never married my mother's mother. Mother was born to Erma Holloway while he was separated from his wife, Beatrice. He and Beatrice reunited, and soon afterward my maternal grandmother moved away to St. Louis and left Mother with Papa Holloway. I knew Beatrice as Grandmother Cullins and her children as my aunts and uncles. Mother and her siblings never thought of themselves as half of anything. We've always just been family. Grandmother Cullins was fifty-five when she died of stomach cancer in 1951.

All of my grandfathers outlived their wives. While I was nurtured by a cadre of well-educated and loving women, I spent a lot of time around the men on both sides of my family. And they heavily influenced the woman I became. The independent streak that I'm sure I inherited from my grandfathers would land me at Central in the days ahead, and the determination I witnessed in all of their lives would help me survive the toughest days there.

No one was more determined than my Big Daddy. He was Porter Walls, my father's father. He had mahogany skin and a medium build and stood about five feet five inches tall, on the short side for a man. He had only a third-grade education, but he could read and write and was one of the smartest businessmen I've ever known. He owned and operated a pool hall and restaurant in a red cinder-block building that extended about a half block at the intersection of 18th and Pine streets, a short walk from my house. Big Daddy enjoyed looking like a businessman, so his preferred attire was a suit and hat when he wasn't in the kitchen. He also smoked cigars.

Daddy had helped his father build the business and worked there part-time. Big Daddy worked at Arkansas Tent and Awnings during the day, while his sisters ran the café. But he split his nights and weekends between the café and pool hall and poured all of his energy and every extra dime into building his business.

I was grown—a thirty-five-year-old married mother of two, to be exact—before I truly understood the source of his drive and persistence. It was 1977, and *Roots,* the television miniseries based on Alex Haley's novel, had a grip on America. People everywhere sat glued to their televisions night after night, and many black men and women for the first time began digging into their own family trees. I was deeply moved by the drama, which chronicled the life of a West African captured from his native land and sold into slavery in the southern United States. All of a sudden I, too, was filled with questions about my southern family.

My questions started with Big Daddy, who happened to visit me in Denver a short time after the series.

"Tell me the story of the Walls family," I said to him one day when I caught him alone.

Big Daddy looked up at me, surprisingly annoyed. "Why do you want to know all that?" he snapped.

Big Daddy was usually a warm, patient man, and he and I were close, having spent much time together throughout my childhood. But he knew what I was getting at, and he was no fan of all the modern talk about slavery and our people needing to discover their African roots. Just a couple of generations removed from the humiliation and degradation of slavery, he was not eager to remember. The past was the past, Big Daddy figured. No need in digging up long-buried bones. He paused, and finally, peering straight into my eyes, he said:

"Look, all you really need to know is my grandfather owned land."

The seriousness in Big Daddy's eyes told me he had nothing more to say. What, if anything, he knew of slavery in his family, he wasn't willing to share. But he was proud that somehow in the shadow of the nation's most brutal system of oppression, his family had managed to accumulate valuable land. That knowledge, that pride, would push him toward his own dreams of owning a business. Eventually, about the time I became a teenager, Big Daddy opened a second restaurant and pool hall on the outskirts of Little Rock, retired from his day job, and became his own boss.

Historical records show that Big Daddy's great-grandfather Richard was born during slavery. It is unclear how Richard's son Coatney came to own more than 360 wooded acres in Cornerville, the town where the Walls family first settled about seventy-five miles south of Little Rock. But when Coatney Walls died, the land was divided and passed on in equal shares to his heirs—Big Daddy and each of his seven younger siblings. All but one of his siblings eventually sold their land, some of which Big Daddy acquired. He would end up with 100-plus acres of the inherited land.

In many ways, Big Daddy was ahead of his time. He seemed to have an innate understanding of economics and how much it influenced power. All he ever wanted to be was a businessman, a powerful man, and as he saw it, that didn't include getting married and raising a family. That, he once told me, happened quite by accident.

Big Daddy had volunteered for World War I, but when he arrived in France in 1918, the war was ending. He soon returned to Cornerville and went to visit Henrietta, the girlfriend he'd left behind. He saw an infant playing outside and moments later learned the child was his son. This wasn't the life he had planned, but he did the proper thing and married Henrietta. The couple eventually moved to Little Rock and had four more boys and two girls. Their third-born was Cartelyou, my father.

Big Daddy worked hard at the awning company and put aside whatever money he could. At home, he ruled with an iron fist and pushed his children to work hard, too, particularly the older boys. The older two sons could hardly wait until they were grown enough to take the train out of Little Rock and move on to lives of their own making. But Cartelyou stayed, working at his father's side, soaking in his father's work ethic and values.

Cartelyou was fifteen when his mother, just thirty-nine years old, died of pneumonia. He grieved mightily and clung especially to one of his younger sisters, Juanita, who even as a child was a natural nurturer. It must have seemed like a sign of some sort when his other sister, Margaret, introduced him to one of her friends, a petite, fair-skinned beauty with a fateful name: Juanita. Juanita Cullins was a fellow student at Paul Laurence Dunbar, Jr. and Sr. High School, the premier black high school in Arkansas. It was love at first sight, and on February 3, 1942, the teenagers eloped with another couple to Benton, Arkansas. They were married by a Justice of the Peace.

Cartelyou was shipped off to World War II on December 7 that year. Eleven days later, I was born. To support us, Mother got a job downtown at M. M. Cohen Department Store, where she worked as a seamstress and clerk, mostly altering customers' newly purchased clothes. She could assist in waiting on customers, but as a black woman, she was not permitted to touch the cash register or receive credit for a sale. Likewise, black customers could shop in the store but were not permitted to try on clothes or return them. Mother, as soft-spoken and dignified as she was good-looking, never complained.

When Daddy returned from the war, she mostly stayed home. She also continued her education at Philander Smith, though she stopped short of graduating. When money was tight, she helped out by getting a job, usually doing secretarial work.

Big Daddy often babysat me, and I loved spending time with him. He was quiet but attentive, much like my father. He lived just two doors down from his business, but I always wanted to be near him. My favorite place to hang out was the restaurant, where I had access to all of the cold drinks and candy I wanted. But the pool hall was off-limits to me. At night, it attracted some unsavory characters, who often carried half-pints in their pockets and quick-trigger attitudes ready to fire. When I got sleepy, I stepped outside, climbed into the backseat of Big Daddy's car, and stretched out, feeling safe and protected. Every time I opened my eyes, it seemed, I could see through the car window the silhouette of Big Daddy, a cigar clenched between his teeth and a pool stick in hand, standing in the darkness, checking on his grandbaby.

As I grew older, Big Daddy let me tag along when he went to the meatpacking houses along the riverfront downtown to buy discounted boxes of ribs and fish for the barbecue dinners and fried catfish plates that had helped to make the restaurant and pool hall a popular neighborhood gathering spot. As soon as Big Daddy opened the door of the meat house, I could smell the thick scent of raw meat. A round white man wearing a sleeveless shirt and dingy white apron stood behind the counter. His bare arms looked beefy and pale. I sauntered behind Big Daddy as he walked straight up to the counter. My grandfather seemed to stand taller there, placing his order just like the white customers coming in and out. I watched quietly as Big Daddy exchanged a few amicable words with the white man, who soon left to fill Big Daddy's order without a hiss or word of disrespect. When it came time to pay, Big Daddy dug into his pocket and pulled out a huge wad of cash. He always carried his cash in his pocket that way, as if he didn't quite trust anyone else with his hard-earned money. Big Daddy then unfurled a few bills into the hands of the white man, nodded a silent thank-you, and turned to walk away. I trailed behind him proudly, thinking to myself that Big Daddy must be a rich, important man to get such respect from white folks.

Big Daddy's personality and style were as different from those of Grandpa Cullins as was his appearance. But both men deeply respected each other, so much so that each addressed the other as "Mr. Walls" or "Mr. Cullins." They shared a love of baseball—and, more specifically, the Brooklyn Dodgers. Their lifelong allegiance to the Dodgers began, of course, when the team signed Jackie Robinson in 1947 and became the first team since before the turn of the century to integrate professional baseball. Jackie was their hero, and he became mine, too. When the Dodgers played the Yankees in the 1955 World Series in New York, Big Daddy and Grandpa Cullins made the cross-country journey together to cheer for their team. They also made regular trips together to St. Louis to attend baseball games—a sign of economic freedom that few black men of their era enjoyed.

Whenever the Dodgers played in St. Louis, six or seven of us—Mother, Daddy, Grandpa Cullins, and various other relatives—piled into the car for a road trip to the game. Big Daddy was usually working. We most often left late at night and traveled until morning without stopping because hotels and restaurants through-out the South didn't admit black customers. Daddy meticulously mapped out the eight-hour trip so that we could stop along the way at relatives' homes for bathroom breaks and rest. If we slept there, the children who lived in the home gave up their beds to the adults and joined the rest of us on blankets spread across the floor. Likewise, our home in Little Rock often felt like Grand Central Station because we had so many relatives stopping through on their cross-country road trips. I always gave up my bed and made pallets on the floor.

On one of those trips to St. Louis with Grandpa Cullins, we stopped in Newport, Arkansas, at his cousin Gabe's house. Cousin Gabe was a worm farmer and a gracious host. His wife spent much of the morning preparing a full breakfast spread for us to eat be-fore we got back on the road. The smell of homemade biscuits, grits, bacon, and eggs filled every room and drew us all into the kitchen. But I took one look at the inch-thick dried mud caked on Uncle Gabe's hands and under his fingernails, and suddenly, no matter how much my stomach growled, I was no longer hungry.

In St. Louis, we had plenty of extended family and always stayed with them. If Grandpa Cullins or my father couldn't make the trip, I traveled to St. Louis by train with Mother, who was also an avid baseball fan.

Back home in Little Rock, my entire family looked forward to watching baseball teams from the Negro Leagues square off in the city's Triple-A stadium in Fair Park before an enthusiastic all-black crowd. Mother and I usually caught the bus about four blocks from home. As the bus rolled down 13th, past the Lee Theatre and Pine Street, where a big crowd was always waiting, it seemed every colored person from the West End was headed to the game. I was in elementary school then, and those trips to the park were like going to the circus, especially when the Indianapolis Clowns played. The team mascot was a clown that kept the crowd thoroughly entertained. Mother loved the Birmingham Black Barons. I'd hear her and Daddy talking about the team's outstanding center fielder, Willie Mays, who later became a Hall of Famer in major league baseball and one of the greatest players of all time.

It never occurred to me as I grew up to question, even in my mind, why colored folks could go to the park only on certain days, why we had to climb to the back of the bus, or why stopping at a gas station to use the bathroom in most areas of the South wasn't even an option. Those were just the rules, and I learned to follow them like I learned to walk, by observing those closest to me and following their guidance until I knew the steps well enough to venture out on my own. The world I knew best—a black world full of protective family, neighbors, and my church community—felt safe. There, I knew I was loved and accepted, even when a few of my darker-skinned playmates took to calling me "high yella" because of my light complexion. The name-calling could get rough sometimes from my playmates, who assumed that I thought the white tint in my skin somehow made me better than them. That mystified me then. I would come to understand it later as one of the more destructive legacies of slavery. The lighter-skinned slaves (sometimes the master's offspring) received slightly more favorable treatment, such as house jobs, while the darker-skinned slaves were relegated to the fields, fostering a divide that persists today. But in the mind of a child, the skin color separation just seemed silly. My family members were every hue, from pinkish white to the color of the rich brown earth, like Daddy and Big Daddy, whom I adored.

Daddy and Big Daddy were my protectors. Mother was, too. When the ugliness of that other world—a white world as foreign to me as Russia—surfaced in my presence, my parents and grandfather tried to explain. They wanted to make sure I understood that I was not the problem.

I must have been in elementary school the first time I felt the sting of a white woman's words. Mother and I were headed downtown on one of our many bus trips when a white woman stepped onto the crowded bus and made her way to the back of the white section. She quickly scanned the bus and rolled her eyes.

"These nigras are all over the place," she blurted as she took a seat.

The anger on her face and the huffiness in her voice told me her words were not nice, and somehow I knew they were directed at me, at those of us sitting in the back. I looked up at Mother, with a face that all my life has shown exactly what I'm thinking. In that moment, my eyes probably asked: What does she mean? What did *we* do wrong?

At first, Mother said nothing, as if she didn't even hear it. Then, ever so discreetly, she pulled me closer to her and whispered: "Carlotta, we must be patient with ignorance and never, ever bring ourselves down to their level."

I would hear those words many times, too, from Daddy, like when he didn't respond or seem overly deferent to a white man who uttered something disrespectful: *You are a Walls. You must never, ever stoop to the level of ignorance.*

I came to believe that *they*—mean and intolerant people—were the ones with the problem and that I must never, ever *stoop* to their level. That lesson would shield me in the years ahead when I came face-to-face with the ugliest side of that foreign world.

Until then, I played by rules I knew. I'd never seen the game played any other way.

Then came New York.

I could hardly believe my ears when my parents told me near the end of my third-grade year in 1951 that I'd be going to that great city for the summer. Daddy's younger sister, Juanita, had invited me to spend my three-month break from school with her family. I realize now that she was likely offering much-needed relief to my parents, who by then had a second daughter—my sister, Loujuana, two years old at the time. But at age eight, I felt as if a fairy godmother had waved a magic wand and granted me a dream summer vacation. I had heard Mother brag about New York practically all of my life. Her eyes seemed to light up when she talked to her friends about the time she'd visited New York with her sister in 1944, stayed out too late one night, and almost got locked out of one of the gated apartment buildings in Sugar Hill, the ritzy section of Harlem that sits high, overlooking what is now Jackie Robinson Park. From the 1920s when wealthy black men and women began migrating there through the 1960s, Sugar Hill was home to some of the nation's most well-known black scholars, writers, activists, sports figures, and entertainers: W. E. B. Du Bois, Roy Wilkins, Langston Hughes, Zora Neale Hurston, Duke Ellington, Joe Louis, Thurgood Marshall. Aunt Juanita's first apartment in New York was there, too. She managed to find a room with a kitchen in a building on Convent Avenue for $4 a week when she realized that the housing her government co-workers had recommended on 113th in Harlem wasn't quite to her liking.

I was just two and Daddy was away at war in 1944 when Mother left me in the care of another aunt and took the trip to New York. She accompanied her sister Loualice, who didn't want to travel alone to the big city to meet her husband, J.W., a navy man whose ship was heading back to the States and would dock there briefly. Aunt Juanita rented Mother and Aunt Loualice an apartment in another Sugar Hill building. By the time Uncle J.W. arrived, he had hatched a matchmaking plan: Aunt Loualice and Mother would bring along Mother's single sister-in-law, Juanita, and he would bring along a single friend so that all of them could go out together. When Uncle J.W. stepped off the ship, he had with him a handsome young soldier named Alfredo Andrade, a Portuguese Creole whose parents were from Cape Verde, off the western coast of Africa. The two singles were introduced and quickly became a couple. They married a year or two later and stayed in New York.

When the two of them invited me to New York to visit for the first time, the anticipation of seeing the high-rises and bright lights and getting anywhere near Mother's Sugar Hill left me so excited about my trip that I couldn't even bother being scared.

My parents used their connections to get a free pass and summoned their friends to keep watch over me along the way. They included Herman Freeman—Uncle Herman to me—who worked as a redcap at the Little Rock station. He wasn't my real uncle, but he was married to my mother's close friend. My parents also were good friends with the head cook on the train, Aubrey Yancy. My classmate's father, Mr. Murchison, a porter on the route to St. Louis, had agreed to be my guardian for most of the trip. As protective as my parents were, they trusted that I was in good hands. The connections among black rail workers throughout the country back then operated like a modern-day Underground Railroad, assuring the safe transport and comfort of one another's family and friends.

Shortly after Memorial Day that year, Mother and Daddy packed a huge suitcase and sack lunch, drove me to Union Station in downtown Little Rock, and put me on a train bound for a two-day journey to what seemed like the other side of the world. Just before I climbed on board, Daddy and Mother reminded me to mind my manners: Be polite. Don't ask for anything. Just wait. Mr. Murchison would get me a pillow and take me to the whites-only dining car for a meal before it opened or after it closed. With that, I climbed on board and made my way to the last seat in the railcar for black passengers, next to my railroad guardian.

For hours at a time, I sat with my face pressed against the passenger window and watched as the brilliant sunshine faded into night. Excitement churned on the inside. My head was so full of thoughts that I could hardly sleep. What would the city look like? Where would we go? What would I see? Would I meet any movie stars?

Finally, the train pulled into New York's Penn Station, and I followed the flow of the crowd up the stairs. There, just inside, Aunt Juanita and Uncle Freddie were waiting. I felt like a real-life Alice in Wonderland as I stepped off the train into that vast space. I had landed in a different world, and the thrill of it rushed through me like a current. Penn Station was at least twice as big as the Little Rock station. Throngs of people scurried about in all directions. There was a palpable sense of energy and purpose. My uncle and aunt greeted me warmly and ushered me through the station, which seemed like a city unto itself. My head snapped back and forth as my eyes and ears tried to take in all the faces, hues, and languages mingling in one place. In a blur, I saw crowds of people standing and staring up at a gigantic board that listed a seemingly endless number of trains going to places I'd never even heard of. We whizzed by a couple of water fountains and public restrooms, one for men and another for women. That's when it struck me: There wasn't a "Whites Only" sign anywhere in sight.

Outside, we climbed onto a bus headed to my aunt and uncle's apartment. It amazed me that we just plopped down wherever we pleased. Not once did the bus driver look back and order us to the back of the bus when white people needed a seat. This was the freedom up north I'd heard so much about. I could tell already that being colored seemed to mean something else up here—or maybe it meant nothing at all. Here, colored men and women seemed to walk with their backs a bit straighter, their heads higher, as though they had as much right as anybody else to occupy this time and space. Here, colored men and women also seemed about as likely as anyone else to be called "mister" or "ma'am." My parents had ingrained in me all of my life that people of all races were equal in the eyes of God. Here, in New York, I was getting a glimpse of life through His divine lens.

Aunt Juanita and Uncle Freddie had three children of their

own—Camille, who was five; Renata, two; and Michael, an infant. My aunt didn't seem the least bit overwhelmed by the prospect of adding another child to her brood for three whole months. She was a short, deep-brown-skinned woman with a happy disposition, always bubbly and sweet. She stayed home with us during the day while Uncle Freddie worked as a hospital lab technician. He was thinly built, with wavy black hair and skin on the light side of honey. He spoke Portuguese and Italian and patiently played my interpreter and tour guide as we cruised the streets of New York. The family lived in a three-bedroom apartment in a dark redbrick building at 62nd Street and West End Avenue. The complex was among the city's first public housing units, built primarily for veterans returning from World War II. It was brand-new and wonderful, nothing like the crumbling urban tenements that still stand in most major cities today. Their apartment was on the fourth floor, so we frequently took the elevator, which was as exciting as an amusement park ride to me. I'd hop off and on and ride over and over again. From the bedroom window, I could look out and see across the Hudson River into New Jersey. Sometimes, on stifling nights, I'd get out of bed and stand in front of the raised window to try to catch a breeze and watch the boats cruising down the river. The lights looked like stars, dotting the landscape on the other side of the water.

We walked about four blocks to Central Park to picnic, visit the zoo, play ball, or ride our bikes. I even lost a fingernail there, showing off on the bike. I wanted to show my family and the many spectators how well this southern girl could ride, but I momentarily took my eyes off the path and was pumping so fast that I missed a curve and slammed into a nearby water fountain. Fortunately, aside from the fingernail and a few scrapes, the only thing seriously hurt was my pride.

I spent most of my time on a concrete playground in the courtyard of the apartment complex. Aunt Juanita took the children outside to play there practically every day, but some mornings I couldn't wait and went ahead of her. She joined the other mothers on a bench, and I continued playing, running from the sliding board to the swings and jungle gym. It was the strangest thing to see small patches of dirt and trees sprouting from all that concrete.

There, in the courtyard, a group of us regularly encountered an old man, always alone, nodding on a bench. He was usually dressed in a black suit and a hat that fell slightly over his face as he slept. I thought he was a drunk, a wino, like some of the men who worked for Grandpa Cullins. For some strange reason, we kids thought it would be fun to hide and throw rocks at him. We did, and we giggled each time the man eventually stood and stumbled away. Nearly forty years later, I would learn the identity of that man when I brought my son and daughter to New York to visit Aunt Juanita. I walked with them to the courtyard and told them stories about the old drunk I used to see there. As I moved closer to the bench to point out the spot where he always sat, I noticed a plaque with a name engraved on it. My mouth dropped open, and a rush of shame flushed through me when I read the name inscribed there: jazz great Thelonious Monk. The plaque pointed us to a small house next to the apartment complex, where Aunt Juanita still lives today. Little did I know that for those three months when I was eight years old, Thelonious Monk was my neighbor.

The summer of 1951 was full of firsts for me, grand and small. It was there that I first encountered the awful smell of lamb simmering on a Sunday afternoon, which left such a bad impression that a decade passed before I got the nerve to try even a lamb chop. I heard for the first time my new friends ask for "soda" or "soda pop" instead of a "cold drink," which we said back home. I sat in a soda shop and watched a server make the drink before my eyes and serve it in a glass with a straw instead of a bottle. I saw firemen open a fire hydrant and neighborhood kids dash through the blast of water in their clothes again and again under the fiery sun. I also visited the amusement park at Indian Point with Uncle Freddie and his parents, who were Portuguese and Cape Verdean and spoke little English. They were visiting from their home in Rhode Island where Uncle Freddie had grown up. How we all managed to squeeze into that tiny three-bedroom apartment and communicate that summer, I don't know. But the beauty of it is that somehow, we managed. And I'll never forget that trip to Indian Point.

Now home to three controversial atomic energy reactors, Indian Point was then a popular park spread over more than two hundred acres. It included carnival rides, a swimming pool, and picnic grounds. We were going on a picnic, and I could hardly wait to get on the rides. A ferry took us to the park, but there were two stops. Our stop was first, and the next one was Bear Mountain State Park, another expansive park near West Point, the U.S. military academy. After the ferry left Indian Point, it would travel to Bear Mountain and dock there for the rest of the afternoon. Just as the ferry was about to make its first stop for us to get off, Mr. Andrade, Uncle Freddie's father, needed to go the bathroom. Uncle Freddie warned: "Dad, just make sure you're back within five minutes. We're getting off here."

The ferry docked temporarily, and after five minutes of waiting for Mr. Andrade to return, we got off. Five more minutes passed and then ten, and still no Mr. Andrade. As we stood waiting just beyond the dock, we watched the gangplank to the ferry rise slowly, and then the boat pushed away deeper into the water and glided out of sight, off to Bear Mountain. Mrs. Andrade looked terrified. She spoke rapid-fire in her native tongue. Uncle Freddie tried to calm her.

"I'm sure he's here," he said. "He probably got off before us. We just need to look around."

We walked around for what felt like hours. No Mr. Andrade.

But here's the catch: We had the picnic basket of food, and Mr. Andrade had the money. Uncle Freddie didn't have a dime, and neither did his mother or Aunt Juanita. So we ate our picnic lunch and played the free games, but all of us kids were angry because we couldn't get on the carnival rides. That had been the main reason for going to Indian Point.

About three-thirty in the afternoon, it was time to return to New York City. We stood and watched as the ferry came around the bend and docked. The gangplank went down, and the rest was like a scene from Ellis Island. Mr. Andrade, who apparently had gotten lost on the way from the restroom, came running down the plank. His wife ran to meet him, again speaking quickly in her native language. Tears streamed down both of their faces. They were hugging and crying, so happy to see each other. You would have thought they had been separated by an ocean for years.

Among my other New York firsts was pizza. Little Rock didn't have pizza, but my friend Peggy, who had visited New York one summer with her grandmother, had told me all about it.

"Make sure you try the pizza," she reminded me again and again.

I couldn't wait to tell her that it was every bit as delicious as she had described.

I also tasted Cream of Wheat for the first time and marveled over the Rockettes, Ellis Island, and the Statue of Liberty. I visited Radio City Music Hall, where I saw a thrilling Technicolor remake of the box office hit *Show Boat* and its unforgettable classic, "Ol' Man River." I even took the train to Harlem to spend the weekend with my great-uncle Callon Holloway (Uncle Buster). I felt like a real city slicker when I sat on the stoop with him and his friends at night, sometimes as late as midnight. They would set up a card table and chairs under the streetlamp at the corner nearest his apartment and then gather around for games of dominoes, checkers, and cards, mostly pitty-pat. Uncle Buster also took me to the

Polo Grounds and to Ebbets Field, where I saw our beloved Brooklyn Dodgers play the New York Giants.

But among the more memorable experiences of that magical summer in New York were the times I spent with the white boy who became my best friend. His name was Francis, and that was the first thing that struck me as funny. In my book, Francis was a girl's name. He had pale skin and strawberry blond hair, and like me, he enjoyed playing stickball and tops. We met on the playground in the courtyard of Aunt Juanita's apartment complex, and from that day on, we played ball together, chased each other around the playground, and giggled over the silliest things. Most astonishing of all, no one even seemed to notice. I guess I took to him because he wasn't one of the most popular kids. And like me, he was an early bird. Some mornings, it would be just the two of us, swatting our little pink ball back and forth to each other with our narrow sticks. Francis and I weren't close enough to share secrets, like my friends Bunny, Peggy, and I did back home. There wasn't really anything all that extraordinary about my friendship with him, except this: Here in this brand-new world, an ordinary friendship between a little black girl and a little white boy could exist, free of the boundaries that defined such relationships back home.

Summer zoomed by, and then one day I returned to the apartment to find Aunt Juanita standing atop a large navy blue suitcase trimmed in white leather.

"Look what came in the mail today," she announced excitedly, pointing to the matching two-piece luggage set.

My parents had sent me Samsonite's latest suitcase—Silhouette, the model was called. I'd seen television and magazine advertisements touting the bag's strength as a model stood on top of it, but I grimaced when I saw my aunt acting out those ads. Fortunately, the luggage was every bit as durable as the ads claimed.

A short time later, my new suitcases were packed and I was on the train, headed back to Little Rock, no longer the same girl. I'd tasted the sweetness of freedom and seen more than my eight-year-old mind could fully understand. But everything that the Jim Crow South had tried to make me believe about my people and my place in life had been flipped upside down. Suddenly, the world had opened wider. It was just a matter of time before I was ready to step out of the one I knew.

CHAPTER 2

The Playing Field

Softball was as much a summertime staple as homemade ice cream around my neighborhood. Practically every evening before sundown, a group of us—my good friends Herbert Monts, Peggy Cyrus, Marion Davis, and Reba Davis and whoever else we could round up throughout the day—gathered for a game. If we ended up with fewer than ten people, we played in the street. But most days we rallied enough players for a real game—five or six members per team—and headed across 15th Street to a huge vacant lot. It was shouting distance from my back door, and it became our Ebbets Field—in more ways than one.

Just a few years after Jackie Robinson broke the color line in Major League Baseball at that historic New York stadium, a group of us schoolkids crossed that line, too, on a vacant lot in west Little Rock. Our motives were purely practical: The black kids needed more players to fill our teams. So, as we gathered on the field one day, we just began recruiting the white kids passing on their bikes.

"Want to join us?" one of us called out.

Before long, we had a group of regulars: J.R., Connie, Billy, Jay, and Pete. The adults stayed out of our way, and there wasn't a moment of trouble or awkwardness. I was keenly aware, though, that what was happening on our field was, to say the least, different. Aside from those three months in New York, I had never played with white kids before. I'd seen my white neighbors in passing, standing in their doorways, sitting on their porches, or riding their bikes along our dusty roads. We usually acknowledged one another with a polite nod or even a "hello." But they were lumped together in my mind as simply "white people," as nameless and faceless as shadows to me, as I'm sure I was to them.

Things were quite different among my black neighbors, which included a mix of professionals—a doctor, lawyer, Philander Smith College professor, and high school teacher—as well as postal, railroad, and construction workers, like my dad and Sam Mumford. Mr. Mumford, the one Grandpa Cullins claimed was the grandson of former president Zachary Taylor, often worked on construction jobs with my father. He lived about a block away, and every morning, about six a.m., he would walk to our house to meet Daddy. When I made it to the kitchen, Mr. Mumford would be sitting at the table with a cup of coffee and the newspaper. He always helped me with current events, especially when I got to junior high school. By then, I was taking civics and had to bring in a current news topic for discussion.

"So, what's happening in the news today?" I'd ask.

Mr. Mumford would look up from the paper and launch a discussion about whatever had caught his attention on the news pages that day. Thanks to him, I left home each morning feeling more prepared for my civics class.

The neighborhood was full of people like Mr. Mumford. Even the families that didn't have children my age welcomed us into their homes. The Duncans, an older couple who lived across from us on Valentine Street, had the first television on the block, and I sometimes stopped by to watch my favorite television show, *American Bandstand*. They had helped to raise their three granddaughters—Alexine, Norma, and Billie Jean—all of whom were at least ten years older than me. The oldest of them, Billie Jean, had babysat me.

I especially liked spending time with another neighborhood couple, A.B. and Doll Fox, who were in their fifties and lived across 15th Street, next to the field. They were the surrogate grandparents of the neighborhood, the first to stop over with home-cooked food if someone was sick and the first to offer hugs and help if misfortune struck one of the families. They were the ones who somehow managed to stay connected to everybody's lives. I watched boxing matches with Mr. Fox, an industrial arts teacher and real Renaissance man, who also played the cello. Some of our neighbors called him "Professor," which he didn't like because he didn't have a doctorate. Though he had graduated from Kansas State Teachers College and pursued postgraduate studies, he still didn't believe he had earned the privilege to be addressed with such esteem. But the title fit him perfectly. Mr. Fox was a smart man and by nature philosophical. He was always teaching, even when we didn't realize in the moment exactly what we were being taught. As I was about to enter junior high school, Mr. Fox warned: Always be prepared because you will be tested every day. The thought at first intimidated me because I thought he was talking about written tests. But more conversations with him revealed that he was sharing a deeper lesson about life and making good decisions. His wife, Doll, loved to bake, and she kept homemade goodies around their house. She knew my father had a huge sweet tooth, so she usually sent me home with slices of pound cake or sweet-potato pie for him. Her sugar cookies were my favorites, particularly because they were always burnt around the edges. Cookies that looked too neat and fussy never seemed to taste as good. Nobody in the neighborhood could bake like Mrs. Fox.

Our neighborhood was full of kids about the same age, and the black parents saw it as their moral duty to keep watch over us all, correct us, and, if necessary, report any misbehavior to one another.

While my parents were generally mild-mannered folks who rarely raised their voices, I knew that nothing could result in serious trouble at home quicker than embarrassing them or bringing shame to the Walls name by acting up in public. The black kids rode bikes, walked to the corner store, and swam together in the segregated swimming pool at Gilliam Park, a small recreational area operated by the city for Little Rock's black residents. We also knew and respected one another's parents as our own. But when it came to our white playmates, we knew nothing more than their first names.

On our playing field, though, everything was level. Our teams were integrated, and every one of us, black and white, played hard. For the most part, we also played fair. We knew how one another hit, caught, and ran. We knew who played dirty and who could steal a base. And none of us was above boasting when the game ended in our favor.

"We'll whip you again tomorrow," I proclaimed many times after victory.

I imagined myself Jackie Robinson and always played first or second base. I was somewhat tomboyish and one of the better players. I also was usually among the first ones picked for a team. Occasionally, when we needed an extra player, I called my cousin Robert Henry Harris, who lived with his grandmother on the other side of town during the summer. It would take him about forty-five minutes to get to the field on his bike, but we just made small talk to kill the time. Robert Henry, who often saw the Cardinals play when he visited his father in St. Louis, was a pretty good center fielder. But when his team began winning too often, the losers started complaining and demanded a new rule: No one from outside the neighborhood was allowed to play in our games. In those moments on that field, there was no black or white, just winners and losers and kids being kids. The only outsider was a too good center fielder who had seen too many professional baseball games up in St. Louis.

Away from the field, though, the boundaries were clear and un-spoken. When it was time for a game, a few of us black kids might walk over to a white neighbor's yard and just stand there, close to the road, until a parent spotted us. We knew better than to even knock on the door.

"There's a colored kid in the yard," we'd hear one of the white parents yell.

Soon, our white playmate would come running out, ready to play. There were times, too, when a white neighborhood kid walked over to my yard and just waited.

"Some white kid is outside," Mother called out to me.

I grabbed my mitt and dashed outside.

Most days, we played so hard under the blazing Arkansas sun that we had to stop for water breaks. The black kids would all run over to one of our yards and turn on an outdoor water faucet, usu-ally connected to a long green hose. We'd take turns sipping from the cool stream pouring from that pipe. I suppose the white kids ran to their yards or homes, too, because they seemed to disappear like ghosts. Then we'd all meet back up on the field and play until hunger got the best of us or the grown-ups called us home.

Except for the white kids on our teams, the rest of us had known one another practically all our lives. Most of us were stu-dents at Stephens Elementary. It was the neighborhood elementary school, and it was named in honor of Charlotte Stephens, the first black teacher in Little Rock. She had taught English and Latin for sixty years—more than any other teacher in the school district's history—mostly at Dunbar, where she also served some of the time as the librarian. Stephens Elementary was the physical and cultural center of the neighborhood, a place that drew practically everyone together for holidays and special occasions. In my early days there, the school was an old, multistory building that sat atop the hill on W. 18th Street. Big wood-burning stoves in each room provided heat in the winter, and we relied on Mother Nature and the help of big fans to keep the rooms comfortable in early summer. None of the schools and only one or two homes I'd visited were air-conditioned back then. The school's wooden floors were cleaned religiously with linseed oil, which left a thin shine and light oily scent. But the old building was replaced a couple of years after I arrived by a one-story California-style model, similar to the building that sits in the same spot today. From as early as I can remember, I walked up that hill every day alone or with other schoolmates to class. Parents felt safe enough to let us go, and I certainly didn't feel a need to have Mother or Daddy tag along.

I was a sixth grader at Stephens in May 1954 when news about the historic *Brown v. Board of Education* broke. I read about it in the *Weekly Reader,* a popular children's newspaper. My teacher, Mrs. King, explained that the highest court in the land had decided it was unfair and against the law for black and white children to attend separate schools. Black children would finally have access to the same opportunities the white students had, she told us. Being a kid, I thought she meant we'd see some changes—new books, at least—right away. I was disappointed when, as far as I could tell, nothing changed that year. The next year, I moved to the all-black Paul Laurence Dunbar, Jr. and Sr. High School, which had been named for the internationally renowned black poet.

Some days, I caught a ride with a family member or rode the city bus to school to Dunbar. But most of the time, I walked the two-plus miles. I'd pass Roselawn Cemetery and cross the bridge over the Union Pacific Railroad track. Then, there it was—to my left, just one mile from my house, the all-white Little Rock Central High School. From that angle, I could see only the huge football field and stadium. That grand school building, with a campus that spread across four square blocks, loomed just beyond in the distance. The stadium was so close that on Friday and Saturday evenings during football season, I could see the bright lights shining from Central's football field in the neighborhood. That stadium and field house were the envy of schools everywhere.

But the school's reputation extended far beyond its championship football teams and sports facilities. Mr. Fox had taken classes at the University of Kansas with Jess Matthews, Central's principal, so when I visited the Foxes, I always got an earful about the school's academic success and first-rate programs. The school had a stellar reputation for sending its graduates to the top-rated colleges in the country, often on scholarships, Mr. Fox told me. It also had a huge two-thousand-seat auditorium, professional stage, and state-of-the-art lighting for students interested in theater. Students interested in biology and science had access to a fully equipped greenhouse.

Sometimes, as I passed Central, I wondered what it would be like to be a student there and have access to all of that and more. I was a serious student who made A's and B's and spent a good bit of time thinking about my future. I had recently begun dreaming of becoming a doctor after reading about Madame Curie, the first woman in France to receive a doctorate and the only woman to receive the Nobel Prize twice. She wasn't a medical doctor, but she was a brilliant scientist whose discoveries in the field of radiation changed the world. I liked that her discoveries helped prove to the world the scientific capabilities of women. I'd heard one of my uncles say that he once wanted to become a doctor, so I figured that would be a good field for me. I didn't know of any women doctors and certainly not any black ones, but Madame Curie had inspired me to take a chance. I loved science, and I liked the idea of helping people, of changing the world. I was sure that Central would have everything I needed to reach those goals someday. Maybe there, I thought, I could even get a new biology or chemistry book—one that I could write my name in. At Dunbar, all of my books were hand-me-downs from the white schools. By the time I got them, a white kid's name usually was already scrawled across the front cover. Some of the books were so shabby and worn that they were missing pages. My ears would always perk up when I heard the white kids on our neighborhood softball teams talking to one another about new lab equipment coming to their school or a new book a teacher had promised. New books and resources for the white kids usually meant newer hand-me-downs for the black kids, always far better than anything we had.

I frequently heard complaints about the outdated textbooks, limited supplies, and inferior equipment at the black schools from the relatives and family friends who worked there. Practically everywhere I turned at Dunbar, I was under the watchful eye of an aunt, uncle, or family friend who was on staff. Among them were my Aunt Eva, the librarian; Uncle Silas, who taught auto mechanics; and Mr. Fox. My seventh-grade gym teacher also became my Aunt Whaletha when she married my mother's brother Med, Jr. the summer after I took her class. I'd hear the adults talking among themselves about the injustice of it all, with white schools always getting the best of everything.

The disparities between Dunbar and Central can be traced to their beginnings. In 1927, the Little Rock school district spent $1.5 million to build Little Rock High School, which was renamed Little Rock Central High School in 1953. News reports called the school the most elaborate and expensive high school in the nation. School officials had poured so much of the system's resources into the construction that little was left to build a school for black children. But private financing came forth from philanthropists John D. Rockefeller and Julius Rosenwald for the construction two years later of Dunbar, then called the Negro School of Industrial Arts. Rosenwald, part-owner of Sears, Roebuck & Company, worked with Booker T. Washington from 1912 to 1932 to build almost five thousand schools for black children throughout the South. Dunbar, which cost $400,000 to build, still sits in the same spot. It is one of a few Rosenwald schools that are still operational.

The architects of Dunbar had contributed to the design of Central, so the schools look quite similar. Both are regal-looking old buildings with columns and concrete steps that lead to a grand entrance. Their brick-and-stone facades reflect the art deco style popular in the early twentieth century. But the schools have always been far from equal. Central, with one hundred classrooms spread across six hundred thousand square feet, served as a senior high school and junior college. Meanwhile, Dunbar, with thirty-four classrooms spread over two hundred thousand square feet, operated as a junior high, senior high, and junior college. While Central's first library was stocked with eleven thousand library books, Dunbar's first library had only five thousand books. Central had both a gymnasium and a stadium, but Dunbar had neither until 1950, when a gym was added. The boys and girls basketball teams practiced and played at large halls or centers located in the black community, including the Masonic Temple, YMCA, and Arkansas Baptist College. At reunions over the years, I've heard athletes talk about having to walk as far as sixteen blocks for football practice. I've also seen documents showing that Central's first principal in 1927 made a salary of $500 per month, compared with the $344 per month paid to Dunbar's principal. By 1954, the school district was spending $102.25 per child on white students but only $67.75 per child on black students.

Despite the discrepancies, though, Dunbar was far more modern than the one-room shacks where black children were educated throughout much of the South. Its all-black staff was highly educated and helped to create an academically rigorous curriculum that in 1931 resulted in accreditation from the North Central Association of Colleges and Schools. Most white schools in Little Rock, with all of their resources, had not achieved such status. Many of Dunbar's teachers had advanced degrees and often spent their summers taking classes at northern universities. What they lacked in resources, they made up in creativity and dedication. Educating black children was more than a job back then; it was a mission—one that for most of the teachers was rooted in the teachings of historically black colleges and universities created in the wake of the Civil War to educate freed slaves. They were schools like Philander Smith College, which had many alumni among Dunbar's staff.

The twenty-four-acre campus of Philander Smith sat right in the heart of black Little Rock. Before the construction of Interstate 630 in the late 1970s, the school was walking distance from the black business district on West 9th Street. Students and staff from the campus could walk a short distance to patronize the array of black-owned and -operated businesses, which included barber and beauty shops, restaurants and cafés, doctors' and lawyers' offices, taverns, a cab stand, a liquor store, an insurance company, and more. Then the interstate sliced a path right down the middle, leaving the university and businesses on opposite sides of a busy federal highway. But Philander Smith was a vibrant part of the black community. It instilled in its students an obligation to give back to that community. In that spirit, the Dunbar staff pushed us to excel, expected it, and drilled in us that when we stepped outside the schoolhouse doors, we not only represented our families and our school, but also represented the race.

My biology teacher, Edna Douglas, was one of my favorites. She had taught Mother, and she was a worldly woman who traveled extensively out of the country during the summer. She wove stories of her travels into her lectures and left us captivated with her descriptions of the people and places she had seen. Mrs. Douglas did more than teach science. She took us to those faraway places and made them more than just dots on a map. She engaged me in the world beyond Little Rock and made me want to see more of it. A good education was the door to the broader world, she told her students. And when we stepped into that broader world, she said, we represented the best of Dunbar and of colored people everywhere.

Dunbar's reputation as a top-notch school attracted black students from all over Arkansas who stayed with relatives to attend. Some were from well-to-do families who wanted their children to have access to the best possible education. Others were from rural areas that had no schools for black children. Not only did my parents graduate from Dunbar's high school, but Mother also graduated from the junior college. After World War II, Daddy spent a year at the junior college on the GI Bill, too. They never lost their tremendous affection for their alma mater. To this day, I usually accompany Mother to the school's big biennial reunions, which draw hundreds of proud and accomplished former students and staff to rotating venues throughout the country.

I, too, have fond memories of Dunbar. I was an honor student and active in a number of extracurricular activities. I was captain of the girls basketball team, a class representative on the student council, a member of the Junior National Honor Society, captain of the cheerleading squad, and a member of the choir. I also served as vice president of the student council two years in a row. In my day, women were never selected to be president of the council.

I was in the seventh grade at Dunbar when the school district announced plans to build two new high schools, Horace Mann for black students and Hall High for whites. Dunbar was to convert exclusively to a junior high school when the new high schools opened in fall 1956. Word of the new black high school circulated quickly among my junior high school peers, and we were excited about it. I didn't realize then that the new schools were part of an overall plan that had been unanimously approved by the school board in May 1955 to respond to the Supreme Court decision that I had read about the previous year in the *Weekly Reader.*

The school system's plan called for a deliberately slow process of desegregation that would be phased in over six years. It would start with a small number of black students entering Central High School in the fall of 1957. Selected black students in the following years then would enter previously all-white junior high and elementary schools in phases two and three, which would be implemented through 1963. The proposal would come to be known as the Blossom Plan, named for Virgil T. Blossom, superintendent of Little Rock public schools. Under Blossom's plan, desegregation of the schools would follow the city's residential patterns. As one school board member suggested, the plan would provide "as little integration as possible for as long as legally possible." Mann would be built on the predominantly black east side of the city and remain all black. Hall High would be built on the other side of the city in a more affluent white area, and no black students would be admitted. Central was surrounded by working-class white and racially mixed neighborhoods and would become the first testing ground for school integration in the city.

I watched Mann rise slowly from the dirt when my friends and I carpooled or took the bus to Gilliam Park to swim during the summer of 1955. I couldn't help thinking that in a few years I would be a student there. Even then, I thought it made no sense that I would have to travel even more than the two miles I traveled to Dunbar when Central High School was so close to my home. But high school was on the back burner. I was just looking forward to returning to Dunbar for eighth grade. In August of that summer, though, a brutal crime nearly two hundred miles away in Money, Mississippi, rattled me to the core.

I first heard the name of Emmett Till whispered from the lips of adults, speaking in hushed tones around my house about the horrible thing the white people did to that little black boy in Mississippi. My parents subscribed to the *Chicago Defender,* that city's black newspaper, and it was there that I first read the full, terrifying story. As I followed the story for weeks in the black press, I couldn't get the images out of my head. How Till, a fourteen-year-old Chicago boy visiting his great-uncle in Money, Mississippi, walked to the white-owned Bryant's Grocery on August 24, 1955, with some friends after a long day in the cotton fields. How the teenager, unfamiliar with the deadly taboos of the South, may have whistled at a white woman while leaving the store. How Roy Bryant, the store owner and the white woman's husband, showed up four days later with his half-brother at the home where Till was staying and dragged him away. How Till's battered and mutilated body was pulled from the Tallahatchie River a few days later. How the body had been weighed down by a seventy-five-pound cotton gin fan attached by barbed wire.

As horrible as those images were in my imagination, nothing could have prepared me for the real-life pictures I saw when Mother's September 15, 1955, issue of *Jet* magazine arrived at our home. As I flipped open the magazine and turned to the story about Emmett Till's memorial service, I gasped. The photo of his badly disfigured corpse was right there, in black and white. Part of me was so horrified that I wanted to turn the page quickly or throw the book down, but I couldn't take my eyes off his bloated, monstrous face. It was one of those moments when legend meets reality. I had read stories before about the lynching of black folks in Mississippi and other areas of the Deep South. I'd even heard my relatives tell the story of a lynching in downtown Little Rock. A woman who appeared to be in her early forties sat on her porch about five blocks from my home every day, just staring at passersby through sad, empty eyes. Her mind was never quite right, my folks said, because her brother had been lynched on Broadway when she was still in her mother's womb. To me, such stories were tragic yet distant history. But I *knew* Emmett Till. I'd never laid eyes on him before the magazine photos, but in the handsome face of the boy he had been before his murder, I saw my cousins, my friends, my classmates. He was just one and a half years older than me and as real to me as the black playmates I met on the softball field every day.

I imagined that Emmett was probably a popular teenager, eager to show off his big-city ways to his small-town southern friends, like my cousin Robert Henry, whose prowess on the field near my house (and no small amount of envy) had gotten him kicked off our neighborhood softball team. I imagined that the country store where Emmett may have acted on the dare of his friends that summer day looked like Mr. Thompson's shop, the white-owned store across the street from Uncle Teet's house. And what teenager hasn't said or done something silly to impress others? But Emmett's death said to me that for a black child, a little too much confidence, a joke, saying or doing the wrong thing, in the wrong place, at the wrong time, or just being the wrong color could cost him his life.

Because of what happened to Emmett Till, Mississippi became a fearsome place in my mind, and I wanted never to set foot there. That must have been the case with the adults in my family, too, because from that moment on, Daddy mapped out our road trips so that we never even passed through Mississippi. Those were the days before the interstate highway system, and sometimes we might have gotten to our destination quicker by going through Mississippi. But we weren't taking any chances.

Somehow, though, I still did not see Little Rock through the same eyes as I saw Mississippi. Yes, Little Rock was the South. Yes, I had to sit in the back of the bus and climb to the black section in the balcony when Peggy, Reba, and I walked to the Lee Theatre for the Saturday afternoon show. Yes, I'd heard white folks make degrading comments. And even though I had relatives who lived in the predominantly white neighborhoods on the west end, around the 202-acre War Memorial Park, I knew I couldn't swim there because the pool was for whites only. Yet in my mind, my hometown was not as bad as Mississippi. Till's murder had set the bar for racial evil in my mind, and compared with that, Little Rock was somewhere on the other end of the spectrum—or so I thought. At that point, I had always played by the rules. I'd never stepped out of my so-called place. That would come a few years later, and I would be shocked and saddened to see my hometown for the first time as it really was.

In some ways, though, Little Rock was indeed more progressive than many areas of the South. The city's public libraries had been integrated without any trouble in January 1951. And despite the limitations and motivations of the Blossom Plan, the Little Rock school district was among the first in the South to respond in any way to the U.S. Supreme Court decision mandating school desegregation. But black residents in Little Rock were growing restless of being treated like second-class citizens. With the massive show of black togetherness and power taking place in Montgomery, Alabama, at the end of 1955, some black residents were also starting to feel empowered.

I recognized the infectious power of the Montgomery movement one day in early 1956 when my cousin Delores and I decided to ride the bus downtown. As we stepped on board, we noticed Alexine Duncan, one of the granddaughters of the older couple who lived across the street from me. Alexine was in her twenties and had spent some time in Denver, Colorado, where her father operated an upscale men's clothing store. Like me, she had traveled up north and lived another way. Delores and I waved hello and we sat across from her in the middle of the bus, where the black section began. The bus grew more and more crowded as it traveled down Park Avenue. Suddenly, at one stop, a white passenger boarded, and the driver looked up into his rearview mirror at Delores and me and shouted over his shoulder:

"You two girls, get up!"

We knew he meant for us to go to the back and clear that row for white passengers. Without question, we were about to comply when I heard a sharp reply from across the aisle:

"Oh, no, you don't! You stay right there!"

Delores and I froze in our tracks and looked up. It was Alexine. She was fuming. Her arms were folded across her chest, and she was staring the bus driver down. We had a right to sit there, she demanded. Hadn't he heard about the Montgomery bus boycotts?

I had felt such pride reading about how the black people of that city were refusing to ride public buses to protest the system's segregated practices. I eagerly followed the news stories and photos in black newspapers and magazines, showing how fifty thousand black men and women there were working together, walking and carpooling to work, church, and everywhere else they had to go, while empty buses crisscrossed the city. I knew the whole story—how a small act of defiance by Rosa Parks had ignited the boycott. What a gracious lady. I imagined that she was just bone-tired that day when she quietly refused a white bus driver's order that she give up her seat to a white passenger. I had sat on the bus next to many black women like her in Little Rock. They would be headed home from jobs cleaning, cooking, and sewing in white people's homes and businesses, so tired they could barely keep their eyes open. When I saw that iconic black-and-white photograph of Rosa Parks being fingerprinted after her arrest for taking such a bold stand, I thought of all the hardworking women she had lifted by keeping her seat. And she became my forever she-ro.

I knew that Alexine was probably thinking of Rosa Parks and feeling the call of history to take her own stand. But as she grew louder, refusing to back down even after the bus driver threatened to call the police, I grew more frightened. I wanted to disappear. I wanted to run off the bus. I wanted to tell her that I knew she meant well, but that I just wanted her to be quiet—please—and let me go to the back of the bus. I've never been the kind of person to make a scene, and that was the last thing I wanted right then. But it was too late. The next thing I knew, the police were climbing aboard to escort Alexine off the bus. Delores and I got off, too, and quietly walked back home.

I never talked to Alexine about what happened that day, but I always felt horrible that she had landed in the hands of the police for standing up for me on that bus. Little did I know that another integration battle was heating up in my hometown. And soon, I would take my own stand.

CHAPTER 3

Birth of a Tiger

B y the spring of 1957, my days at Dunbar were winding down. My ninth-grade year was almost over, and high school was just around the corner. The idea of going to the brand-new Horace Mann had grown on me. I looked forward to moving with my friends there. Just the idea of attending a school where everything was new—the building, the classrooms, the labs, the lockers—was exciting.

Then one day before the end of the school year, I was sitting in my homeroom class when the teacher made an announcement: Central High School would be integrating in the fall. If our homes fell within certain border streets and we were interested in attending, we should sign the sheet of paper circulating around the room. Three years after the U.S. Supreme Court had ordered schools to integrate, it was really about to happen in Little Rock. But you wouldn't have known that there was anything special about this moment. No one asked a question. No one offered a comment. No one passed notes or even whispered to one another. If there was any excitement, uncertainty, nervousness, or fear in the room, none of my peers or our teacher expressed it. The announcement was treated as just another administrative task.

It caught my attention, though. My address put me in Central's attendance zone, so I had a quick decision to make. My mind weighed the options. Central High, that grand building looming in the distance as I walked to school practically every day, now would open its doors to me. I'd heard so much about it. I knew I could get into Philander Smith or Arkansas AM&N, but I couldn't help wondering how much wider my options for college would be if I attended Central and suddenly had all of its resources available to me. Plus, Central had competitive athletic teams, and it was just a mile from my home, much closer than Mann. My decision was made. When the sign-up sheet got to me, I eagerly wrote down my name. There were other names on the list, but it didn't occur to me to note who they were.

When I made it home from school that afternoon, I didn't even mention my decision to my parents. It wasn't a calculated choice to keep the news from them, but it just never came up. I know that sounds strange, but I've always been independent. I also tend not to make a big deal of things, even at times when something really is a big deal. In my mind, I had done what my parents would have expected. They had told me all of my life that a good education was paramount and that I should always strive for better. Central clearly seemed the better choice for me, so my decision didn't stick out in my mind as one that needed much discussion. I must say, though, I was also just naive. I thought I had made a simple decision to go to a different school. I had no idea how much my life and the lives of those closest to me were about to change.

As the school year ended, my thoughts were consumed with planning my summer. I knew the Brooklyn Dodgers would play the Cardinals and that my family would drive to St. Louis for the game. I wondered how many Arkansas Travelers minor league games I'd get to see and which Negro League teams would come to town. I knew we'd at least catch all of the big games on the radio. By then, Daddy also had bought our first television so that we could see some of the games, too.

These were good financial times. Construction jobs were plentiful, and for several years Daddy had been earning enough money to splurge on a few luxuries, like the TV. He also was putting the finishing touches on a new wing he had added onto the back of the house. The renovation started at the old kitchen, which he widened and opened into a new den. A door from the den led into a large master bedroom with an entire wall divided into his and her closets. My parents needed the extra space for their expansive wardrobes. The room was spacious and bright, with lots of light streaming in from a pair of horizontal windows close to the ceiling. Among my favorite features of the room were its light oak hardwood floors, which I had helped Daddy lay.

Daddy taught me lots of practical skills, including some tasks that fathers of my generation were more likely to teach their sons. I helped out when he mowed the yard and trimmed the bushes. He would even have me watch while he changed a tire on the car. Mrs. Fox, our neighbor, didn't drive, so when Daddy drove her to the grocery store, he taught me how to shop. You don't just pick up any jar of olives, he would say. Sometimes you want this brand or that one. Sometimes quality matters more than price. When he worked in Big Daddy's café, I was his gofer, setting up tables and delivering orders to the cook. He taught me how to make chili-mac (homemade chili with macaroni or spaghetti added), one of the mainstays at the café. And when he worked the cash register, I sat on a high stool while he showed me again and again how to count money and give change to customers quickly. I was just thirteen when he first taught me to drive. He and I would hop into his truck and head to a deserted back road somewhere in town, then he'd hand over the wheel. Daddy was a patient and diligent teacher, always had been. I was barely past the toddler stage when he began waking me up at five a.m., before he went to work, to go over my ABCs and numbers. I'd roll my red wagon full of ABC blocks to him and dutifully recite my alphabet and numbers. The house would be as still as the dawn, with just Daddy and me puttering around. When it was time for him to go to work, he'd kiss me on the cheek and head with his metal lunch box out of the door. My teenage friends were crazy about Daddy, too, especially the guys, some of whom found it difficult to communicate with their own fathers, who tended to be more rigid and stern. Herbert, one of the regulars in our neighborhood softball games, once told me that he always enjoyed talking to my father. He said that Daddy was playful and down-to-earth, that Daddy really listened and never talked down to him.

Daddy had a big soft spot in his heart for his daughters. Mother did, too. Nothing revealed that more than when the two of them decided during the summer to give their dream bedroom to me. They hadn't even moved in yet when they surprised me with the news. Now that I was going to high school, they told me, I would need a quiet place to study. I could hardly believe my ears. For the first time in my life, I had a room of my own. I knew how much my parents wanted and needed a bigger bedroom, but they were willing to wait at least a few more years until I left for college. Their sacrifice and generosity spoke eloquently to me about what they considered important: My education meant far more to them than their own desire for comfort.

When it came to taste and style, my parents were two of a kind. They didn't have much, but whenever they pulled themselves together for a night on the town, they looked like a million bucks— Daddy in his Italian-designed hat, dress suit, and shoes and Mother in something flowing with glittery jewels around her neck. There was nothing pretentious or haughty about Mother. Daddy just loved spoiling her, and whatever Mother wanted from him, she generally got. He didn't believe in buying things on credit, so he often worked two or three jobs at a time, whatever it took to provide for his family. His family was his pride. You could see it all over his face, especially when he stepped out with his glamorous wife on his arm.

That sense of style extended to our home. As my parents made changes here and there, our house took on a more open, modern look, inspired—I'm almost certain—by Mother's many magazines. She had subscriptions to the most popular ones of the day—*Look, The Saturday Evening Post, Life,* and, of course, *Ebony* and *Sepia.* The latter three were her favorites. *Ebony* and *Sepia* were general-interest publications, heavy with photos and uplifting stories, but they were black-owned publications that focused primarily on black success. They particularly showcased the glitz and glamour of the few black movie stars and entertainers of the time. Mother was a huge fan of crooner Billy Eckstine, and her black magazines kept her in close touch with the likes of him, Nat King Cole, and the Lena Hornes of the world. Mother had that kind of movie-star presence about her, too. One of her best friends, Tyralese, used to say Mother entered a room like Loretta Young. Young, a popular white actress, had her own television show back then, and when she entered the stage with a sweep of her flowing evening gown, Aunt Tyralese would say: "There goes Juanita."

Mother's touch was noticeable everywhere that summer as she finished the transformation of our house. Out went the plastic-covered sofas and chairs, and in rolled more contemporary replacements. I spent many evenings curled up in the cup-shaped white leather swivel chair in front of the television, a black-and-white model with the largest screen I'd ever seen. It was an RCA, and it sat on a fancy black swivel table in the new den. For the expanded kitchen, my parents added a bar with red-padded stools that each sat on a chrome base. When I plopped down many mornings on those bar stools with my piping hot grits and scrambled eggs, I felt as if I were in one of those California diners I'd seen on television.

Sitting in front of the television had become one of my favorite pastimes. With no homework during summer, I could spend as much time as I wanted watching my favorite shows, *Amos 'n*

Andy, I Love Lucy, and Esther Williams in her swimming movies. I especially loved *Father Knows Best.* After watching an episode one day, I turned to Mother and asked: "May I call Daddy 'Father'?" She just laughed. She had long ago put an end to my calling her "Mama." She said it drove her crazy the way I dragged out that four-letter word. "Mother" seemed more fitting, more elegant. But "Father" never stuck, never felt quite right. There was an earthiness, a closeness, a kind of warmth, to "Daddy."

Daddy was a prankster who kept us all laughing. But he was wise, too, and very much the traditional head of our household. The truth be told, my home life wasn't much different from those of the white families I saw depicted on-screen every day in what became known as the golden age of television. I didn't see families that looked like mine—happy black families—on TV, but we were a stable clan with two loving, doting parents. Daddy worked, Mother primarily took care of the family's domestic needs, and we children got to be just children. I knew our lives weren't as perfect as those we saw on TV, but whatever problems my parents may have had, they did their best to keep them from my sisters and me. Our home was peaceful, full of laughter, and often, full of extended family. Some of my favorite family times were spent in front of that black-and-white television, watching a broadcast of a Dodgers game. On those Saturdays, Mother, Daddy, and I would gather in the den with whatever relatives and friends had joined us, usually my uncles and their wives or girlfriends. I'd cook hamburgers, while my sister Loujuana, then eight, played with her dolls. All the while, the newest member of our family, my youngest sister, Tina, who was two at the time, ran from one family member's lap to another.

In previous summers, my love of baseball had extended to playtime. But for the first time since our neighborhood softball games began, the kids in my community didn't meet on our playing field in the summer of 1957. All of us—black and white—had practically grown up together on that field. Some of us were finally headed to high school. I wondered if any of the white kids among us would be going with me to Central, too, but I never got to ask them.

I couldn't have imagined that we would never again come together on that field.

Perhaps they were already feeling the tension. By then, community tensions over the school system's plans to integrate Central had started bubbling to the surface, though I was still mostly oblivious to it. I kept busy with family, friends, and, of all things, potato chip sales. In June and July each summer, I sold bags of potato chips to raise money for Y-Teen camp, a two-week program sponsored by the local YWCA. And I must say, I was pretty good at it. I hiked through the neighborhood, knocking on doors with my chips in tow. I took the chips to church and, of course, to every family gathering until I made my sales commitment. Going to camp was a great sales motivator. I loved camp. It was two weeks of freedom with some really good friends. My best friend, Bunny, always joined me on the trip. Her real name is Dorothy Frazier, and we've been friends for as long as I can remember. Her grandmother lived just a block away from my house and across the street from White Memorial Methodist Church, which both of us attended. Bunny's father had died in World War II when she was a baby, and she lived with her mother and stepfather, who was a doctor. I also enjoyed spending time at camp with another good friend, Jeannette Mazique, who lived about forty-five miles away in Pine Bluff. Jeannette and I had met through our fathers, who sometimes worked construction jobs together. Because we lived in different cities, we didn't get to see each other regularly until camp. Bunny, Jeannette, and I rode the bus with the other Y-Teens to a camp in Clear Fork, Arkansas, just outside Hot Springs. I didn't realize then that it was the only site in our area that admitted black campers. It was beautiful and serene, several acres of woods surrounding a sparkling lake. Rustic cabins sat nestled among the woods. We rose early most mornings to hike, explore the woods, compete against other cabins in games, and participate in arts and crafts projects, such as making key chains and lariats. At night, we enjoyed cooking out and singing around an open campfire. I could hardly wait. But camp was at the end of July, still a few weeks away.

In the meantime, I spent many of my days at the Dunbar Community Center, a city-run recreational spot that had become a sort of gathering place for black Little Rock. It was a short bus ride from my house, and something fun was always happening there. In the evenings and on weekends, black fraternities, sororities, and other groups regularly held meetings and adult parties in the center's huge hall on the main level. A smaller room upstairs drew families and church groups for afternoon receptions. But during the day, the center belonged to the city's youths. It was always full of children and teens, playing games and cards while the latest sounds of rock and roll blared from the jukebox—Chuck Berry, Little Richard, the Platters, Elvis Presley, Fats Domino, you name it. Occasionally, some of the popular artists passing through Little Rock played daytime gigs at the center. One afternoon, I made my way there to see the duo Mickey & Sylvia perform their latest hit, "Love Is Strange." I was headed in the door when I spotted Ernest Green, a friend and former Dunbar student. Ernie was two years older and about to enter his senior year at Horace Mann. His mother had been my first-grade teacher. The two of us greeted each other, chatted for a moment, and then he asked:

"Are you going to Central?"

"Yep," I responded proudly.

He told me that he had signed up, too, but that none of his friends wanted to leave Mann in their senior year. One of them, Lottie Holt—who would later become Lottie Shackelford, the first woman elected mayor of Little Rock—had just achieved her longtime goal of becoming editor of the *Bearcat,* the school newspaper. Ernie asked if I knew of anyone else who had signed up for Central, but I didn't. My friend Peggy, who lived two blocks from me, had told me she had no interest in going to Central. She was having too much fun at the new Mann.

Ernie looked concerned. "We need to contact a few people and see if they want to go with us," he said.

We agreed and headed into the center.

"See you at Central," I said.

A few weeks later, I stepped outside my home to meet the postman, as usual, and was surprised to find a letter for me from the Little Rock school district. I read it quickly and ran inside to show Mother confirmation of my admittance to Central. She smiled approvingly and congratulated me. That's the first time I remember any communication with her about my decision to go to Central. Even then, there was no big discussion, but I could tell she was happy for me. The card instructed me to show up at Central on a certain date in August to register for fall classes. Now, I was getting excited.

But just two days into August, misfortune struck my family.

I was standing on the porch that day when Mother stepped to the front door and called me inside. The distress on her face and her red eyes told me right away that something was wrong. Papa Holloway was gone, she said. Our patriarch—the man who had raised her, protected her, and kept the ground beneath her steady in those early days after her mother left—was dead. His oldest son's wife, Aunt Helen, had found him unconscious, lying among the corn in his expansive garden. I heard Mother say something about him hemorrhaging. I'd never heard that word before. I hugged her as she wept inconsolably. My heart ached, too.

Papa's death dulled the excitement I had felt in the days before. But as relatives chatted in our home after the funeral on August 7, I heard Mother tell some out-of-town relatives:

"You know, Carlotta will be going to Central in the fall."

There was pride in her voice, which lifted my spirits.

However, when word got out that I was going to Central, not everyone in my family agreed with my decision. I couldn't understand why Aunt Eva, the Dunbar librarian, didn't seem particularly excited when I told her. That was unusual for her because she was such a high-spirited, fun-loving person. I'd learn through the family grapevine much later that she wanted my parents to withdraw me from Central and send me to Mann. She didn't understand, I'd heard, why I needed to go to "that school."

Aunt Eva and all the other staff members at Dunbar were a proud bunch, and rightly so. They had given up their summers and holidays to add postgraduate degrees to their résumés. They had labored in a school system that still paid them less than a generally less educated white teacher. They had invested their skills and hearts in preparing black children for a world that would require them to be twice as good and work twice as hard. And they had produced stellar students, despite the discrepancies in resources. Those dedicated black educators knew where their loyalties lay. But they weren't at all confident that their white colleagues at Central would be able to look past the skin color of black students, see and nurture the future doctors, lawyers, scientists, and entrepreneurs we could become. So while the Dunbar staff may have understood and supported the justice of the U.S. Supreme Court decision in *Brown,* if they were a tad chilly to the practicality of it—their sons and daughters, nieces and nephews, being the first to go over to that school—they believed they had good reason. Nothing was ever quite so black and white.

Of course, as a stubbornly determined teenager, I couldn't fully understand why all of my relatives weren't just thrilled that I was preparing to attend one of the top high schools in America. Hadn't they always preached to me about the value of education? Hadn't they always encouraged me and shown by example that I should open myself to opportunities for advancement? So the concern and reluctance among a few of them to embrace my decision fully didn't sit too well with me back then. It smacked of hypocrisy. With maturity, I would come to understand the gray that sometimes sits between right and wrong, and I would come to appreciate that their concern was more out of love than anything else.

But at the time, I just tuned them out. Thankfully, Mother and Daddy would not be influenced, either. So as registration day grew closer, I called Gloria Ray, a classmate at Dunbar. We had taken typing together and were members of the Honor Society. She was a serious student—she wanted to be an atomic scientist, for goodness' sake. I suspected that if anyone else was considering Central, she was on the list. I was right. Gloria told me that she was indeed planning to attend and had received the same card about registration day. She agreed to pick me up.

As planned, Gloria and I rode together to Central for the first time. We considered the day so routine that we went without our parents. Our parents were very protective and would have demanded to go along if they'd had any inkling of trouble, particularly Gloria's father. Harvey Ray was much older than my parents and had already retired from the U.S. Department of Agriculture. There, he'd founded the Arkansas Agricultural Extension Service for Negroes. He had received a degree in horticulture under Booker T. Washington at Tuskegee Institute and worked as Washington's assistant. Her mother, Julia, worked as a sociologist for the state of Arkansas. Gloria's siblings, an older brother and sister, were already grown. Gloria was the baby of the family.

She parked the car about a block away from Central, and we made our way to the front of the school. It was a clear, sunny day, and as we moved closer, I was filled with awe. I had never been this close to the front of Central before, and the yellowish brick and white concrete building was even bigger and more elegant than I had imagined. As I stood ground level and stared up at that great entrance, I felt tiny. Concrete stairs flowed up from two sides and seemed to go on forever. The building seemed at least five stories high, and I wondered if there were elevators inside. Gloria and I climbed the steps, headed for the main entrance on the second floor. At the top, we passed beneath four white, life-size statues of Greek gods and goddesses. Each bore an inscription that seemed to carry a message about the place: "Ambition," "Personality," "Opportunity," "Preparation."

At first, when Gloria and I stepped inside the school, we didn't know which way to go. The closed doors of the auditorium faced us just a few steps away, and signs pointed toward the main office to our left. We followed the signs to the office. We had barely made it inside the office door when a woman behind the counter quickly rose from her seat and approached us. I announced that we were there to register for the fall semester. She introduced herself as Miss Opie, the registrar. She smiled and handed each of us a card that said we had to attend a special meeting at Superintendent Blossom's office with our parents before we could register. Gloria and I looked at each other, completely baffled. Miss Opie was firm, not the warm and fuzzy type, but pleasant enough as she explained that everything would be okay; the superintendent just needed to meet with us before the opening of school. None of the other administrative workers even looked our way. Gloria and I thanked her, then turned and walked back out of the office and down the steps, headed for her car.

The two of us weren't quite sure what to make of what had just happened. It was silly, we agreed, for school officials to instruct us to show up for registration, only to give us another card requiring us to attend another meeting. Why did we need to meet with the superintendent, anyway? Why was it necessary to bring our parents? And who else would be at the meeting? Gloria and I grumbled all the way to the car. As we got closer, we noticed a car parking just behind Gloria's car. An attractive, honey-colored woman wearing a dress and heels hopped out and began hailing us over to her. I recognized her right away. It was Daisy Bates, president of the Arkansas State Conference of NAACP branches. She and her husband, L. C. Bates, co-owned and -operated the *Arkansas State Press,* the black newspaper I had delivered on my paper route in elementary and junior high school. Mother worked occasionally as an NAACP volunteer from a space at the newspaper's 9th Street office, where she sold memberships and collected poll taxes. Mrs. Bates and Mother got along well. In some ways, they were cut from the same cloth—both pretty, ladylike southern women who placed great value in their manner and appearance. But where Mother was soft-spoken and quiet, Mrs. Bates was outspoken and opinionated. And in L. C. Bates, a longtime newspaperman, Daisy Bates had found a partner and kindred spirit willing to use the editorial pages of their newspaper to take a stand for civil rights and to rally against police brutality, the mistreatment of black war veterans in the city, and other injustices against black residents.

Mrs. Bates greeted Gloria and me and immediately began asking questions. She wanted to know all of the details—whom we saw, what had been said, how we were treated, whether we were allowed to register. We told her about the meeting with Superintendent Blossom and showed her the card. That was the beginning of my almost daily contact with the woman who soon would become my adviser, mentor, and biggest public defender. I didn't question why Mrs. Bates had come to meet us at the school or even how she knew Gloria and I would be there. It would have been impolite to ask. The way I was raised, children stayed in their place, and it was not my place to ask a woman of her authority why she was there and whether she was expecting trouble. At fourteen, I was old enough to understand the historical significance of my enrollment in Central and the NAACP's interest in it. It was the NAACP and its brilliant attorneys, after all, that had fought for the ruling in the *Brown v. Board of Education* case in the first place. I also knew some white folks wouldn't like the idea of black students going to Central. But I really believed that what the U.S. Supreme Court said should happen *would* indeed happen because it was now the law of the land and because the law was just. I believed, too, that my presence at Central would allow my white peers to see that beyond the color of our skin, we all wanted the same thing: a fun and unforgettable high school experience, the best education possible, a jump start for our futures. I had no clue that while I was counting down the days until I started my new school, enraged white parents and other citizens—including the Arkansas governor, who had gotten my parents' vote in the last election—were organizing to keep me away.

I'd been too caught up with the events of summer to pay much attention to the local newspapers, which were full of stories about the activities of the Capital Citizens Council and the Mothers League, which were organizing to stop the integration of Central. Both groups had begun holding meetings and even lobbying Governor Orval Faubus for a delay in implementing the Blossom Plan. The groups must have been emboldened by a poll indicating that 85 percent of the white population in Little Rock opposed school integration. Telephone calls poured into the offices of Blossom and Faubus from white callers who threatened violence if black students were allowed to enter Central. One of the most vocal segregationists was Reverend James Wesley Pruden, the founding pastor of Broadmoor Baptist Church and an active member of the Citizens Council. He ran newspaper ads to help whip up the public frenzy. The ads asked questions that seemed to reveal the underlying source of all the fear: Would black boys and white girls be allowed to dance together at school dances? Would black boys and white girls be paired in romantic love scenes in school plays? The mere thought that their white daughters would be in such proximity to black boys petrified white mothers and fathers throughout Little Rock. Superintendent Blossom obviously was feeling the pressure because he would raise that overtly sexual issue when he met with us students and our parents face-to-face at the August meeting.

Mother and I left home early that August evening to make sure we made it to the meeting in Blossom's downtown office on time. Punctuality was always important to Mother and Daddy. Even now, I try to arrive at least fifteen minutes early for appointments. That practice paid off when we arrived at the school administration building that day, because we were among the few who got seats. Several folding chairs had been lined up facing Blossom's desk, but most of the crowd behind us was forced to stand. By the time the meeting began, about thirty-nine students and our parents were crammed shoulder to shoulder in that small space. It didn't take long to feel the temperature rising, as though all of those bodies sucked up every bit of fresh air.

I felt a bit anxious, unsure why we were all there. What was there to discuss? Hadn't the Supreme Court said that black students should have the same educational opportunities as our white peers? Central was my neighborhood school, and I'd made my choice. I knew I was a good enough student to make it there, but I wondered whether the purpose of this meeting was to discuss our qualifications. I looked at Superintendent Blossom, who sat stoically behind a large wooden desk. He was a big white man, about six feet three inches tall and at least 250 pounds. His dark hair was slicked back lightly, and a pair of black glasses framed his serious eyes. His large hands rested atop his desk. Blossom's serious expression didn't change when he started to speak. He had called us there to go over the rules, he explained. Black students would be allowed to attend Central, as expected, he said, but it would take time on both sides to adjust. We might hear some name-calling, he said, but we were not to retaliate in any way. For our own safety, he added, we had to leave the school grounds as soon as our classes ended. That meant we would not be allowed to participate in any extracurricular activities—no varsity sports, clubs, chorus, band, or even the Student Government Association. We also could not attend any after-school parties or sporting events. Central had a championship team whose winning streak had lasted over a year, and I'd been looking forward to attending the games. I could just imagine myself with my classmates in the stands in Central's college-size football stadium, cheering and chanting for the Tigers, bursting with school spirit and pride. It had always been that way for me at Dunbar, which didn't have a football stadium and had to play at Central.

Blossom could not be serious, I thought. Sure, I was a serious student, but I'd always maintained a full roster of extracurricular activities, too. That was the fun part of school. My family encouraged my getting involved in school. It helped to make me well-rounded, they said. Now I was expected to give up all of it? What about baseball? And basketball? What about cheerleading, the student council, and the National Honor Society? Weren't those the rewards of working hard in school? Wouldn't those kinds of activities give black and white students with equal talents and interests a chance to work together and get to know one another? The superintendent had no idea how involved I had been at my old school or how good I was at sports, I thought. When my white classmates got to know me, when they saw me play, they would want me to join their organizations and athletic teams. I was sure of it. So part of me just tuned Superintendent Blossom out. In my mind, this was just formality. Blossom was saying what he believed he had to say. But I was certain things would be much different when I got to Central.

As I sat in that room taking it all in, I was still under the impression that the decision to attend Central High School had been all mine, that I'd sealed the deal when I signed the sheet of paper in my homeroom class at Dunbar. I had no idea that Little Rock school officials had been given the biggest say, that *they* had approved me. I would learn decades later that by the time we black students showed up at Blossom's office with our parents that day, every one of us had been thoroughly vetted. So Blossom indeed knew exactly what kind of student I had been at Dunbar. I imagine that I, as well as all the others in the room that day, had been put through a kind of Jackie Robinson test. Baseball historians say that Jackie Robinson, though clearly talented, was not the best player in the Negro Leagues. But he became the Dodgers' top choice for his historical role because he also possessed the kind of character and temperament that would enable him to withstand the racist attacks sure to come. Likewise, the black students in that room were not just the best and brightest students academically, but we were student leaders from working- and middle-class families whose backgrounds had been deemed acceptable by the school system's white leaders for the moment at hand.

I snapped out of my own little world when I heard Blossom specifically address the boys in the room. The room was full of black teenage boys, listening intently as the superintendent put them on notice:

"You are not to date—or even look at—our girls," he said.

I distinctly remember his using the word *our*. The girls weren't just white; they were his. They were special. I was stunned. What did that have to do with anything? I thought about my friend Ernie. I also thought for a moment about Emmett Till. I wondered how Ernie and the other guys in the room must have felt. What if they accidentally bumped a white girl? Or, God forbid, smiled at one? Would it be misinterpreted? Would they be reprimanded? Or worse?

Everyone else must have been shocked, too, because no one said a word. The room was so still, it felt as though no one even breathed. The tension was as thick as the heat and humidity. Sweat rolled down faces like so many tears. This came at the close of a meeting that lasted about forty-five minutes. There were no questions or discussion. Even as parents and their children filed out of the room, there was silence, uneasiness.

Mother and I walked quietly to the car. When we stepped outside, an uncharacteristic breeze was blowing. It wasn't exactly cool, but it was fresh air nonetheless. The sweat on my face and hands began to dry. I slowed my stride. Mother wouldn't dare let me know if she was concerned about what she had just heard. She would wait and talk it over with Daddy behind closed doors. I knew that if they felt too worried, they could just put their foot down and say I couldn't go to Central after all. As independent as I was, I had no illusions about who was in charge. But I was pretty confident in my abilities to sway them. I wasn't a crier; I'd learned in elementary school that crying didn't work with Daddy. When I got in trouble back then, it always seemed Mother waited until just before Daddy came home to spank me. A time or two, I was still red-faced, heaving with sobs, when Daddy walked through the door. I looked at him with my most pitiful wet eyes. He leaned close, as if he felt sorry for me, and then he said:

"Young lady, why are you whipping your mother this evening?"

He always took Mother's side. That used to upset me, so I stopped playing the crying bit. But unlike some members of my family who believed to the core in the old edict that "children should be seen, not heard," Daddy would hear me out if I objected to his decision. Sometimes, just a certain look on my face would do it. But after the meeting with Superintendent Blossom, I knew that I would just have to wait to find out where my parents stood. This was grown-folks business, and Cartelyou and Juanita Walls weren't apt to discuss grown-folks business with children. As usual, Mother put on her best June Cleaver face after the meeting. She always wore that composed look, even in the midst of trouble. But from the time I was a child, I've always been able to see right through her. I learned early to read her eyes. They always told me the truth, even when her demeanor or her words did not. And that evening, her eyes told me something was wrong. She was worried.

This was not going to be an ordinary school year. Blossom certainly had made that clear. But even then, I wasn't particularly worried. The advantage—or disadvantage—of youth is that you don't know how much you don't know; you can barely conceptualize those things you've never seen. Youth can give you an unfailing faith that the world will give you back what you give to it, what you expect. Youth can give you untainted hope. So I walked out of that meeting undeterred. If Blossom had intended to change my mind, it didn't work. Even the worry in Mother's eyes didn't give me a second thought about my decision. I was as determined as ever to go to Central.

Come September, I would be a Central Tiger.

CHAPTER 4

Wait and See

Just before Labor Day, my great-uncle Emerald Holloway stopped by the house with a surprise gift for me: cash to buy a brand-new dress for my first day at Central. Everybody in the family knew that Mother was a fastidious seamstress who usually made all of my clothes. But this was no ordinary first day of school, Uncle Em said. The integration of the finest high school in Arkansas would happen just once in our lifetime, and I had to have a dress to match the occasion. Even one of Mother's perfectly tailored creations would not do. I had to have a store-bought dress.

Mother and I took the bus downtown and searched our favorite department stores until we found the perfect outfit: a black skirt set with small, bluish green letters and numbers spread in a random pattern. The blouse had short sleeves, just right for the hot and humid early days of September. The skirt was pleated at the waist, with enough fabric to flow over my crinoline slip. The outfit looked sophisticated and smart, not too dainty. I wasn't a dainty kind of girl. I hung the skirt set in my closet to wait for the big day: September 3, the Tuesday after Labor Day.

Labor Day marked the end of summer vacation, and my family spent the afternoon at Gilliam Park. The pool was the main draw, and it was always so full of people that you could barely swim a clear path from one side to the other. My family cooked hot dogs and hamburgers on a cast-iron pit in the grassy picnic area. Between pool breaks, the teenagers danced to the rhythm and blues and rock and roll blaring from the intercom. About midday, I heard a rumor that Governor Faubus would appear on late-night television news to make a speech about Central, but I was having too much fun to give it much thought. Later that afternoon, though, I checked the newspapers—the *Arkansas Gazette,* the morning paper that we received daily at home, and the *Arkansas Democrat,* the afternoon paper that we sometimes picked up from the newsstand. Neither of them had any information about the speech. My parents didn't seem worried. They liked Faubus. They had voted for him twice before in previous elections. He was a man of the people, I'd heard them say. And unlike his past opponents, he was not a strident segregationist. He certainly was no John Patterson, the Alabama governor who had banned the NAACP from operating in his state and welcomed the support of the Ku Klux Klan. And neither was Faubus a Marvin Griffin, the brash Georgia governor who promised to keep the schools in his state segregated "come hell or high water." Three small school districts in rural Arkansas already had been integrated peacefully in the previous two years with little notice. Faubus had even refused to intervene when white residents in one of the towns—Hoxie, a community with fewer than two thousand residents in northeastern Arkansas—protested the desegregation of their schools and asked the state to step in. My parents and I had no clue that Faubus had made an about-face and was moments away from announcing a bold move that would help to write Little Rock's civil rights history.

I had paid little attention to recent news coverage and was unaware that Faubus had spent much of the summer cavorting with groups of well-known segregationists. In late August, when the Mothers League filed a temporary injunction in Pulaski County Chancery Court to halt the integration of Central indefinitely, Faubus even testified as a surprise witness. He upheld the group's claims that parents were afraid to send their children to school for fear of widespread violence. He said guns and knives had been confiscated from Little Rock students. The injunction was granted, but just days later, a federal district court judge nullified it when the NAACP sent two of its best attorneys—Wiley Branton, a homegrown lawyer who had been involved with the successful integration of the University of Arkansas's law school in 1948, and Thurgood Marshall, the rising star who had argued the *Brown* case before the U.S. Supreme Court. As my family gathered at ten p.m. in front of the television in the den to watch Faubus, none of us expected any earth-shattering news. This was my bedtime, and quite frankly, I was just eager to get to sleep so that I could be well rested for the big day ahead.

About fifteen minutes after the hour, Faubus appeared on-screen. Like Blossom, he was a big man. He wore a dark suit and tie and spoke with a southern drawl typical of white politicians of his ilk. I listened as he droned on the first few minutes about the history of race relations in Arkansas. But at age fourteen, I was a busybody who found it hard to sit still for long periods, especially during rambling speeches. I was about to start daydreaming when the governor said something that caught my attention:

> Now that a federal court has ruled that no further litigation is possible before the forcible integration of Negroes and whites in Central High School tomorrow, the evidence of discord, anger, and resentment has come to me from so many sources as to become a deluge. There is evidence of disorder and threats of disorder which could have but one inevitable result—that is, violence which can lead to injury and the doing of harm to persons and property.

I could hardly believe my ears. Were white men and women in Little Rock really so angry about black students attending Central that they were willing to harm us? I just wanted to go to school and get the best possible education. What was so wrong with that? The thought that people were threatening violence at first made me more angry than afraid. But I found an odd sense of comfort in what Faubus said next:

> Units of the National Guard have been or are now being mobilized with the mission to maintain or restore the peace and good order of this community. Advance units are already on duty on the grounds of Central High School. I have informed Chief Lindsey, director of the Arkansas State Police, of the developments and he is now mobilizing a force to act as an arm of the state militia in maintaining or restoring the peace and order of the community and to act in every way possible to protect the lives and property of the citizens of Pulaski County.

I knew I was a citizen of Pulaski County. My parents paid taxes; they were citizens, too. I honestly believed that I was included in those whom our governor had deployed the Arkansas National Guard to protect. It was shocking to think that a military unit might be necessary to keep the peace on my first day at Central, but I still wanted to go. Somehow, I had gotten it into my head that Central was crucial to my future. I knew that if I could make it there—a school ranked among the top forty in the nation—I could make it anywhere. Things would settle down eventually, once the rabble-rousers realized theirs was a lost cause, I figured. In the meantime, the National Guard would keep me safe—or so I thought. I must have been too caught up in my own thoughts to pay much attention to the last part of the Faubus speech, the part calling for a delay in integrating Central. When I closed my eyes that night, I was confident that I would be at Central the next day and that I would be safe.

It would be my last night of innocence.

The next morning, I woke up to news that the opening of school was delayed. Mrs. Bates had called my parents while I was sleeping with word that the school board was asking the black students to stay at home until further notice. With the disruptive presence of the National Guard and Faubus's call for a delay, the board wanted to seek further legal resolution. My new dress would have to wait. I'd pinned so much of my hope and excitement on this day. Now, all I could do was wait and wonder. It was beyond frustrating. The day seemed to drag with little information from the adults involved. Daddy went to work, as usual, and Mother spent much of the time on the telephone, answering questions from concerned relatives and friends. She also checked in with Mrs. Bates for updates. The neighborhood was dead still. Most of my friends returned to Mann that day, so I couldn't even talk to them on the telephone.

The legal matter was resolved by early afternoon. U.S. District Court judge Ronald Davies, the magistrate who had nullified the initial injunction, ordered the school system to proceed the next day with integration at Central. He said he was not swayed by the sentiments of the segregationists.

"I have a constitutional duty and obligation from which I shall not shrink," he said.

Later that afternoon, Superintendent Blossom called a last-minute meeting with as many parents as could attend and instructed them to send their children to Central the next day alone. The presence of the parents might incite even more trouble at the school, he told them. My parents could have decided right then that the risks were too high and withdrawn me from Central. I'm grateful that they did not. Instead, they remained calm and resolute. In a rare newspaper interview, Daddy later explained to a *Gazette* reporter why he didn't back down:

"Only one thought ever crossed my mind about the whole thing. She had a right to go there. My tax money is not separated from the rest of the tax money. There was no reason for her to pass one high school to go to another."

Daddy believed we were doing the right thing. He and Mother were among the youngest of the black parents sending their children to Central, and they deeply respected the leadership of Mrs. Bates and the other parents involved, particularly Mrs. Green, Ernie's mother, my first-grade teacher. If Central was safe enough for Mrs. Green's son, they figured, then surely it was safe enough for me.

After the meeting with Blossom, Mrs. Bates gave us the good news: School was back on for the next day. Besides Ernie and Gloria, I still wasn't sure who would join me at Central. Several students had changed their minds when they first heard from Blossom that they would have to give up all of their extracurricular activities. I'd just have to wait and see. Sometime after midnight, Mrs. Bates called again to tell my parents to drop me off at eight-thirty a.m. at 13th and Park streets, about a block from the school. An interracial group of ministers would meet us there to escort us to school, she said. We wouldn't have to walk alone.

The next morning, September 4, I popped out of bed without hesitation. It was really going to happen, I thought. The anticipation of walking up those regal steps into Central made each moment seem to tick by slowly. Questions filled my head: Who else would be there from Dunbar and Mann? What would the teachers be like? What about the students? Would I make new friends? Was I ready to compete with them academically? How long would it take me to learn my way around that huge campus?

Finally, it was time to go. Mother and I climbed into the car shortly after eight a.m. and headed down 14th Street to Valmer to 13th and cruised toward Park. We noticed a small group of students and two black ministers whom Mother recognized gathering near the intersection. This was the meeting spot, and Mother pulled to a stop. She looked relieved when she saw Reverend

Harry Bass, who had been my pastor at White Memorial. He now
served as pastor of Wesley Chapel Methodist Church on the campus of Philander Smith. It was one of Little Rock's largest black
Methodist churches and where the Cullins side of my family attended. Mother also knew the other black minister who was there,
Reverend Z. Z. Dryver, the father of one of my friends at Dunbar.
She trusted these men, and I'm sure it comforted her to leave me in
such good hands. Three older white ministers and a young white
man, none of whom I knew, were there, too. I said good-bye to
Mother, hopped out of the car, and made my way over to the
group. As I walked toward them, I saw Ernie, Gloria, and another
student I recognized, Jefferson Thomas, a fellow sophomore who
had been president of the student council at Dunbar the previous
year. I had worked closely with him as vice president, so I knew
him pretty well. There were three other students I didn't know, but
I learned their names pretty quickly: Thelma Mothershed, Minnijean Brown, and Jane Hill, a tall, quiet girl who seemed a bit more
uncomfortable than the rest. We chatted anxiously until one of the
ministers approached and said it was time to get moving. But first,
he said, we needed to pray. We formed a tight circle and bowed our
heads as the reverend asked God to walk with us, strengthen and
protect us. Then the adults put us in formation. Out front were the
four white men: Reverend Dunbar Ogden, Jr., president of the
Greater Little Rock Ministerial Association; his twenty-one-year-
old son, David; Reverend Will Campbell of the Nashville-based
National Council of Churches; and Reverend George Chauncey of
First Presbyterian Church in Monticello, a small town in southern
Arkansas. The students lined up by twos in the middle. Reverends
Bass and Dryver held up the rear. Now, it was time to go.

Slowly and silently, our group began moving in tandem up
Park Street toward the school. I could hear the rumble of a crowd
up ahead. It was loud, like a Dunbar football game–size crowd. I
clutched my notebook and moved with the group through the

sticky September air. With every step, the hooting and hollering grew louder. As we got closer to 14th Street, I glanced toward the Mobil gas station on the other side of the street, and for the first time I saw it—a mob of people that stretched as far as I could see. The sheer size of the crowd was shocking. There must have been hundreds of people—white mothers with faces contorted in anger, white fathers pumping their fists in the air and shouting, white teenagers and children waving Confederate flags and mimicking their parents. Just who were these people? Were they the women who turned up their noses and murmured nasty words at Mother and me on the city bus? Were they the white customers I saw from time to time with Big Daddy at the meatpacking houses downtown? Were they my white neighbors? The scene felt surreal. With everyone screaming and jeering at once, their words sounded muddled, except for one: *nigger . . . nigger . . . nigger.* It shot out of angry mouths like bullets and pierced my ears again and again.

Adrenaline pulsed through my body and quickened the pace of my heart. But I wasn't afraid. The mob was too far away to stop me from getting inside. The front entrance of the school was now in sight, and the military was just steps ahead. I was more perplexed than anything else. I had never seen such raw anger up close before. And this was directed at me. For what? Because I wanted to go to school? I turned away and remembered Mother's and Daddy's words:

They're just ignorant, low-class people. They're just trying to scare you. Do not stoop to their level. You are a Walls. Just take the next step, and the next.

Finally, we were staring into the faces of the Arkansas National Guard. The guardsmen had formed a ring around the school. They blocked the entrance, but I was certain that when they saw us, they would just step aside and allow us through. They were, after all, there to protect us and keep out the troublemakers, I thought. But not one of them budged. Instead, the commander, Lieutenant

Colonel Marion Johnson, whose name I was to discover later, stepped forward. Commander Johnson assumed Reverend Ogden was our leader and began addressing him. The rest of us gathered closely around. I stood to the side of Johnson, who had both hands clutched unnaturally tight around a billy club. His knuckles looked white. Ernie, pressing his lips together nervously, stood beside me. That put him almost face-to-face with the officer. Gloria stood behind me, and behind her, Jane towered over us all. Johnson told Reverend Ogden that on the orders of Faubus, we would not be permitted to enter the school. The commander's words stunned me. There was a huge disconnect in my head. The guardsmen weren't there to protect us; they were there to keep us out. As the message washed over me, I thought:

You've got to be kidding.

Ernie, the only senior among us, spoke up: "You're not going to let us in? Is that what you're telling us?"

The officer repeated his order for us to leave. His men stood resolutely in formation, still blocking us out, their rifles slung across their chest. Our group stood there for a moment, not quite sure what to do. And then the ministers turned and led us silently away. The mob continued yelling in the distance, but this time, I barely heard any of it. I was completely stunned. I'd never missed a day of school in my life. I still could not believe that I was standing just steps from the schoolhouse door, wanting desperately just to go to class, and the powers that be wouldn't let me in. The highest court in the land had said I had a right to be at that school, to learn, just like the white children. What would it take to open those closed ears and change their hardened hearts?

For the rest of the day, I felt out of sync, isolated. I kept thinking that all of my good friends were in school, where I should have been. But as bad as I felt, nothing could compare with the sorrow that came over me when I clicked on the television news that evening and saw in black-and-white what had happened to Eliza-

beth Eckford, a junior who was supposed to be with our group
that day.

I didn't know Elizabeth personally. But, as was common in the
black community, our families knew each other. She and some of
her siblings had attended Stephens Elementary, and her father periodically worked for one of my great-uncles. Her grandfather also
owned a neighborhood grocery store just across the street from Big
Daddy's pool hall and café. But the Eckfords didn't have a telephone, and as Mrs. Bates later described in her memoir, Elizabeth
didn't get the word about our meeting place. Mrs. Bates had intended to try to reach her that morning, and in the hurried pace of
the day, she just forgot. Unfortunately, Elizabeth walked right into
the mob, which surrounded and terrorized her. There she was on
my television screen, walking silently and alone in her crisp black-
and-white dress. Her face looked solemn, and she wore dark sun-
glasses, which I'm sure must have hidden her tears. She was
followed by some of the same angry men, women, and children I
had seen from a distance earlier that day. But they were right on
Elizabeth, shouting at her, spitting at her, clawing at her, not the
least bit concerned that television cameras were capturing it all for
eternity. That iconic image of Elizabeth surrounded by the mob
would circle the globe and outrage the world.

The next day, *The New York Times* would run this account of
the moment when a lone white woman—Grace Lorch, whose husband taught at Philander Smith College—came to Elizabeth's aid:

> The Negro girl . . . sat on a bench. She seemed in a state of
> shock. A white woman, Mrs. Grace Lorch, walked over to
> comfort her.
>
> "What are you doing, you nigger lover?" Mrs. Lorch was
> asked. "You stay away from that girl."
>
> "She's scared," Mrs. Lorch said. "She's just a little girl."
> She appealed to the men and women around her.

"Why don't you calm down?" she asked. "I'm not here to fight with you. Six months from now you'll be ashamed of what you're doing."

"Go home, you're just one of them," Mrs. Lorch was told.

She escorted the Negro student to the other side of the street, but the crowd followed.

"Won't somebody please call a taxi?" she pleaded. She was met with hoot calls and jeers.

Finally, after being jostled by the crowd, she worked her way to the street corner, and the two boarded a bus.

Two others who were supposed to be part of our group, Melba Pattillo and Terrence Roberts, both juniors, also walked separately into the mob that morning. But each of them managed to slip away. I didn't know Melba, but Terrence had been president of the student council at Dunbar while I was vice president in my eighth-grade year. That would have been ten black students who showed up with intentions to enter Central. But after that morning, Jane Hill, the tall, quiet girl who had made that first terrible walk with us, never returned.

That left nine of us.

None of us had any idea how long it would be before we were allowed to go to school. One day turned into two days, which turned into a week and then another. When I wasn't at home, the nine of us often could be found at the home of Mr. and Mrs. Bates. The couple lived on West 28th Street in a middle-class neighborhood that was a collage of small wood-and-brick houses. The Bates home was a yellowish brick ranch model with a large picture window facing the street. To the national civil rights leaders who came to town to assist in the case and the reporters who covered it, the house on West 28th Street became the unofficial headquarters for the nine of us trying to enter Central. We were interviewed there, we met politicians there, and we heard words of encouragement and lectures about the importance of our mission there. It became our home away from home, and Mr. and Mrs. Bates were our trusted guardians. Mr. Bates was tall and lean, with a narrow face, deep brown skin, and short gray hair. He was much older than his wife, grandfatherly to me, very low-key, gentle, and reassuring. While he was a longtime activist who used his newspaper to advocate for civil rights, it was Mrs. Bates who rose to the limelight. She wouldn't be caught anywhere without being perfectly made up, head to toe, but pity the man who mistook her ladylike ways as a sign of weakness. She was tough to the core, with razor-sharp edges. And she demanded respect. Her objection to the treatment she received from an attorney for the Little Rock School Board during a court hearing in a separate case a year earlier had made front-page news. The NAACP was in court in 1956, attempting to force the school board to speed up its plans to desegregate. But during questioning, Mrs. Bates stopped the attorney in his tracks:

"You addressed me several times this morning by my first name," she told him. "That is something that is reserved for my intimate friends and my husband. You will refrain from calling me Daisy."

The attorney retorted: "I won't call you anything, then."

Mrs. Bates shot back: "That's fine."

The next morning, all of Little Rock read about the gutsy NAACP president in a front-page story in the *Gazette*.

Over the weeks that my cohorts and I were out of school, Mrs. Bates became our point person—the one who arranged media interviews and often the one who spoke for us. She was ahead of her time as far as the media was concerned. She was naturally at ease under the glow of television lights and quick to fire off the perfect quote. I didn't understand then how necessary the media was to this greater good the nine of us had been anointed to carry out. I was just one who never liked a whole lot of hoopla. So from the start I was uncomfortable with the constant throng of people always around us, asking questions, taking pictures. No matter the time of day or night, it seemed somebody was always at the Bateses' house. Journalists. Politicians. NAACP fieldworkers. Sometimes the guests bunked in the couple's basement. Sometimes they even stayed next door at the home of Dr. Garman Freeman, a dentist who was also married to a dentist. Theirs was an entire community of like-minded people. Dr. Lee Lorch, head of the math department at Philander Smith, and his wife, Grace, the white woman who had helped lead Elizabeth to safety on September 4, lived just across the street.

When I could, I'd slip away from them all, find a quiet corner somewhere, pull out my books, and at least try to look busy—a tactic I began using to deflect attention. When the nine of us were together as a group, I tried to be inconspicuous and just fade into the background. I never liked the feeling of being on display. I think Mrs. Bates eventually came to understand that about me and just let me be. I always appreciated that about her, and I've come to understand and appreciate her even more now that I'm older. She took a lot of the heat off our parents. They weren't hounded by the press and got to stay mostly in the background. For that leadership, she was already paying a heavy price—threatening telephone calls every day, a cross burned in her yard, and a rock slammed through her picture window in the middle of the night with a message that promised dynamite the next time. And the nine of us hadn't even made it inside the school yet.

After the first week of our missing classes, Mrs. Bates arranged for our teachers at Central to send homework packets containing our schoolwork so that we could at least make a valiant effort to keep up with our classmates. I saw my schedule for the first time when I received a homework packet. I was enrolled in English, geometry, biology, Spanish, gym, and speech. The Lorches pulled together a group of Philander Smith professors and other teachers to tutor us and help with our schoolwork. Dr. Lorch was particularly helpful to me because I struggled with geometry, which seemed so different from algebra. I occasionally took the bus to Philander Smith in the afternoon or evening when he was available to work with me. When I finished my schoolwork, I turned it in to Mrs. Bates, who arranged to get it to our teachers. What happened to it after that, I don't know. I wouldn't have been able to keep up without the help of Dr. Lorch and the other tutors. But I missed going to school. I missed the daily interaction with teachers, the give-and-take in the classroom that sometimes helped the textbooks make sense. I wondered how long it would be before I got to meet the teachers face-to-face and whether they would resent my presence as much as the mob that continued to gather each morning outside the school. I grew more and more anxious that I was falling behind in school, especially since no one seemed to have any idea how long the wait would be. I think all nine of us felt that way. Clusters of us had known one another before our fates thrust us together, but during all of those meetings and meals at the home of Mr. and Mrs. Bates, the nine of us began getting to know one another as friends.

On television, we often heard ourselves referred to as "the nine" or "the Little Rock Nine" in the same way that people sometimes identify twins, as if they have no separate identities. But we were growing more comfortable around one another, and I was starting to get a real sense of the distinct personalities. Ernie was the oldest, coolheaded and serious. His status as the lone senior seemed to catapult him into the position of our leader. He was usually the one Mrs. Bates and the press grabbed to speak for the group. Melba and Minnijean were the gregarious ones, both outgoing and outspoken. They were also good friends, singers, and quite comfortable in front of the cameras. Terry was a young intellectual who was always at the top of his class. But he also had a fun side, a dry, witty sense of humor that kept me in stitches. Elizabeth seemed painfully shy. She had expressive doe eyes that seemed to reveal a hint of sadness. She could barely even make eye contact when she spoke. There was a sweet innocence about her and an easy, trusting nature. Thelma was quiet, too, but she seemed the most fragile among us. Aside from being physically small—just about five feet tall and less than one hundred pounds— she had a heart condition that made everybody want to protect her. Jefferson was a sophomore, like me, and everyone's pampered baby brother, a bit naive, but athletic and smart. He was always joking around and somehow seemed to find humor in even the most serious situations. He also loved music and had an unbeliev- ably large and varied record collection. Gloria was the other soph- omore. She was mature and dignified, petite and dainty. She also had what most teenagers envied: her own car. I had a December birthday, which made me the youngest of the bunch, but from the time I was a little girl, people always said that something about me seemed old. Maybe it's my way with all kinds of people. I don't know. But I got along well with everybody, and in the days ahead, I would be called in to referee when some of the personalities began to collide.

Mrs. Bates understood the anxiety the nine of us felt about being out of school, and she tried her best each day to assure us that things would be resolved soon. Thurgood Marshall was com- ing to town to represent us, she said. That really excited me. He was already high on my list of heroes. Even before successfully pre- senting the *Brown* case in the Supreme Court, he had argued a case in Little Rock that involved my uncle Byron Johnson. He was among a group of black teachers at Dunbar who had demanded equal pay with the white teachers in the 1940s. The NAACP and Marshall took on the Little Rock School Board in that case and won. I knew we were in good hands.

Judging from what I was reading in the newspapers, we would need someone of Marshall's status to battle our hardheaded governor. By now, I was reading the newspaper practically every day. The adults involved were spare with the details, when they talked about the case at all. But the local newspapers and the black press helped me keep up with what was going on. I followed the legal wrangling, which seemed nonstop. Just three days after the National Guard blocked our entry into Central, the school board was back in court, asking for a suspension of its own desegregation plan. Davies took just four minutes to refuse the request. His message was clear: Integrate now. Then, following up on an investigation ordered by Davies, the U.S. Justice Department filed a petition asking the court to force the governor to remove the National Guard and comply with the desegregation order. The department's investigation had found no credence to the governor's claims that he called out the National Guard to keep the peace based on evidence that violence would erupt at Central if black students were admitted. The investigation determined that Faubus had acted purely as a segregationist with the sole purpose of keeping out the black students. Davies scheduled the courtroom showdown on that matter for September 20.

Meanwhile, it was hard to miss the political maneuvering, too. Thurgood Marshall and others had begun urging President Eisenhower to get involved. Initially reluctant, the president responded to a telegram from Faubus objecting to the "extreme stand" from the federal court. The two men decided to meet at Eisenhower's summer home in Rhode Island on September 14. The nine of us happened to be meeting with Mrs. Bates at her home that day when we saw a television report about the meeting. We gathered around the television in the basement and watched as Faubus and Eisenhower emerged from the meeting smiling. The men shook hands for the cameras. I sighed with relief. It appeared that a favorable agreement had been reached. With excitement, I pronounced to the group:

"And now, we'll go to school on Monday!"

But Mrs. Bates quickly shot back: "Well, not so fast."

Experience had taught her caution. As it turned out, she was right. Despite Eisenhower's declaration that the two had engaged in a "constructive discussion," the men had reached no agreement. Nothing changed. We'd have to wait nearly another week for the September 20 court hearing.

I had never been inside a courtroom until that day. My friend Bunny, who was home from the private school she attended in North Carolina, went along to offer her support. I didn't know what to expect, and as we walked inside, I could feel my palms getting sweaty. The courtroom was still, dark, and quiet. I could almost hear myself breathe. I took a seat near the front. When the judge entered, he sat behind the large mahogany desk before us. He was small and serious. But my eyes stayed mostly on Mr. Marshall. Bunny and I were mesmerized by this attorney who had the swagger and aura of a movie star. I had never seen a black professional with more confidence. Here was a black man striding up and down this courtroom with the certainty that this was where he belonged. Tall and lean, with closely cropped black hair, he was as handsome as he was smart. And he did not tread lightly. I suppose I had been conditioned to expect diplomacy, perhaps even deference, from a black lawyer practicing in a room full of white people. It was the southern way. But not this man. He spoke his mind, and he did so unapologetically, indignantly. He commanded respect, and respect is what he got, especially from Judge Davies.

I added Judge Davies to my list of civil rights heroes that day, too. He treated Mr. Marshall with the respect he deserved, a respect that might not have been as forthcoming if one of the white southern judges had been presiding. Davies was destined, it seemed, to become a part of this chapter in history. Eisenhower had appointed him to the federal bench in North Dakota two years earlier, and Davies was dispatched to Little Rock on a temporary assignment in August 1957. One of the first cases to hit his desk would become the most high-profile and significant of his career.

In stature, Davies stood barely five feet tall. But he was fearless and unfailingly fair in the face of segregationists willing to try just about anything to have their way. Faubus and his attorneys even questioned whether Davies had the proper authority to preside over the school desegregation case since his jurisdiction was North Dakota. But Davies rejected their challenge and kept right on moving. Like Marshall, the judge didn't mince words. In one of the earlier hearings, he told Faubus: "The testimony and arguments this morning were, in my judgment, as anemic as the petition itself. . . . In an organized society there can be nothing but ultimate confusion and chaos if court decrees are flouted, whatever the pretext."

Faubus didn't attend the September 20 hearing. Instead, he sent his attorneys. But they soon grew frustrated after Davies overruled them several times. Before the hearing was over, they gathered their papers and announced that they were leaving. It caused quite a buzz in the courtroom. Judge Davies slapped his gavel on the desk.

"The hearing will continue," he said.

I was so proud of Ernie and Elizabeth, who were called to testify. They answered questions thoughtfully and articulately about why they wanted to attend Central and what happened when we had tried to enter on September 4. And of course, Mr. Marshall did not disappoint. He gave a rousing closing argument. In one simple but powerful moment, he turned and pointed at Ernie, Minnie, and me, shook his head, full of righteous indignation, and said:

"These young people should be in school."

Judge Davies didn't take long to render his decision: The National Guard had to go. Faubus could no longer use the troops to block our entrance into Central. With that, Davies banged his gavel once more, and court was adjourned. The room was filled with supporters, who filed quietly out of the courtroom. But I was absolutely jubilant. I'd just seen everything I'd learned about the Constitution, the judicial process, and justice come to life. Justice had been served. I assumed that meant our ordeal was finally over. I turned to Mrs. Bates and said:

"This means we can go to school!"

Her caution again caught me off guard.

"We'll see," she responded, not sounding excited at all.

I was disappointed. I didn't understand her lack of enthusiasm.

That night, Faubus went on a statewide radio broadcast and announced that he was withdrawing the troops from Central in compliance with the federal order. He lambasted Davies and the Department of Justice. He also took one more swipe at the NAACP. He urged the group to back off of its integration plans in favor of a voluntary "cooling-off period." And he threatened the possibility of bloodshed.

I went to bed that night feeling completely deflated. The weekend was yet ahead. Anything could happen. Bunny was headed back to school in North Carolina. The National Guard was gone. And the governor was peddling fear. After what I'd seen of that mob outside Central, I couldn't be sure that his threat wasn't real. I had no idea whether my parents were thinking that, too.

Outdoors, a storm raged, casting a gloomy pall over the entire city. The weather was mimicking my mood. The big day was set for Monday, September 23. But a world of doubt lay between this moment and that one. Mrs. Bates was right. I'd just have to wait and see.

CHAPTER 5

D-Day

When I opened my eyes the morning of September 23, the first thing I noticed was the sun. It streamed into my bedroom through a pair of bare, horizontal windows near the ceiling. After such a wet and gloomy weekend, this was surely a good sign. The National Guard troops were gone, and the court order still stood. Once again, I put on my new, store-bought dress.

The plan was to meet at the home of Mr. and Mrs. Bates and wait for instructions from the city police, which now had the responsibility of protecting us. When Mother and I arrived by seven forty-five a.m., several of the other students and their parents were already there. The front yard and living room were abuzz with media, snapping photographs, shooting television footage, conducting interviews, and darting here and there. As usual, I skirted past them with little notice and joined the cluster of students. Soon, our long wait would be over. By eight a.m., all nine of us were there. We chatted anxiously about our "first" day of school—which classes we had, which ones we feared, what our teachers might be like. I think all of us recognized what *could* happen. We'd seen the mob outside the school. Elizabeth had even been close enough to feel its wrath. But I didn't want to talk—or even think—about the danger. None of us did.

The police called a little while later and instructed Mrs. Bates to transport us to a side entrance of the school, away from the crowd gathering out front. It was time for us to go, Mrs. Bates said. We hugged our parents and headed out. I was excited to be finally starting school. Each day out had been worrisome for me. Despite trying to keep up with the homework, I couldn't help wondering what I was missing by not being in class, and I worried about falling behind. I would work extra hard and do whatever it took to make up for the lost time, I promised myself. Before heading out the door, I glanced back at Mother, and she had that look on her face again—the smile that didn't match the worry in her eyes. The nine of us then piled into two cars, driven by NAACP officials, for the short ride to Central. As we drew closer to the side of the school, I could hear the muffled sounds of a crowd beyond the car's closed windows. Though the school building mostly blocked my full view of the crowd gathered out front, I knew the mob was back. They were not going to give up their fight easily. But neither was I. The cars carrying us rolled up to the curb, one behind the other, and pulled quickly to a stop next to the side entrance. The drivers hopped out and yanked open the car doors. Suddenly, the chants and jeers of the crowd sounded deafening:

"Two, four, six, eight, we ain't gonna integrate . . ."

I stepped out of the car and moved swiftly behind the other students. I had no time to think or worry about what the crowd was saying or doing. Just take one step and then another, I told myself. In no time, all nine of us were at the side door. We rushed through a set of large double doors, which closed quickly behind us and shut out the light. No one made a sound, but we kept moving rapidly through the darkness. I just followed the footsteps up some stairs and then up another set, into the light. Next, there was a long hallway, and we stopped just outside the main office, where we were met by a primly dressed white woman with graying hair and glasses. She seemed very professional and pleasant enough as she handed us our schedules and pointed the way to our classes. I would come to know her as Elizabeth Huckaby, my English teacher and the vice principal for girls. As my eight comrades and I were preparing to head to our classes for the first time, the crowd outside was growing steadily and working itself into a frenzy. The chaos had started even before we arrived. News photographers and reporters captured the upheaval that unfurled when four black journalists who had been with us at the Bateses' home made it to the scene just moments ahead of us.

Alex Wilson, editor of the Memphis-based *Tri-State Defender,* and Moses Newson, on assignment for the *Baltimore Afro-American,* led the way, inching toward the rowdy crowd to cover the scene. They were followed by James L. Hicks, editor of the *Amsterdam News* in New York, and Earl Davy, a freelance photographer who often took photos for the newspaper owned by Mr. and Mrs. Bates. Two white men began following them.

"Go home, you son of a bitch nigger!" one of them yelled.

A few more white men leapt in front of the journalists with outstretched hands to block their path.

"We are newspapermen," Wilson retorted.

"We only want to do our jobs," Hicks added.

But the taunting only continued. The crowd quickly swelled, and mayhem broke out. Someone threatened a lynching. Others lunged into the black journalists, kicking, punching, and spitting at them. The attackers slammed Davy's Graflex camera to the concrete sidewalk and chased him, while another group attacked Newson and Hicks until they were finally able to escape. But Wilson, a veteran journalist and former war correspondent, stood his ground. He had seen this kind of hatred up close as he traveled throughout the South covering civil rights, including the Emmett Till trial in the fall of 1955. As Wilson picked up his wide-brimmed hat and straightened himself, one of the ringleaders ordered him to run. But Wilson, a lanky ex-marine who stood six feet four inches tall, refused. Incensed by this man's proud composure, the mob grew more virulent in their attack. Finally, one of them delivered a crushing blow to the back of Wilson's head with a heavy object believed to have been a brick. The tall black man tumbled to the ground. In his own account of the incident, Wilson later wrote that a vision of Elizabeth Eckford "as she with dignity strode through a jeering, hooting gauntlet of segregationists" had flashed in his mind and given him the courage to face the mob on his feet. But Wilson never fully recovered from the beating. He developed a nervous condition widely reported as Parkinson's disease and died three years later at age fifty-one.

I was horrified when I saw the attack on the evening news. As leery as I was of the press, I felt a kind of kinship with the black reporters who were risking their own lives to tell our collective story. They were accomplished professionals, but in the wooded hamlets and Klan territory throughout Mississippi, Alabama, and on this day Little Rock, they were as reviled as the subjects they traveled miles to cover. But they kept coming and kept writing, long before the mainstream press jumped on board. Mother read her black newspapers and magazines with a kind of religious devotion. That's how she kept up with what was going on with our people, she said. When I read the news accounts of the attack on Mr. Wilson and his colleagues over the following days, I realized that the four of them had unwittingly become decoys for the nine of us. There was much speculation then about whether there was some kind of agreement for those four men to distract the crowd while the nine of us entered the building, but Wilson and his colleagues all denied it. I was never told of any such deal, either. Of course, as a fourteen-year-old, I likely wouldn't have been privy to such information anyhow, but I've never believed that those four journalists were doing anything in that moment other than their jobs.

Eventually that morning, someone in the crowd recognized that while the journalists were being savagely beaten, the nine of us were entering the school building. The hysteria immediately shifted our way. By then, though, the doors already had shut behind us. Benjamin Fine, the *New York Times* reporter who had catapulted our story to the front page of his newspaper weeks earlier, gave this account:

> "They've gone in," a man shouted.
>
> "Oh, God," said a woman, "the niggers are in school."
>
> A group of six girls, dressed in skirts and sweaters, hair in ponytails, started to shriek and wail.
>
> "The niggers are in our school," they howled hysterically.
>
> One of them jumped up and down on the sidewalk, waving her arms toward her classmates in the school who were looking out of the windows, and screamed over and over again:
>
> "Come on out, come on out."
>
> Tears flowed down her face, her body shook in uncontrollable spasms.
>
> Three of her classmates grew hysterical, and threw their arms around each other. They began dancing up and down.
>
> "The niggers are in," they shrieked, "come on out of the school. Don't stay there with the niggers. Come on out . . . come on . . ."

Unable to get to us, the crowd began turning on the white journalists covering the scene. Among those attacked were a *Life* magazine reporter and two of its photographers, whose equipment was yanked and smashed. As that sickening spate of violence unfolded, I was likely stepping into my first class of the day, Mrs. Huckaby's English class, where I was oblivious to the commotion outside. Because Mrs. Huckaby was a vice principal, her class was just down the hall from the main office, not far from where I had ended up after first entering the school. I just followed her down the hall, and as soon as I walked into her classroom, she directed me to a desk in the first row, two seats from the door. She didn't smile

readily, and she wasn't particularly warm. I would come to understand that it had nothing to do with me; she treated everyone the
same. But I could tell from the outset that she was fair. She didn't
tolerate any name-calling, and at the first sight of any snickering or
taunts, she shut it down immediately. She also kept her eyes on a
small group of boys in the back who were most likely to cause
trouble. She wouldn't hesitate to file a disciplinary report, she
warned, and since she was an administrator, her threat carried
weight. In the weeks and months ahead, her sense of fair play
would cause trouble for her among the segregationists, who considered her too sympathetic to us, and thus, the enemy.

As I slid into my chair in her class that morning, I could feel all
eyes fastened on me. That was one of the things I hated most—
being the center of attention. My insides knotted with dread. I
wished to be invisible. I stared at my desktop, the worn hardwood
floors, Mrs. Huckaby's face, anywhere to avoid the hot gaze of my
classmates. Mrs. Huckaby didn't miss a beat, trying to go on with
class as though this were a regular day. But there was nothing regular about this. I tried mightily, but I couldn't concentrate. Why
wouldn't they stop staring at me? This was not at all how I had
imagined feeling on the first day inside my new school.

Finally, the bell rang, but momentary relief turned quickly to
even more serious dread. Hundreds of students spilled from their
classes into the halls. The noise level was louder than the loudest
football game I'd ever attended. Every face in the crowd was
white, and they all seemed to be staring at me, sneering at me. A
group of slick-haired boys with their black leather jackets and
white T-shirts with cigarettes rolled in them—poor imitations of
James Dean and Elvis Presley—purposely walked too close,
bumped me hard with their shoulders, and swaggered off, laughing at "that nigger." The word was slung at me so often that day
that my heart turned almost numb. I tried to tune out their words,
their stares, and their finger-pointing, but to no avail. A few stu-

dents looked my way sympathetically, almost as though they were ashamed of their schoolmates' behavior. But they also seemed afraid to smile, afraid to say hello, afraid to be seen showing even minimal empathy. Their sympathetic eyes quickly looked away as soon as they met mine. I yearned to see a kind face, something or someone familiar. Where were the other black students? I saw no sign of them anywhere. I felt so completely alone. Somehow, I made it to my second- and third-period classes and each time was assigned to the first row, a couple of seats from the door. By third period, my nerves were starting to settle a bit. This was geometry, the class I most feared, and I knew I didn't have another moment to waste. My teacher, Margaret Reiman, was a strict disciplinarian who, like Mrs. Huckaby, didn't tolerate any nonsense. Her stern face and voice set the tone. She would put up with no disruptions, she announced firmly. We had much work to do, and she moved quickly into the business of class. The atmosphere was calm for about the first twenty minutes. Then came a knock on the door. I was close enough to see a uniformed officer standing on the other side. Mrs. Reiman walked to the door and stuck her head out. I kept my eyes on the two of them as they talked briefly. As my teacher stepped back into the class, I searched her face for clues. Was something wrong? But her face was blank as she announced:

"Carlotta Walls, get your books and follow the gentleman outside."

Get my books? My heart sank. I knew I was leaving again for the day.

"Follow me," the officer said, turning quickly and stepping speedily down the hall.

This time, the hallway was empty and quiet, except for the officer's heavy footsteps. As I tried to keep pace with him, my mind turned back to geometry. I couldn't afford to miss another math class. This was my weakest subject. I didn't know anyone yet, so how would I be able to make up the next day's assignment? I'd missed far too much already. The thoughts and questions in my mind made the trek to the office seem short. Once I stepped inside, though, all thoughts about geometry ceased. I could tell right away that something was seriously wrong. My eight comrades were already gathered there with their books. They looked frightened and confused. Before I could ask any questions, another officer commanded: "This way!"

Even with my long legs, I almost had to trot to keep up. I had no idea where we were going or why, but we were in a hurry. It was a labyrinthine descent—around a corner and down some steps several times until we arrived in the mechanics classroom three floors below on the ground level. The classroom was an enclosed garage. Two police cars sat parked inside the garage on a ramp. An officer waiting there instructed us to get in quickly. Then, someone handed us several blankets and told us to lie low and hide.

"Put your foot to the floor," my driver was told. "And don't stop for anything."

Now, I was terrified. We were on the run from something, but what? As I lay crouched on the backseat, I lifted my head from under the blanket. I had to see what was going on. If I was going to die, I wanted to see it coming. I heard a loud grinding noise and realized that the garage doors were opening. Streaks of light gradually filled the garage. Then, suddenly, the two police cars shot out of the garage into the light and sped down a gravel drive, past the Campus Inn, the on-site diner where the white students hung out for burgers and Cokes at lunch. I prayed no one was crossing the sidewalk there, or they surely would have been killed. As we whizzed down 16th Street, past the stadium, away from the school, I craned my neck but couldn't see anything more than the back of the school. The four of us in the back were too frightened even to speak. The officer sped down streets and whipped around corners until he had dropped the other three students in the car with me at their homes. I was the last one to be dropped off. By the time he rounded the corner and pulled to a stop in front of my house, my heart was sprinting.

"Thank you," I said politely as I hopped out and headed up the front steps.

Mother met me at the door. This time, she didn't even try to hide her fear. Her face was as pale as a sheet of paper, and her eyes were red. I'm certain that her jet black hair started graying that day. She threw her arms around me.

"Are you okay?" she asked repeatedly.

News of the mob had been on the radio all morning, she said. Wild and erroneous reports about students being beaten and bloodied had even made it to the airwaves. Newscasters were saying the crowd had grown to more than one thousand people and that police could no longer control them. That's when I realized why we had left in such a hurry. Relatives had been calling all day, and their message was unified: Get Carlotta out of that school!

I retreated to my room and took off my new dress. Maybe, I thought, the darn dress brought bad luck. I slipped on my "after-school" clothes, plopped down on the living room sofa, and stared out of the picture window at the dirt road in front of the house. My eyes fell on my church up the road. I wondered: Where was God in all of this? Was it He who had spared us from the wrath of that mob? What if they had gotten inside? Would they really have lynched us? I couldn't understand their fury. All this because they didn't want their children to sit next to me in school? I had heard white parents complain in television interviews that school integration could lead to race mixing and interracial marriage. Was this the source of their rage? If so, it seemed silly to me. I wasn't even old enough to date yet. Would my first day at Central be my last? There was nothing left to do but wait.

While I waited for word about what would happen next, I had no idea that at 6:24 p.m., Little Rock mayor Woodrow Mann was sending a telegram to President Eisenhower—one that ultimately would help to influence the final outcome. The city and state police had tried valiantly to control the mob at Central, Mayor Mann wrote, but the situation ultimately was determined to be too unsafe for the nine of us to remain in school.

"In the final analysis it was deemed advisable by the officer on the ground and in charge to have the colored children removed to their homes for safety purposes," he wrote.

News reports painted a picture of a city out of control with random mobs roaming the streets, terrorizing any black residents they could find. In black neighborhoods throughout the city, lights were off, curtains were drawn, and streets were still and quiet.

The same day, President Eisenhower released a statement:

I want to make several things very clear in connection with the disgraceful occurrences of today at Central High School in the city of Little Rock. They are:

1. The federal law and orders of a United States District Court, implementing that law, cannot be flouted with impunity by any individual, or any mob of extremists.

2. I will use the full power of the United States, including whatever force may be necessary to prevent any obstruction of the law and to carry out the orders of the Federal Court.

3. Of course, every right-thinking citizen will hope that the American sense of justice and fair play will prevail in this case. It will be a sad day for this country—both at home and abroad—if school children can safely attend their classes only under the protection of armed guards.

4. I repeat my expressed confidence that the citizens of Little Rock and of Arkansas will respect the law and will not countenance violations of law and order by extremists.

President Eisenhower also issued an emergency proclamation barring anyone from blocking the school and interfering with the federal court's desegregation order. But the next morning, I awakened to news reports that the mob had again gathered outside Central—one thousand people strong. I spent the day indoors, glued to the television. The telephone rang constantly, but I no longer moved to try to answer it. At the first ring, Mother or Daddy would yell from wherever they were in the house, "I'll get it," and then dash to make it to the phone before my sisters or me. Sometimes they just stood there quietly for a few seconds and hung up without saying a word. But sometimes, I could see the anger on Daddy's face as he slammed down the receiver. Neither of them ever said a word to me about those phone calls, but they didn't have to. I knew what was going on. I knew it was those nasty men and women from the street, and I could only imagine the vile words they spat into the phone. I hated to see the worry I was causing Mother and Daddy. This was a particularly low day for me. When would it all end? Would we ever get inside and get to meet our classmates at Central without the circus atmosphere? Would they ever get to know us and realize that they had nothing to fear?

This time, Mayor Mann sent a more urgent telegram to President Eisenhower. At 9:16 a.m., he wrote:

"The immediate need for federal troops is urgent. The mob is much larger in numbers at 8 a.m. than at any time yesterday. People are converging on the scene from all directions. Mob is armed and engaging in fisticuffs and other acts of violence. Situation is out of control. . . ."

President Eisenhower followed up on his promise that his actions would be "quick, hard, and decisive" and signed an executive order to use military force to protect the nine of us. That night, I watched with my family as the president announced on television that he had called out the troops of the 101st Airborne Division to ensure that the federal school desegregation court order was carried out.

"To make this talk, I have come to the president's office in the White House," he began. "I could have spoken from Rhode Island, where I have been staying recently, but I felt that, in speaking from the house of Lincoln, of Jackson, and of Wilson, my words would better convey both the sadness I feel in the action I was compelled today to take and the firmness with which I intend to pursue this course until the orders at Little Rock can be executed without unlawful interference."

My spirits perked up. More than one thousand paratroopers were already on their way to Little Rock from Fort Campbell, Kentucky, President Eisenhower said. He also announced that he was placing the Arkansas National Guard under federal orders. The media called the move historic, the first time a U.S. president had called on the military to enforce a federal school desegregation order. But my first thought was: What took so long? The restless teenager I was then, I figured the federal government should have swooped in when Faubus first snubbed the orders of the nation's highest court. I don't feel much differently now, but I am tremendously grateful that President Eisenhower stepped in when he did. I strongly believe it was his military background—the general in him—that gave him the fortitude and forthrightness to stand up to a loudmouthed governor who ultimately would go to his grave arguing that his decision to use the National Guard to keep us out of Central was right. But that night, I listened carefully as President Eisenhower got to the heart of why he was using the U.S. military to enforce the law:

"The very basis of our individual rights and freedoms rests upon the certainty that the president and the executive branch of government will support and ensure the carrying out of the decisions of the federal courts, even, when necessary, with all the means at the president's command . . . Unless the president did so, anarchy would result."

In that moment, I wasn't thinking so much about history or the Constitution or the everlasting impact of the president's words. I rejoiced for the simplest of reasons: Finally, I would be able to return to school—and with the protection of the U.S. military, no less.

Later that night, Uncle J.W., a World War II veteran, called to tell me about the 101st Airborne. They were America's military elite, also known as "the Screaming Eagles," he explained excitedly. They were renowned for their heroism during the Normandy invasion and the Battle of the Bulge in World War II. Now, they were coming to Little Rock. Now, I surely would be in good hands, he said.

There have been few moments in my life prouder than this one. I believed so strongly, with all the naïveté of my youth, that the system of governance I had learned about in school would prevail and that the U.S. Supreme Court order somehow would be upheld. And through it all, I never even considered backing away from my decision to attend Central. I'd been taught all my life not to be a quitter, so quitting just wasn't in my nature. If my parents ever considered pulling me out of Central during those scary first days, they never told me. I'm sure they had tough questions for Mrs. Bates behind closed doors. I'm sure all of the parents did. To this day, I don't know exactly what went on in those private meetings between her and them. I just know that in my presence, my parents never wavered in their belief that I had a right to attend Central. And if it took the power and might of the U.S. military to make it happen, well then, so be it.

For the first night in a long time, I slept peacefully.

I woke up extra early on September 25. A mix of nervous anticipation and excitement jolted me out of bed before sunrise, even though I wasn't sure I would be going to school. When I went to bed the night before, the word was we were going to wait another day before returning to school, despite the presence of the troops.

Mrs. Bates had called my parents around ten p.m. the night before and told Mother that she had not yet heard from Superintendent Blossom with a plan. Sometime before daybreak, though, Mrs. Bates showed up at our door with different instructions. We were to meet at her house by eight a.m., she told my parents. Superintendent Blossom had called her after midnight to say that the military troopers would meet the nine of us at her house later that morning and escort us to school. To make sure we all got the message, Mrs. Bates drove to each of our homes. Blossom had rounded up two black men who worked as principals to accompany her. Their first stop at one a.m. was the home of Gloria Ray. Gloria's father, on edge from all the threats and mob violence that week, met the unexpected guests at the door with a shotgun. And he was in no mood to hear about his baby going back to Central.

"I don't care if the president of the United States gave you those instructions," he barked. "I won't let Gloria go. She's faced two mobs and that's enough."

Everybody was on edge, Mrs. Bates later wrote, but the remaining parents, including mine, responded a bit calmer. Of course, I wasn't aware of any of this when I first popped out of bed and went to Mother for an update. Yes, I was going to school, she said, revealing—as usual—just what I needed to know, nothing more. I got dressed quickly and grabbed a bite to eat. I couldn't wait to see what this elite military unit looked like. Mother and I pulled up outside the home of Mr. and Mrs. Bates as other students and their parents were getting out of their cars, too. The place was already swarming with reporters, photographers, neighbors, and NAACP officials. I joined the other students, making small talk until everyone, including Gloria, had arrived. The parents milled about, chatting with one another, while Mr. and Mrs. Bates worked the crowd, reassuring everybody. This was an important day, the couple told us. We would walk into that school under the protection of our U.S. government. The atmosphere was noticeably lighter. One of the ministers in the room led us all in prayer. Heads were bowed, and tears rolled down many cheeks as the minister asked God to protect and guide us on this historic day. But I was slightly distracted. Of all things, I couldn't stop thinking about whether I would remember the way to the three classes I had attended two days earlier.

The light chatter returned, but it was soon drowned out by the rumble of military vehicles making their way down the quiet residential street. The army was here, someone announced. A wave of excitement rushed through the room. I dashed to the picture window in the living room as the other students also scattered to get a closer look. A convoy of jeeps rolled past the house and idled in the street. Soldiers dressed in helmets and combat gear hopped out and blocked 28th Street on each end. They stood at attention with their rifles. As a large olive-colored station wagon pulled up in front of the house, Mrs. Bates called us away from the windows. It was time, she said. We gathered our books and made our way to the door. I felt more ready than I'd ever been for this moment. As we stepped outside, cameras flashed around us from high and low. Reporters shouted questions and jotted into small notebooks. Neighbors stood in their yards and along the streets to bear witness. One by one, the nine of us climbed into the station wagon. A topless jeep filled with soldiers led the way. Another followed us. This time, we drove at a normal slow pace. Black mothers and fathers, who had been held captive inside their homes for days by the rampaging white mob, spilled onto front porches, yards, and the sides of streets. As our convoy moved up 16th Street in the vicinity of the school, I saw small clusters of white parents and children walking away from the school. I learned later that Major General Edwin Walker, commander of the operation, had met with the white students in the auditorium just before we arrived to explain his mission:

"You have nothing to fear from my soldiers, and no one will interfere with your coming, going, or your peaceful pursuit of your studies . . . ," he told them. "[My soldiers] are here because they have been ordered to be here. They are seasoned, well-trained soldiers, many of them combat veterans. Being soldiers, they are as determined as I to carry out their orders."

A group of the students walked out. Perhaps they were the stragglers we saw exiting the school grounds as we pulled onto the campus. Their faces looked angry and hateful, but this time, there were no loud, hateful words. This time, there was no speeding or trying to hide from the mob. The would-be members of the mob had been dispersed, some forcefully, before we arrived. The U.S. military had tucked all nine of us securely under its wing, and in just a few minutes, we would fly right into the heart of Central, almost daring those hateful men and women to try to put their hands on us now.

For a few precious moments, life seemed to roll in slow motion as our caravan turned left onto Park Street from 16th. Hundreds of paratroopers lined the streets around the school. They stood shoulder to shoulder, their M-1 rifles and bayonets ready. They had been in position since five a.m., the news reports said, cordoning off the school for three blocks on either side. A few students milled around outside, watching the scene quietly, curiously. The streets were graveyard quiet, except for the occasional crackle of the soldiers' walkie-talkies. The soldiers snapped to attention when our station wagon pulled up. This time, we rolled past the side door we had entered on that terrifying first day. Our caravan pulled to a stop right in front of the school. This time, we were going through the front door. Until that moment, it hadn't fully registered that the game of ducking and hiding was over. I could hold my head up. I—we—had a right to walk through those front doors, like anyone else. And the president of the United States had sent our U.S. military to ensure that right.

The car doors swung open. It was 9:22 a.m. My heart thumped

faster than ever before. As I stepped out of the station wagon, the morning sky seemed brighter. The nine of us got into line, mostly by twos. A helicopter hovered above. Several soldiers trotted across the yard to catch up with us. Then twenty-two of them positioned themselves completely around us. I felt safe, protected and proud. In tandem, we began to move slowly, deliberately—off the curb, up the walkway, past the fountain, up the left set of steps, and then up the next set. Finally, I stood at that grand entrance with its heavy wooden doors, surrounded by so much brick and stone.

I took a deep breath. The granite eyes of those four Greek gods and goddesses above my head seemed to peer down at me: Ambition. Personality. Opportunity. Preparation. Walk with me now, I implored.

And with a new sense of calm, I stepped across the threshold.

CHAPTER 6

The Blessing of Walls

To my surprise, getting inside Central was just the beginning of a brand-new struggle: finding a way to survive. So much of my energy had been focused on gaining access to the school that it hadn't really occurred to me what daily life would be like on the inside. I wanted to believe that the cold stares, the name-calling and taunts I had experienced on the first day would soon melt away. That the mobs would disappear for good now that the U.S. military's best stood guard. That the student troublemakers would turn their attention elsewhere. That eventually Central would embrace me.

It wouldn't take long for those hopes to fade.

Ernie and Melba have said that for them, each day was a war. For me, it was more of an internal battle: How do I dodge the heel walker? How do I hold my books to avoid attack? How do I manage to get through the day without using my locker or going to the girls' bathroom? The strain of calculating my every move was consuming. There was no training for us in self-defense or in the ways of nonviolent protest or passive resistance. That came years later for the college students who sparked the sit-in movement at lunch counters throughout the South. Our "training" was on the job. And my earliest lessons came in the hallways between classes.

The noise in the halls of Central was earsplitting the first month. Just imagine a constant stream of about two thousand raucous teenagers wending their way to classes in all different directions over five floors several times a day. Add to the mix nine much-resented black students, and the atmosphere was volatile, even with the presence of our military guards. The soldiers met us at the home of Mr. and Mrs. Bates each day for a while and drove us to school. Then, each of us was assigned a military escort to accompany us through the day. The troopers usually waited outside the classroom door until it was time to move to the next class. But I learned early that while the soldiers were there to make sure the nine of us stayed alive, for anything short of that, I was pretty much on my own. They were in a precarious position, for sure. But it seemed to me that too much just seemed to escape their ears and eyes. Like the spitting, for instance.

The band of boys in the black leather jackets were the worst offenders. They seemed to have come from the woods with their dank, moldy smell and their facial stubble, and they made a sport of spitting on me. If you've ever been hit by a nasty gob, you know how disgusting it is, how humiliating, how infuriating. The first time, the wet slime just came flying out of nowhere, landing on the bottom left side of my face. My military escort usually walked on my right. I was trying to work my way through the crowded halls between classes on my second day inside when without warning I felt something wet hit my face. I flinched. Immediately, I knew what it was. But who had done it? It was useless trying to single out the villain in the sea of smirking faces quickly moving past me. Was it one of the black leather boys? Or did it come from one of their ponytailed female cohorts? In either case, there was nothing I could do to respond. I had already been warned against retaliation by Dr. Blossom before school even started; responding in kind could lead to my expulsion. And no matter how demeaned I felt, tears were out of the question. I couldn't let them see my hurt. I couldn't give them that kind of power. So without a word, I just wiped my face against the sleeve of my dress and kept on trekking.

From then on, I stayed on guard, scanning eyes and mouths as I traveled the halls. I learned to jump back quickly or duck to avoid being hit in the face. But I always carried Kleenex, just in case.

Remembering the lessons learned in the halls became an important part of getting through each day. When the black leather boys or their female sidekicks walked close to me and knocked my books out of my hand, I learned never to bend over right away to pick them up, lest I provide the perfect target to get kicked in the backside and onto my face. The first time it happened, I was completely blindsided. In a kind of one-two move, somebody slinked up to me on the left side and knocked against me hard, sending my books flying out of my hands. I guess I was a pretty easy target because I usually carried an armload of books. I didn't like leaving anything in my locker because it was frequently the target of vandals, as were the lockers of the other eight. The vandals often left crude handwritten notes, like "Nigger go back to Africa." They sometimes took our books and destroyed our homework. So I usually piled into my arms as much as I could carry. After my books went sailing across the floor, I leaned over to pick them up, and somebody else whacked me with a foot in the bottom. I heard laughter in the background as I went down flat on my face. Stunned and embarrassed, I hopped quickly back onto my feet.

Most times, my guard was at a loss to stop an attack before it happened. The troublemakers were quick and sneaky, and they didn't seem at all threatened by the military presence. When I pointed out the assailants, the guard could only direct them to the office. One of my regrets is that I never got to know any of the men who journeyed through those halls with me. Unlike some of the other nine, I didn't have the same escort on a regular basis. I never even learned their names. To this day, I'm still unsure why my escort changed so regularly. The other nine declared I just wore the troopers out walking so fast. Melba got to know her guard pretty well, and she thought the world of her Danny. He had no more power than the other troopers to intervene against the trouble-makers, but he seemed to really look after Melba. He warned her when he sensed trouble ahead. He'd radio for help when the bullies approached her. He seemed to empathize with the scared teenager she was, and he taught her how to be a warrior. A couple of my other comrades got to know their guards, too. It just wasn't that way with me. Maybe I came across as unfriendly or at times annoyed and angry. I wasn't angry at the troopers as individuals. They were probably decent, hardworking guys, and I never lost sight of the fact that they were the reason we had made it into the school in the first place. But the entire situation made me angry. I was angry that I had to face this kind of torture in a hallowed place of learning, angry that the threat to my life was so great that I needed to be escorted to class by battle-trained soldiers, yet those same soldiers didn't even have the authority to stop groups of hateful boys and girls from spitting on me and knocking me on my face. Well, I'd always heard that what doesn't kill you just makes you stronger. If I learned nothing else that year, I learned that. I did grow mentally tougher. I resolved that if the soldiers couldn't protect me, I'd have to do it myself. That's why I didn't have time to chat with them. That's why I raced through the halls most days just short of a sprint, heading to class as if I were late for work. The soldiers had a job to do, and so did I. As I saw it, part of my job was to avoid making the same mistake twice. That one tumble onto my face taught me to carry my books on the side closer to the wall and never next to the open hallway. And when I had to bend over, I learned to turn my backside to the wall as well. Thank goodness for the walls. At times, they seemed the only protectors I had.

The troublemakers found their protection in numbers. They always traveled in groups, and with the many distractions and the high-decibel unruliness in the halls, their antics could easily escape notice. When I walked past one group or another, impromptu chants would break out: *Two, four, six, eight, we ain't gonna integrate. . . .* Then they'd erupt into laughter. Sometimes I'd feel a sharp kick in the calf or a jab in the arm as I passed them. I learned to just hold my peace and hope one of the more compassionate teachers caught a glimpse. There were indeed a few teachers who'd step in, call out a name, and write up a disciplinary report. But many of them just turned the other way. It was as though they stood in their classroom doors with their eyes and ears closed. They didn't want to know anything because to know might have required anyone of decent conscience to *do* something. I didn't waste my breath reporting anything to them. I didn't want to face the frustration that some of my comrades faced when they tried to report violent incidents to teachers and were met with a question: Did any adult witness it? The guards didn't count.

The teachers and the guards didn't stop the verbal taunts in the halls, either, so I found my own ways of dealing with those, too. The insults were regular and plentiful, hurled from every corner of the halls like rocks—*nigger . . . baboon . . . you think you're white . . . coon.* I tried to envision the words as bubbles left floating in the air. Or I imagined in my head a name-calling game colored folks used to call "playing the dozens," in which the one who could sling the most degrading insult ruled. When their words hit my ears, I'd kind of smirk to myself and think: I've heard better from my own people. That's all you got? That much was true. I'd had plenty of practice with name-calling all of my life from my own people, and we can be pretty creative in that arena. So I got good at letting the words just bounce off like balls. But I'd be lying if I said I managed to do so every time. Some days I just wasn't in the mood for any of it. Some days I was so mentally exhausted that I didn't have the energy to guard my heart. In those low moments, when the troublemakers hurled their insults, they smashed my spirit like bricks. It took all of my energy just to stay on my feet and keep moving forward to the next class.

Class offered little solace, though. A whole new set of defense mechanisms was required there. The most common pranks usually involved my desk. A time or two, I plopped down in a puddle of spit or glue, only to look up and find several of my classmates doubled over with laughter. Humiliated, I just did what I could to wipe the stain from my clothes. But from then on, I quickly inspected my seat with my eyes or ran my hand across it before sitting down. Some incidents I couldn't prevent, like the flying spitballs, tiny bits of paper rolled with spit and blown out, usually through a short straw. They stung my face and my neck repeatedly, but it was more annoying than painful, and I refused to acknowledge it. At times I'd hear the sudden flick of a fountain pen, and before I could lean out of the way, a spurt of ink would ruin my clothes. I just added a change of clothes to the stuff at risk in my locker. After the repeated break-ins of my locker, I kept the change of clothes in the office of Mrs. Huckaby, the vice principal.

The daily incidents of harassment kept me on guard everywhere I went in the school. When my class went to the auditorium for assemblies, my assigned seat was next to the teacher. The auditorium was quite a spectacle, grander than any I had ever seen before, except in New York. It was a bright, cavernous space with theater-style seating for two thousand students, professional lighting, and a stage that was 60 feet deep and 160 feet wide. The stage doubled as the gymnasium and basketball court. With so many students together at once in the auditorium for assemblies, I was always on edge. I rarely saw the other black students during those times. The only time I saw any of the other eight during the school day was at lunch. There were two lunch shifts, and every day I sat with the other black students who shared my lunch period. The usual crew included Jeff, Thelma, Ernie, and Elizabeth, but that sometimes varied. We always sat in the same spot, though, at the second table on the far right. I chose a seat with my back to the rear of the cafeteria, which allowed me to face the greater part of the dining room and the doorway to the hall. I always brought my lunch from home, too, so that I could avoid the cafeteria line. None of the white kids ever invited me to join them at their tables, and the truth be told, I never even thought much about it. I looked forward to seeing my friends. It was the only time of the school day that I felt at ease enough to laugh.

By the end of each school day, all nine of us were exhausted. When we climbed into the car to head to the Bateses' home together, it was the first time of the day that all nine of us were together again, and we were happy to see one another. Some of the others shared stories about what had happened to them that day, and being teenagers, we usually found a way to laugh about it. I laughed with my comrades, but I rarely chimed in on the storytelling. I just didn't want to relive any of it. Every ounce of energy I had left, I needed for homework. Sometimes, when one of us had experienced a particularly tough day, the car would fall silent. We'd notice a pair of watery eyes, and we knew. Every one of us just knew. Once we arrived at the home of Mr. and Mrs. Bates, we'd file in through the carport door (hardly anyone ever used the front entrance) and grab a snack from the stash she kept for us in the kitchen—chips, cookies, cold drinks. We'd often find Mr. Bates there, stretched out in his lounge chair in the small adjacent family room in front of the television. He had a calming presence that seemed to add a bit of levity to our days. The nine of us usually headed down to the basement for a casual debriefing with Mrs. Bates. Each of us found a comfortable spot on the sofa, a chair, or the floor to answer Mrs. Bates's questions. She would ask each of us about our day—who did what, when, where, whether we reported the trouble, whether anyone witnessed it, and who, if anyone, responded. At first, I dutifully told her all that I had experienced. But day after day, nothing seemed to change. I know she would have fixed it if she could have, but it seemed to me that she was about as helpless to fix things as we were. So I stopped sharing. For some, those sessions may have been cathartic. For me, it was wasted breath, wasted energy, having to go through the trauma all over again. When my turn to share rolled around, I'd just say, "My day was all right," or, "Things went okay." At home, I'd respond the same way when my parents or younger sisters asked about my day. I just didn't want to worry them any more than I already had.

Some things improved slightly after the first month in school, like the noise in the hallways. I began noticing more teachers monitoring the halls, and they clamped down on much of the hooting and hollering and general rowdiness. Still, much of the kicking, punching, spitting, shoving, and shoulder bumping continued, but the troublemakers got better at hiding their dirty deeds. At least, though, I could hear myself think as I moved through the halls.

There were also other changes in that first month. I read in the newspaper on October 15 that the first cutback of the military troops in Little Rock had been ordered. Federal officials said they were pleased with the "general orderly situation" and were returning five hundred troopers from the 101st Airborne—about half of the unit in Little Rock—to their base in Kentucky. Also, about eighty-five hundred soldiers from the Arkansas National Guard were being released from federal control. The remaining eighteen hundred guardsmen would stay under Commander Walker's direction to keep the streets calm. From my vantage point, everything continued operating much the same. My eight comrades and I still had a military escort throughout the day at Central, and there was still a constant military presence in and around the school. The military continued to meet us at the home of Mr. and Mrs. Bates and drive us to school every day until late October, when a few of the parents who were home during the day took on that responsibility.

At the end of the first grading period in late October, a reporter for a national newspaper called Mrs. Huckaby to ask how the nine of us were faring academically. It seemed the whole world was waiting to see if we could keep up with the white students. That was confidential information, Mrs. Huckaby responded, but added that the reporter should check the following Sunday's newspaper, when the *Arkansas Gazette* listed the students who had made the honor roll. My name was on the list. Despite all of the distractions, I somehow had managed to focus enough on my studies to make the honor roll.

Things at Central were still pretty turbulent in mid-November when the *Gazette* assigned a team of reporters to find out more about daily life at the school. The resulting story didn't even come close to capturing the truth. Much of it was based on rumors and factual inaccuracies, including a teacher who reported to her class that the nine of us would be leaving at Thanksgiving. The comments and actions of the teachers described in the story were quite worrisome. One teacher told a reporter that when she first learned the school would integrate, she thought: Well, it had to be. But she acknowledged having second thoughts. The story also described an unnamed black girl jostling in the hall with a white girl, who then spat on the black student—all of which was witnessed by a teacher, who looked away.

But I was most furious when I read this ridiculous attack: "The Negro girls come in for criticism on another matter of less than earth-shattering significance," one white girl complained. "They dress sloppy. . . . They wear colored socks. No white girl would think of wearing anything but white socks."

With all that was going on, it might have been easy to lose sight of the fact that the nine of us were, after all, just teenagers. What we wore to school mattered to us, as did what others thought of what we wore. My mother made most of my clothes, and even now, when I look back at photographs of those days, I have this completely objective opinion of myself: I looked good. My clothes were neat and stylish. In fact, all nine of us were well-groomed—

our clothes always clean, perfectly pressed, and fashionable. Years
later, when I saw myself in an *Eyes on the Prize* video clip, I
thought back to the comment about my socks and realized it was
too true. I was indeed wearing colored socks, and they matched
my dress!

The *Gazette* story summarized the first three months of integration at Central this way: "not entirely calm, by any means, but
not in turmoil either." Perhaps that was the view from the outside
peeking in, but from the center of the drama, it sure felt like turmoil to me.

Meanwhile, as the days passed, Governor Faubus continued
running off at the mouth, grabbing the headlines any way he
could. First, he speculated publicly that he might not take back the
eighty-five hundred guardsmen who had been under federal control—a threat that went nowhere. Then, in mid-November, he was
quoted in the *Gazette* as saying the only way to break the "desegregation deadlock" was for the black students to make a "voluntary withdrawal" from Central. When I read that, I thought: What
deadlock? The deadlock had been broken when President Eisenhower stepped in and ordered the U.S. military to walk us up the
front steps into Central. And there was no way any of us was going
to quit now. But the governor's comments reminded me that the
segregationists on the outside from the statehouse on down were
still fighting hard to regain whatever ground they believed they'd
lost when the Little Rock Nine made it into Central.

On the other side, Mrs. Bates and the NAACP were just as determined to spin the story the other way—that integration was
working perfectly well, which was less than the truth. All nine of
us felt compelled to send out that unified message—that integration was succeeding. I know I certainly did. I had heard all of my
life both at home and at school that I was a representative not just
of my family, but of the entire race. White folks would forever
judge the race by what each of us said and did, my parents and

teachers had told me. Likewise, Mrs. Bates said, white folks would judge how well integration was working by what the nine of us said and did. So I did what I believed was expected. I played down my suffering. I handled it all with as much grace as I could, as if the nine of us bore all of the responsibility for the success or failure of integration. The message that Mrs. Bates drilled in us rang constantly in my ears:

"This is important. It is history. You are helping to change the way America thinks about our race."

The rational part of me understood the huge significance of that. But at times, the other part—the fourteen-year-old girl who just wanted to go to school without all the histrionics—felt used. That was the part of me that came to resent the interruption of my days to suit the media. The reporters were omnipresent, and I never knew when I would be asked to do an interview. Because I was the youngest, I was usually among the last ones Mrs. Bates called on to make a statement. But there were times when we were all asked to participate. Thanksgiving was one of those times. The national media wanted to check in on how the integration process was going, so Mrs. Bates staged a Thanksgiving dinner. She moved out her living room furniture and set up her dining room table there with a leaf that extended it long enough to accommodate all nine of us and the two of them. The spread was elaborate—a huge golden brown turkey with dressing, cranberry sauce, macaroni and cheese, and other southern favorites. We were all uprooted from our homes and individual Thanksgiving celebrations, dressed in our Sunday best, and driven to the home of Mr. and Mrs. Bates to participate in the made-for-television event. The cameras rolled as the nine of us and the Bateses dined together, all smiles, as though we all lived under the same roof and had no parents or other family members. Then, of course, several of us reassured television viewers that we lived in a great country and that all was well at Central. If some viewers also saw for the first time that on

Thanksgiving colored folks ate baked turkey and dressing on fine china with perfectly pressed table linens, spoke articulately, and demonstrated impeccable table manners, then we had well served our dual purpose.

While the nine of us tried to put the best face on integration for the public, it got even more difficult as the months passed to keep from fighting back. One particular redhead made restraint especially difficult for me. Before I even saw her face, I felt the scrape of her hard leather penny loafers against the backs of my heels.

I got caught up in the crush of the hallway crowd between classes one day, which slowed my stride. With so many people around me in every direction, it didn't seem unusual at first that someone was walking so closely behind me, directly in my tracks. Then all of a sudden a shoe crunched down hard on the back of my right heel. A sharp pain shot up the back of my leg. The person behind me must have been in a rush, I first thought. I walked faster. The person behind me sped up, too. And then, crunch—it happened again. And again. I heard laughter behind me. This was deliberate. I could see the red hair in my peripheral vision, and she was purposely walking on my heels. This time, the pain was intense, like a big razor blade dragged from the back of my lower ankle down to my heel. I wanted to cry out, but I sucked it in and just tried to move faster. Eventually, she shot from behind me to head to her class, and I saw her—a slightly built girl, a bit shorter than me at about five feet seven inches tall, with milky skin and straight, shoulder-length red hair pulled into a ponytail. I didn't recognize her from any of my classes. I kept walking, trying to block from my mind what had just happened as I continued to my next class. The back of my ankle and heel felt raw rubbing against my sock and shoe. It wasn't until later that afternoon in gym class that I was able to inspect my heel without drawing attention to myself or showing that I was hurt. While changing into my uniform in the dressing room, I leaned over and peeled back my sock.

Spots of blood had soaked through. I felt the tears rising from my throat, but I choked them back, pulled up my sock, and headed out to the gym. I'd have to remember to bring Band-Aids next time.

The redhead became one of my regular tormentors in the halls. She'd wait for me almost every day, usually after lunch, and before I knew it, she was on my heels. I walked as fast as I could in those crowded halls. If she was going to rip the skin off my heels, I'd make her work for it. I told Mrs. Bates about it. Nothing changed. Then, one day in one of my low moments, instinct kicked in. The same girl skirted up behind me to start her routine, and instead of speeding up, I stopped dead in my tracks. She slammed into me. I whipped around to face her. I could tell that she was surprised. Suddenly, the mouthy redhead who'd acted so fierce was silent. Completely silent. I wanted to sock her but thought better of it. I just stared her down and let my eyes do the talking. Other students stared and walked around us. She hissed and scampered away. That turned out to be a rather good day.

I wish I could say that was the end of the heel walking, but the redhead was soon back at it. Sometimes others followed suit. Occasionally, I reported the incidents. On December 3, I reported that a female student I didn't know tried to trip me as I entered the cafeteria. A week later, two boys outside of school purposely bumped into me hard enough to spin me around. Mostly, I just did what I could to avoid them, stay out of trouble and on guard. One day, my defensive posture had a surprising result. As I headed to class, I noticed five or six of the black leather clan in my path ahead. I knew that one of them would slink next to me and throw out an elbow as I passed. I came up with a quick plan: I'd throw out my own elbow to block it. I'd have to time it just right. Inching closer, I carefully moved my books to the right, next to the guard, to free my left arm. On cue, one of the boys stepped out of the group and took a couple of steps next to me. This time, I was ready. I threw out my elbow to protect myself before feeling his blow. For some reason, though, his elbow hadn't moved, and to his astonishment—and mine—he felt the sharp point of my elbow jab hard into his arm. He jumped back, red-faced.

"You see what that nigger did to me!" he yelled.

I kept walking, hoping that the teachers monitoring the halls at that moment were as blind as they had been all the times I'd been tortured in the same halls. Fortunately, I never heard anything about it. But one of my comrades wouldn't be so lucky.

It was December 17, the day before Christmas break. When I walked up to the lunch table, I noticed that Ernie had just gotten there, too. He looked more frustrated than usual and threw his books and lunch sack on the table. Minnijean was in trouble, he said. She'd dumped a big bowl of chili on the head of a boy who had been hassling her repeatedly in the lunch line. He and Melba had seen it all when a group of boys called Minnie names and blocked her path as she tried to make her way to her table with her lunch, Ernie said. Before he could encourage her to ignore them, he said, he watched the chili slide from Minnie's tilted tray onto the boy's head. The entire cafeteria came to a standstill for a moment, and spontaneously, the black cafeteria staff erupted in applause. An administrator then appeared on the scene and whisked Minnie to the main office. Ernie said he hadn't seen Minnie since. The word was she'd been suspended. I felt bad for Minnie. She had been pushed to the breaking point, and I knew that it easily could have been any one of us. We were all tired of life in the pressure cooker, and at one time or another, every one of us had felt just one notch away from blowing. I nibbled on my sandwich for the rest of lunch; none of us felt much like talking. We were worried about what this would mean for Minnie, what it would mean for us all.

I learned later that Minnie indeed had been suspended and would have to reapply for admission when we returned from Christmas break in January. By the end of the fall semester, 4 stu-

dents had been expelled from Central for causing trouble. Another
153 students withdrew, likely to avoid integration. About two
dozen of them enrolled at Hall High School, the all-white school in
a ritzier section of Little Rock, and a few of them eventually returned to Central.

The news about Minnie's suspension put a damper on the beginning of the two-week break from school, but I looked forward
to the time off. Finally, I would be able to let down my guard,
laugh freely, and enjoy my family and friends. Two days before
Christmas, I did just that when the nine of us and our parents gathered at the Dunbar Community Center for a huge holiday celebration in our honor. The party was sponsored by the Washington,
D.C.–based headquarters of Delta Sigma Theta Sorority, Inc., a
national service-oriented group of professional women and college
students. The large upstairs room sparkled with red and white,
from the festive lights and decorations to the dozens of women
dressed in the colors of their sorority. I wore red and white, too, a
taffeta dress in a polka-dot print. It was especially nice to see
Mother and Daddy dressed in their holiday finery, enjoying themselves like old times. Before Central, they often got all spruced up
for a night on the town, but much of the fun in their lives as a
young couple seemed to have dried up. I missed the laughter that
had been ever present in our home.

Near the end of the party, a Santa presented each of us with
gifts and encouraging letters mailed from around the country by
the organization's members, who thanked us for our bravery and
courage. I'll never forget that evening. It came at a particularly low
point and reminded us all that no matter how isolated we sometimes felt at Central, we were not in this fight alone.

As 1957 wound to a close, I realized just how much of the
world was watching us. I picked up the *Gazette* one day and saw
a story that said the Associated Press had ranked the Little Rock
Nine and our integration battle as the top story of the year in the

nation—even bigger than the passage of the Civil Rights Act, the first major civil rights legislation since Reconstruction. According to the editors who compiled the list, our story was even bigger news than President Eisenhower's stroke. Among world events, our story placed second, just behind the Soviet Union's launch of *Sputnik I* and *Sputnik II,* the world's first artificial satellites and the beginning of the space age. The same list also named Mrs. Bates "Woman of the Year" in education—recognition she shared with several other women, including Althea Gibson in sports, Ingrid Bergman in entertainment, Lucille Ball in business, and Eleanor Roosevelt in public service.

All too soon, the holidays were over and school was back in session. I had but one wish for the new year: that life at Central would somehow get easier. But it didn't take long for that wish to fizzle. On the first day of school after Christmas break, classes were interrupted for what students had been told was a fire drill. It seemed strange when the police department showed up and began searching inside, but we later learned that a bomb threat had been made against the school. Such threats would become almost a routine part of our day. Sometimes the threatening calls came after school hours, and the National Guard was called back to duty, no matter what time, to check every inch of the campus.

In late January, we returned to school after a few scheduled days off to yet another bomb scare. When the alarm sounded, the school was quickly evacuated, as usual. Once outside, when we saw the police, we could tell it was a bomb scare instead of a routine fire drill. That usually meant at least a half-hour wait out in the cold. I quickly learned to take my coat with me when we left the building. While standing outside, the white students rolled their eyes or cut mean looks at the black students, as if we were causing this inconvenience.

This time, the search had not come up empty. Dynamite had been found in an unused locker. Superintendent Blossom told the newspaper that the dynamite could not have exploded, but authorities broke the stick into small pieces and disposed of it in the Arkansas River. Blossom maintained that the bomb threats were just a scare tactic intended to force school officials to close Central.

The next day, another anonymous caller phoned in a threat—this time to the switchboard of the *Arkansas Gazette*. The operator described the caller as a "white boy who had muffled his voice." Principal Matthews was summoned, and he called police and gathered some school administrators, who spent two hours searching the lockers again. Nothing turned up. A frustrated Blossom pleaded in the newspaper and on television for citizens to act responsibly and stop this disruption to the academic process. But his words fell on deaf ears because the threats, the searches, and the long waits in the cold continued. Parts of bombs were found in subsequent searches, but none that seemed to pose a real threat.

However, the message from the segregationists was clear: They were not backing off. If anything, they felt even more emboldened by Minnie's suspension. Minnie returned to school in mid-January, and the retaliatory attacks on her were relentless. One of the tormentors drenched her with hot soup. She didn't respond that time, but the taunts continued daily. On the morning of February 6, Minnie had taken enough and retorted by calling a student "white trash," which got her suspended again and ultimately expelled from Central for good.

The same day, I was sitting in Mrs. Huckaby's office when she came up from the cafeteria shortly after noon. She asked what happened, and I explained that I was on the stair landing, headed to the cafeteria, when two boys approached me and the smaller one kicked me. I pointed them out to the guard, who directed the boys to the office.

In an incident report that Mrs. Huckaby filed, she detailed witnessing the same two boys and a group of girls suspiciously hanging around the cafeteria at a table next to where Jefferson,

Elizabeth, and Melba were sitting that day. The white group had finished eating but just sat there, as if they were waiting for something.

"I waited, too, having motioned for the Negro children not to leave," Mrs. Huckaby wrote in the report. "Only when the Negroes rose at the bell did this group rise. I placed myself between the two groups, at the door made a slight delaying maneuver, and motioned for the guard to follow the Negro children."

The manner of the white group was "directly challenging to me," Mrs. Huckaby wrote.

Mrs. Bates somehow got a copy of a confidential school record dubbed "Students Involved in Repeated Incidents at Central High School," which noted some of the harassment by well-known troublemakers. The report shows that 1958 was already off to a very rocky start:

- Herbert Blount (the same boy who had kicked me on the stairs) kicked and hit Terry, and threatened to beat him up after school.
- James Cole sacked Ernie in the shower with scalding hot towels and used abusive language; James also called Minnijean a "nigger-looking bitch" and refused to go to the principal's office when the guard ordered him to do so.
- Darlene Holloway stepped on Melba's heels and pushed Elizabeth down the stairs, for which Darlene was suspended.
- Lester Judkins pretended Ernie tripped him after Kenneth Vandiver struck Ernie.

These were just a few of the incidents that made the list, and most times, I didn't even bother reporting the name-calling and small indignities. My days were so stressful that I didn't entirely feel bad for Minnijean now that she was expelled: At least she was free from the troubles at Central. Mrs. Bates and the NAACP arranged for her to move to New York and live with Drs. Kenneth and Mamie Clark, the renowned African American psychologists whose research using black and white dolls showed the devastating effects of racism and segregation on black children. The findings had been essential to the success of the Supreme Court's *Brown* decision. Mamie Clark had grown up not far from Little Rock in Hot Springs, Arkansas, where she attended segregated schools. Her husband was the first African American to receive a doctorate in psychology from Columbia University in 1940, and she became the first African American woman to do so three years later. They lived in Hastings-on-Hudson, a New York City suburb nestled among the hills along the Hudson River, which sounded exotic and exciting. The couple helped Minnie attain a scholarship to the prestigious New Lincoln High School in New York.

The remaining eight of us, our parents, and Mrs. Bates went to the airport to see Minnijean off. The closest I'd ever gotten to riding on a plane had been the fantasies I conjured up during my family's occasional Sunday afternoon outings there to sit and watch the planes take off. Now, here was Minnie about to fly off into what seemed to me a much brighter future and a wonderful adventure. I felt more excited for her than sad. A link in our chain had been snapped off, but Minnie no longer had to carry the burden of Central. I put myself in her place and wondered what it would be like to fly far away from friends and family and live with famous strangers. The cold wind whistled as we stood near the tarmac, saying our good-byes. We waved and waved as Minnijean turned and walked away, her face reflecting what we all felt—excitement and regret. One of the guys broke into a verse of the Gene Allison hit "You Can Make It if You Try."

No sooner had Minnijean left Central than hateful cards began appearing all over the school: "One Down . . . Eight to Go." Distributing the cards led to the suspension of one perennial troublemaker, Sammy Dean Parker. Another card was aimed at Gloria: "Get Gloria Ray—Out of the Way." Even the principal, Jess

Matthews, was a target: "That White Trash Matthews Named Jess / Sure Got Central in a Mess / The kids—If They're White / He Deprives of Their Rights / He's a Kansas Nigger-Lover, I Guess." I never saw a card bearing my name, but the segregationists were busy in their campaign to get rid of the rest of us, and sign or not, we all knew it.

We knew, too, that the troublemakers were organized in their campaign to punish us physically. One of the cards found around school invited white students to attack us: "GOOD ONLY UNTIL MAY 29, 1958 / BEARER MAY KICK RUMPS OF EACH CHS NEGRO ONCE PER DAY UNTIL ABOVE EXPIRATION DATE / LAST CHANCE, BOYS. DO NOT USE SPIKED SHOES / SIGNED: DAISEY BLOSSOM."

School administrators regularly took similar cards away from students or yanked down the brazen signs scrawled on notebook paper and posted throughout the school. Practically everywhere I walked, I felt like one big bull's-eye.

That's exactly how I felt at lunchtime on March 12 as I headed down the stairs from the third floor and suddenly felt a round blob of something wet smash against me. I had been hit by a tomato. From the second-floor landing, I quickly looked up and saw the guilty party, one of the black-leather boys with his light-colored hair combed toward his smirking face. I felt both furious and humiliated as I headed to Mrs. Huckaby's office to change clothes. Tomato particles dripped from a huge stain on the right side of my skirt and blouse.

There was, however, one place on campus where I could go without feeling that I was such a target: chapel. It was really just a large classroom, filled with desks and chairs, on the main level of the school. But for about twenty minutes each morning before classes began, the classroom became a place of meditation and prayer. The sponsor, Mr. Ivy, had invited the nine of us to join in, and I started each school day there. On any given morning, about thirty white students also attended. There was no interaction between the black and white students, but I knew that at least we had come there for a common purpose: to pray. Mr. Ivy usually asked the white students to lead the program, which generally included a Bible reading, prayer, and hymns—my favorite part of the service, especially the old standard "Amazing Grace." I could often hear Melba's—or, before she left, Minnijean's—melodic voice rising above the crowd. This became my haven, the place where I found the spiritual fuel I needed to get through each day. I felt the presence of God there. In those moments, it never occurred to me to ask God, "Why so much pain?" When I thought about Jesus Christ and the profound suffering he endured, that made my own challenges seem small. I told myself that I could surely go on.

One of the regulars in the service was Barbara Barnes, the most popular girl in the senior class and the homecoming queen. Though we never exchanged words, she always wore a pleasant smile. Many years later, as adults, Barbara and I both ended up in the Denver area, and Barbara contacted me. By then, we were both married with children, and we began meeting for lunch every couple of months to talk, get to know each other, and sort out the shared piece of our past. Her grandfather had been a religious man and a segregationist, she told me. He had wanted her parents to withdraw her from Central that year, but Barbara said she used the Bible to question his beliefs. What about loving your neighbor as yourself and doing unto others as you would have them do unto you? And what about the family's black maid, who had cooked their meals, cleaned their home, and rocked their babies? Didn't he claim to care about her? What if those nine black students were her grandchildren? Surely he wouldn't mind his granddaughter going to school with them, Barbara prodded. Eventually, her grandfather relented. But the kids at school were another story. Barbara got just a taste of what the nine of us experienced daily as she walked to chapel one day with Ernie. A group of thugs approached and slammed her into the lockers; somehow Ernie got away. Barbara was left stunned, terrified, and angry. Imagine living with those feelings practically every minute of every day at school, I told her. She finally understood. Barbara has since passed away, but I've stayed in touch with her husband, Sterling.

Sometimes I've thought about how much easier survival would have been if more people had taken a stand. As I saw it, the students at Central fell into different categories. The smallest group was the easiest to identify, those students who were determined to make our lives miserable: the tormentors, the black-leather boys, their female cohorts, and the other cowardly students who clung to their groups in their evil efforts to push us out. They were the ones who called us derisive names, spat on us, kicked, hit, pushed, and slammed us into lockers and down the stairs. Maybe it was their parents who helped to make up the segregationist crowds that clung to the wrongheaded belief that Central somehow belonged to them and that the nine of us were the interlopers causing trouble by having the audacity to keep showing up.

The second group included those students who were clearly sympathetic, even if they did not outwardly show it or jump to our defense in times of trouble. You could tell by the kind eyes that on our worst days seemed to say: "I'm really sorry this is happening to you." Sometimes they offered a shy smile in the hallways or in class or slipped a quiet note of support to one of us undercover. Gloria has talked fondly about Becky, a kind white girl with whom she exchanged notes during one of her classes. In their notes, Becky and Gloria established a sort of friendship, swapping tales about regular teenage stuff. On paper, they were just girls who shared the same interests, but the parameters of their relationship were clear. When Gloria wrote one day to ask whether she should speak if she saw Becky in the halls, Becky responded: "No, please don't." They both knew the consequences for Becky would be great. But Gloria has always felt grateful for those few moments in class when Becky helped her to feel accepted, as though she had at least one ally among her white classmates. The kindness of students like Becky sailed under the radar because to be detected was to draw harassment their own way, to be dubbed by the loud-mouthed segregationists a "nigger-lover" and thus the enemy. In this battle, the segregationists forced everybody to choose sides. If you weren't with them all the way in words and deeds, there was no middle ground. You were against them. Even administrators as methodical and "by the book" as Mrs. Huckaby, Mr. Powell, and Jess Matthews ended up on their hit list. The segregationists were taking names, and they were determined to make the lives of their enemies as miserable as they tried to make all nine of ours.

The majority of students at Central fell into the third group: those who kept silent. They wanted all the "trouble" to end. They did not torment us, but they didn't extend themselves to us in any way, either, not even quietly. They did not want to be associated with one side or the other. They chose to remain neutral, as if remaining neutral in the face of evil were an acceptable and just choice. They turned away. They rendered us invisible. They are most likely the ones today who, when asked about the Class of 1957, try to reinvent history. Things at Central weren't as bad as the nine of us have said, they have recalled in recent years. The mobs weren't as big, they say, the bad guys and gals weren't as bad, and the atmosphere wasn't as tense. Well, of course that is how they remember the Central journey these fifty-plus years later. When I was suffering in those hallowed halls, they turned away. They did nothing. They said nothing. They *chose* not to see.

There was another group, a small group, for sure, but in my mind the bravest of all: those teachers and students who at times were openly kind, who seemed to look beyond skin color and see nine students eager to learn, eager to be part of a great academic institution. Mr. Bell, my biology teacher, was one of them. He was young, but he seemed worldly and wise. His mother taught me

Spanish, but even her body language said she resented my presence at the school. Her son, however, had fought in the Korean War and had seen life far beyond Little Rock. He kept an eye on me in class and kept the troublemakers at bay. He didn't single me out, but he called on me about as regularly as he called on my classmates. He even encouraged me to participate in the science fair. He chose to see me.

There were others, too. The yearbook from my tenth-grade year includes kind notes from more than a dozen white classmates who risked harassment for taking even that small step. My exchanges with some of them have disappeared from my memory, but their words will forever remind me that there were moments in the midst of chaos when black and white faded and we were just teenagers. Liz Dolan's locker was a couple of doors down from mine, and we also were in the same gym class. Sometimes, as we stood at our lockers, the two of us swapped tales about our favorite show: *American Bandstand*. Liz was a dancer on the Little Rock version of the show, and as she hurriedly gathered her things in the evenings, she'd mention that she was rushing to get to the local television station. I'd wish her good luck and compliment her the next day on her dance moves. Robin Woods, a junior, was Terry's friend first. Terry had come to class one day with no book, and as he sat there looking lost, Robin pulled her chair next to his and offered to share her book. She wrote in my yearbook:

Dear Carlotta,
    This has been a memorable year for all of us—just wish you didn't have so many unhappy ones. Remember I am for you. Good luck to a really great girl. . . .

Then there was Jenny Lee Ball, a dark-haired girl who always wore her shoulder-length hair pulled back in a ponytail. She was on the student council, and we also shared gym, which usually involved some type of team activity—softball, basketball, or even gymnastics. For obvious reasons, the gym teacher set up the teams in the early part of the school year, which seemed to work fine. But eventually the teacher chose team captains, who got to select their own teams. Whenever Jenny was captain, she always chose me. Maybe the gym teacher had encouraged her to do so; Jenny was, after all, a student government representative. I'll never know for sure. But my name wasn't the first one Jenny called, and neither was it the last. And there wasn't a hint of scorn or regret when she boldly called out my name. When our team got into the huddle to discuss our gymnastics formation—a pyramid that first day— Jenny included me in the discussion. What was I good at? Where should I fit? Was I strong enough to help hold down the bottom? I remember Jenny as befriending me, though I can't think of a specific thing she said or did that was particularly special. But I guess that was the point. I saw nothing in her eyes and heard nothing in her tone that suggested she thought I was special or different. She just treated me with the same consideration and dignity she showed everybody else. That's all I ever really wanted. That's all every one of us wanted.

And each time I encountered a rare soul who seemed to recognize that, I considered it a real blessing.

CHAPTER 7

Star-Studded Summer

When the segregationists failed to force the remaining eight of us out of Central with their telephone threats, sidewalk taunts, and courtroom battles, they began targeting our parents. And they hit where it hurt—our parents' pockets and pocketbooks.

I first noticed that something strange was going on with my father when he began arriving home from work in the middle of the day on a regular basis. More and more often, when I made it home from school, Daddy was already there. Before, he had rarely made it home before supper.

During the spring of 1958, Daddy landed a job as a subcontractor on a new grocery store chain opening in Little Rock. He was hopeful because this was a major construction job expected to last for months. That meant steady work and steady income. For his first day on the job, he left home around sunrise, as usual. But when I returned from school that day, he was already home. He and Mother were deep in conversation in their bedroom.

"They laid me off," I heard him say.

It had happened again. Daddy would get a job, and then a few hours or a few days later, he would be told for no apparent reason that his services were no longer needed. Daddy was a meticulous brick mason who had never had trouble finding or keeping work—until now. I knew this had to be part of the segregationists' scheme to punish him and anyone else involved in the integration of Central. They had already targeted the *Arkansas Gazette* in a well-publicized campaign to hurt the newspaper's profits. The *Gazette* had featured editorials that supported integration with the argument that it was the law of the land. The newspaper's coverage of the events at Central seemed more balanced than that of its local competitor, the *Arkansas Democrat,* which favored segregation. But to the segregationists, there was no middle ground and no such thing as neutral; the *Gazette* was the enemy. Just months earlier, during the Christmas season, unnamed organizers had announced a boycott against businesses that advertised in the paper. The intention of the campaign was clear: to impact the newspaper's bottom line by taking away its primary source of revenue—advertising dollars. When the *Gazette* got wind of the boycott, it published on its front page this unsigned letter that had been circulating throughout the community in the days before Christmas:

> Plans are in the making for a massive crusade to be launched against stores whose ads appear in the *Arkansas Gazette.*
>
> The *Gazette* has played a leading role in breaking down our segregation laws, destroying time-honored traditions that have made up our southern way of life, and at last bringing upon the people of Little Rock the most insufferable outrage ever visited upon an American city. The people thus outraged have awakened. They have discovered that this infamous *Gazette* has a source of revenue. They have further discovered that your store contributes to the *Gazette* source of income with frequent ads.
>
> A crusade, using not one approach but many, lasting not one day or month but many days and many months, is to be launched not only against the *Gazette* but against your store as long as it advertises in the *Arkansas Gazette.*

Each ad you place in the *Arkansas Gazette* is to be a positive notification to every outraged white person that your store ignores their feelings and does not care for their business.

As negroes try to push their way deeper into the white schools and white society, race relations will continue to be inflamed. This will prove a perfect atmosphere to carry on this crusade.

There is a rising tide of race feeling—in fact, a revolution is beginning in the South and in Little Rock. Your store and all stores that advertise in the *Arkansas Gazette* will be placed on one side or the other. This is your notice to make your own choice.

> Sincerely,
> An Indignant Group

The newspaper also had run a front-page rebuttal, calling the letter a "vicious and deliberate distortion" of the paper's position. While the newspaper was the "immediate target," editors wrote, it was not the only one. I now knew that firsthand. I'd heard talk among my comrades that some of their parents had lost jobs, too. Jefferson's father was laid off from his longtime job at International Harvester, which manufactured agricultural machinery, construction equipment, and other products. I often saw Mr. Thomas at the Bateses' home during the day. Gloria's mother, Mary Ray, also was having trouble at work and eventually would be forced out of her job. So was Elizabeth's mother. They all suffered quietly, but when Melba's mother, Lois Pattillo, was informed that her contract as a seventh-grade English teacher at a North Little Rock junior high school would not be renewed the next year, she bravely decided to go public with her struggle. Mrs. Pattillo, a divorcée who was the family's sole breadwinner, wrote a statement and called the newspapers. On May 7, the *Gazette* ran her story on the front page, and it was picked up by media around the world. The resulting publicity ultimately helped Mrs. Pattillo get her job back.

My father wasn't quite as fortunate. He still could not land a decent contract in Arkansas. My grandfathers helped out as much as they could. Grandpa Cullins mostly took small jobs as the primary contractor on construction projects for black churches, schools, and businesses. That allowed him to bypass the racists, and he was able to hire Daddy to work for him. Big Daddy also gave Daddy more work hours in the café/pool hall. And Mother went back to work. Still, my parents were struggling financially. Mother began paying more attention to price tags in the grocery store and buying just the essentials. The occasional splurges on clothing, furnishings, and out-of-town trips also came to a halt.

Then, one day my parents told me that Daddy would be going to Los Angeles, California, for the summer to work. He had heard that plenty of good-paying construction jobs were available there. The news was bittersweet. I was happy that Daddy, who took such pride in his work, finally would be able to do the kind of work he enjoyed and make the money he deserved. But I would miss him. When Daddy was away for even a day, I always felt less secure.

Ernie's graduation helped to take my mind off Daddy's departure. I was so proud of my friend. His graduation said to the world that even under the most extreme circumstances, black students could perform as well as any others. Ernie had persevered through a hell that only the nine of us knew, and he'd completed all but this final walk across the stage. I wanted to be there to support him and was disappointed to learn that we would not be able to attend. Each graduate was given only six tickets for family members. School officials had already banned any nonwhite journalists from the graduation ceremony for security reasons, and they were not apt to make any special arrangements for the other seven of us black Central students. As expected, there had been a higher than usual number of threats. In such a volatile atmosphere, anything could happen.

On May 27, a Tuesday evening, about forty-five hundred parents, guests, and school officials gathered at Quigley Stadium for the big event. Hundreds of National Guard troops were there, and practically every police officer and detective on the Little Rock force had been called to duty. Some were assigned to keep watch over the homes of Superintendent Blossom and Central's principal, Jess Matthews, who were at graduation and feared their properties could become bomb targets. I gathered with my family in the den just before eight p.m. to listen to a radio broadcast of the ceremony. That familiar knot in my stomach tightened as I listened, hoping that those with hateful intentions wouldn't ruin Ernie's special night. Governor Faubus and his crew of die-hard segregationists already had proclaimed the first year of integration at Central a dismal failure. Who knew if one of those loonies would make it a self-fulfilled prophecy with some final, desperate act?

Ernie was among 602 graduates to receive their diplomas that night. About fifty minutes into the ceremony, his name was called. It seemed as though all of Little Rock—maybe even the entire nation—was holding its breath. This was the most publicized commencement in history, and all of the attention boiled down to this moment. There was not a sound. No laughter, no cheers, no applause, none of the celebratory expressions that had accompanied the names of the other graduates. Just silence. I exhaled as I imagined Ernie proudly walking across that stage—the first colored student ever to do so. Surely all those ghosts of our history—those unnamed colored warriors who'd risked torture by their white slave owners to learn the words in their Bibles, who'd braved the woods, the waters, the whips, and the snarling dogs and died without ever reaching brighter shores—surely they were helping to lift his head and straighten his shoulders now.

The next day, under President Eisenhower's orders, the Na-

tional Guard was withdrawn. A newspaper report estimated that
the cost of federal protection for the Little Rock Nine that school
year had been a whopping $3.4 million. That was a staggering fig-
ure in 1958, more than twice the amount it had cost to build Central thirty years earlier.

The media also took note of one special guest who had attended the graduation with Ernie's family: Reverend Martin
Luther King, Jr. At the time, Dr. King was clearly on the rise, having achieved acclaim as leader of the successful Montgomery bus
boycott. He had not yet achieved the legendary status that would
come in the years ahead; he was just another man in the crowd.
The mention of Dr. King in the newspaper made me flash back to
the first time I met him. He had come to Little Rock to speak and
was staying at the home of Mr. and Mrs. Bates, who invited the
nine of us to meet him. I brought my friend Bunny along, and
meeting Dr. King remains one of the highlights of her life, as it is
mine. But I have to chuckle because to this day, my most vivid personal memory of one of the world's most revered leaders is not of
eloquent words or a suit-and-tie moment. It is of him dressed
down, eating barbecue, and drinking beer around a card table in
the basement of Mr. and Mrs. Bates's home.

Dr. King's quiet presence spoke to the national significance of
Ernie's graduation. Now, for Ernie, Central was history. He was
heading to Michigan State University in the fall. For me, Central
was history, too—at least for a while. Summer had officially arrived, and not a moment too soon.

Within days of Ernie's graduation, the eight of us took a plane
to Chicago to be honored by the *Chicago Defender*. It was the first
plane ride for most of us, including Mother, whom Mrs. Bates had
selected as chaperone for the trip. Minnijean met us there, and we
were all thrilled to see her again and to vacation together for several days in this city we all had read and heard about but had never
seen.

We stayed downtown in an integrated luxury hotel. Gloria and I roomed together, Minnie and Melba, Elizabeth and Thelma, and the three guys. The newspaper honored the nine of us with the Robert Sengstacke Abbott Award, named for the founder and editor of the *Chicago Defender,* who was the most successful black newspaper publisher of his era. He had been an early advocate of civil rights for Negroes and had used the pages of his newspaper to encourage colored men and women in the South to move north to pursue a better life. The banquet in our honor was held at the Morrison Hotel, a forty-six-story tower that at the time was the world's tallest hotel and a longtime Chicago landmark. It was razed just seven years later. All nine of us were overwhelmed by the grandeur of the place but even more by the size and enthusiasm of the crowd. More than five hundred people gathered in the Cameo Ballroom to be part of the ceremony. I could hardly believe that so many people in this great city had come there to see us. In Little Rock, we had drawn crowds for sure, but most of them wanted to wring our necks, not hug them. Here, people stood to their feet to applaud us. I saw in their faces a reflection of pride, of something far beyond this moment. They called us brave and told us we were heroes and that they had been pulling for us. For the first time, it really hit me—the magnitude, the scope, of what the nine of us had done. It wasn't just about each of us having access to the best education available in Little Rock. It was about parting once closed doors for colored children everywhere. It was about the sons, daughters, grandchildren, nieces, and nephews of the men and women in the Cameo Ballroom this night. It was about the crowds of people who would fill such rooms in city after city that summer as we traveled throughout the country to meet our supporters and pick up awards.

John Sengstacke, editor of the *Chicago Defender* and nephew of the newspaper's founder, invited us to his home, a mansion on the South Side of Chicago. I had never met colored folks who lived like this. I was amazed to see a house full of black servants. We were ushered into the basement, which included a family room with a theater. But as awestruck as I was by Mr. Sengstacke's home, I was equally smitten by his handsome son, who was about my age. The Sengstackes also invited us to their summer home in Michigan City, Indiana, about an hour from downtown Chicago. There, we were again entertained royally with a host of activities far beyond our realm of experiences, including a boat ride on the family's private lake. In those few days, the nine of us shared more laughter and fun than we had the entire year at Central. We felt like teenagers again, carefree and silly, not nine symbols to be either admired or loathed. Little did we know this was just the first stop in what would be a star-studded summer.

In July, we took another plane ride, this time to Cleveland. Mrs. Eckford, Elizabeth's mother, chaperoned. The NAACP was awarding us its prestigious Spingarn Medal, presented for outstanding achievement. The award was named for Joel Elias Spingarn, a lifelong civil rights advocate, one of the early white leaders and later board chairman of the NAACP. Spingarn was a professor of comparative literature at Columbia University and one of the founders of the publishing house Harcourt Brace & Company. His desire was to draw attention to the distinguished achievements of the American Negro with an award that would inspire the ambitions of young people in the community. Spingarn left $20,000 in his will to ensure that the award, a gold medal, would continue into perpetuity. Mrs. Bates and the nine of us were the first and still the only group ever to receive it. I still feel extremely humbled to be mentioned among the great politicians, scientists, historians, scholars, athletes, authors, entertainers, civil rights advocates, and Nobel Peace Prize winners who have been recipients. They include many men and women whose lives I had studied at Dunbar: W. E. B. Du Bois, George Washington Carver, James Weldon Johnson, Carter Woodson, Charles Chesnutt, Mary McLeod Bethune, Marian Anderson, A. Philip Randolph, Paul Robeson, Thurgood Marshall, Ralph Bunche, and Jackie Robinson. In 1957, the year before we received the award, it was presented to Dr. Martin Luther King, Jr.

The ceremony was held July 11, 1958, in the banquet hall of a downtown hotel, and once again, the room was packed. In one photo used by many news organizations from that night, all nine of us are wearing the medals, attached to royal blue ribbons trimmed in gold. All of us are smiling broadly, except Elizabeth and Ernie, who must have been just tired. The other girls are all wearing solid pastel dresses; mine is plaid. Terry is mugging for the camera, and my face is turned toward him, smiling more at him than the camera. He probably had uttered something witty. I think all of us were just overwhelmed by the attention and unsure how to handle this new spotlight.

Sometime after that photo was snapped, Terry and I decided to have a bit of fun with one of the reporters covering the event. I was standing with Terry in the rear of the banquet hall when I saw the reporter making his way toward us. It was too late for me to make a discreet move in the opposite direction, which I usually did when I saw a reporter headed my way. So I stood politely next to Terry, a young intellectual even then, as he answered a question related to the award. When the reporter asked for his name, Terry responded with a straight face, "George Washington."

Scribbling quickly, the reporter turned to me. "And your name?"

"Martha Washington," I replied, continuing Terry's lame joke.

Without even a hint of suspicion, the reporter scampered off to his next subject. At first, Terry and I cracked up, but before leaving the room, we thought better of our little joke, especially when we imagined what Mrs. Bates and our parents might say. We tracked down the reporter and gave our real names. That remains one of my funniest memories of Cleveland.

Before leaving the city, the nine of us were treated to dinner at the legendary Dearing's Restaurant, known for its "Original Golden Brown Fried Chicken." The popular eatery had an array of food that reminded me of home: ribs, shrimp, homemade rolls, and pastries. It was comfort food, but this was a well-appointed, black-owned restaurant (complete with white linen tablecloths) that also drew white residents of the city. Like the events that took place the summer I was eight years old, these experiences opened the gates to a life far more progressive and sophisticated than anything I had ever experienced in Little Rock.

Soon after returning to Little Rock, the nine of us were off again with Mrs. Bates to New York for a whirlwind week, sponsored and hosted by the AFL-CIO Hotel Employees Union #6. Our host, James Marley, and his assistant, Betty Bentz, escorted us around the city, delivering us where we needed to be and making sure we were suitably dressed and on time for our appointments. We were even accompanied by the union's photographer, Mildred Grossman, a tiny lady who didn't seem at all weighed down by the ton of photo equipment she lugged around. She seemed different from the other professional photographers we had encountered. She tried not to be intrusive, though she snapped photos at every turn. In later years, when I learned her history, I would understand why she seemed so empathetic toward us. She knew what it was like to be singled out unjustly. She had been among thirty-three New York schoolteachers fired from their jobs for refusing to sign a loyalty oath, disavowing membership in the Communist Party during the McCarthy era. She became a union photographer and traveled the country, capturing some exclusive inside shots of their workers, their campaigns, and their leaders, networking with some of the nation's most renowned political and social figures. She ultimately won a lawsuit against the New York school system and was ordered reinstated to her teaching job. She returned for one day and retired. I had no clue when I met her that summer just how brave and honorable she was, but she earned my respect with her ability to keep up with nine giddy, adventurous teenagers.

First stop in New York was the office of Roy Wilkins, executive secretary of the NAACP, one of the early civil rights leaders I'd learned about at Dunbar. In his presence, I was a starstruck fifteen-year-old, watching a storybook figure suddenly acquire flesh and bones. Later, we met New York mayor Robert F. Wagner, Jr. We had lunch with the secretary-general of the United Nations, Dag Hammarskjöld, and 1950 Nobel Peace Prize winner Ralph Bunche. Another day, we had Coke and cookies with Governor Adlai Stevenson at the Waldorf-Astoria, where he lived. We attended a fund-raiser at the Abyssinian Baptist Church in Harlem, where Adam Clayton Powell, Sr. had been the pastor. His son Adam, Jr., then a prominent congressman, was with us there, along with Thurgood Marshall. They were a charming pair. When it was time to plead for financial support for the NAACP from the audience, Mr. Marshall joked:

"Now, folks, let's put in dollars. The sound of change hitting the plates makes these kids nervous."

Later the same day, we visited Concord Baptist Church in Brooklyn. During dinner, Melba got a chicken bone stuck in her throat and was unable to talk to the congregation as planned. But honestly, by then most of us were a bit tired of being paraded around. I remember thinking I would have gladly taken that chicken bone to avoid being called on to talk.

One of the most memorable evenings in New York was hosted by Drs. Kenneth and Mamie Clark, the psychologists who had taken in Minnijean when she was expelled from Central. They had a lovely home at Hastings-on-Hudson, and Broadway stars Ossie Davis and Ruby Dee were waiting to meet us there. What a nurturing, down-to-earth couple the actors were. They had children our age and related to us very much as protective parents, inquiring about our well-being. Later, we went to see David Merrick's

new Broadway play, *Jamaica,* starring Lena Horne and Ricardo
Montalban. Horne's role as the sassy Savannah would earn her a
Tony nomination. Ossie Davis also starred in the production, and
he arranged for us to meet the other actors backstage after the
show. I loved Lena Horne. She was warm and engaging, not to
mention stunning. I knew little then about her politics—how she
had refused to perform for segregated audiences during World War
II, how her friendship with outspoken activist and actor Paul
Robeson had left her branded a Communist and blacklisted in
Hollywood in the 1950s, how she again and again aligned herself
with civil rights causes. But the more I learned about Lena Horne
in the ensuing years, the more I admired her. After the show that
night, I just knew that I felt a connection to her, perhaps because
she reminded me so much of my mother. The way Ms. Horne carried herself—the way she threw her shawl around her shoulders
with the grace of an onstage performance—that sure enough was
Mother.

I could tell that Ms. Horne and Mrs. Bates connected, too.
They were two of a kind, both elegant and ladylike, yet feisty and
committed to racial justice.

After meeting with the performers, the nine of us students and
our adult chaperones ended the evening at Lindy's restaurant,
home of the "World Famous Cheesecake," in Times Square.
Owned by Leo "Lindy" Lindermann and his wife, Clara, the
restaurant was a popular hangout for Broadway and vaudeville
stars. There, like everywhere we went, the staff catered to us as
though we were stars, too. It astounded me that day after day we
met internationally renowned entertainers and politicians, yet they
treated us as if *we* were the celebrities. It felt unreal and at times,
for me, a bit uncomfortable.

The photographer, Ms. Grossman, tried to capture it all. She
accompanied us everywhere. On Coney Island, when we got on
the roller coaster, she hopped on, too, right in the front seat, and

she turned to snap photos of us as our cars raced up, down, and around the tracks. She also caught a picture of me on the ferry, leaning over the deck of the boat at the Statue of Liberty. That shot made the cover of the *Voice,* the magazine of the local union that sponsored our trip. The symbolism was striking: a fifteen-year-old member of the Little Rock Nine stretching for a clear view of the Statue of Liberty, the great promise of America's democracy.

And then our glorious week was done.

I didn't head back to Little Rock just yet, though. Gloria and I were going to separate summer camps in the New York area. Mrs. Bates had received invitations from several organizations for us to participate in summer camps, and she did her best to match our interests. Thanks to a generous sponsor, I was set to spend a month at Camp Minisink, a wooded campsite in the Shawangunk Mountains near Port Jervis, New York. The New York City Mission Society ran the camp, which offered youths, mostly from Harlem, the chance to experience the outdoors and nature far away from the concrete city. The Mission Society operated a year-round community center in Harlem; it was to Harlem what the Phyllis Wheatley YWCA was to Little Rock, a trusted community institution with an endless roster of fun programs aimed at developing young potential.

Camp Minisink was similar to the Y-Teen sessions I'd attended at Camp Clearfork in the Ouachita Mountains of Arkansas, but on a grander scale. Everything, it seemed, was larger—the lake, which flowed as far as the eye could see, and the woods, which spanned more than six hundred acres. But there had been a kind of sameness at Camp Clearfork; all of the campers were primarily colored teenage girls growing up in and around Little Rock. At Minisink, we were a mix of boys and girls, middle-class and poor, Hispanic and Negro. Our days and evenings were spent doing typical outdoor camp activities—hiking, boating, playing games, competing, cooking, cleaning, and singing around the campfire.

We took turns bussing our meal tables and swapping pieces of our dialects and culture. My friends used to laugh at how I said "water." I guess I subconsciously threw in an extra "r," as in "war-ter." And my new northern buddies just found that hilarious. I, of course, had no idea what was so funny because I've never had much of a southern accent—at least, I've never thought so. But I had my share of fun, too, with their dialects from Puerto Rico, the West Indian islands, and those other worlds within the U.S. bor-ders—Miami and the Bronx.

For the first time, I was learning about foods I'd never tasted, trying out dances I'd never seen, and hearing stories about how other kids lived. Finally, my soul and spirit could rest. The other campers all knew my story, and some were naturally curious. But they didn't pester me with questions about Central. I was just one of them.

Program director Gladys V. Thorne, whom we affectionately called Thorny, kept us in line. She was a little dynamo: short, no more than four feet six inches tall, round, and in constant motion. She wore her long black hair pulled back into a bun, and she was the spitting image of actress Juanita Hall, a black woman who played a Pacific Islander and sang "Bali Ha'i" in the Rodgers and Hammerstein film *South Pacific*. The movie was out in theaters that year, and Thorne joked about the special treatment and dou-ble takes she got from moviegoers certain she was the star. Thorne was fun. She felt comfortable hanging out with us teenagers, but she stressed discipline and commitment and ran a tight ship. I've always liked that in people.

After the first two weeks of camp, there was a break of several days before the next session started again. Since I couldn't return to Little Rock, I went home to Harlem with another fifteen-year-old camper, Paula Kelly, who became a fast friend. Her family lived in a two-bedroom flat in a vibrant Harlem community. We walked the neighborhood, shopped—or, rather, browsed in neighborhood stores—and sat outside on scorching days to watch children play in the open fire hydrants. Then we returned to Camp Minisink for another two weeks.

Paula, who attended Fiorello H. LaGuardia High School of Music & Art and Performing Arts, was just the kind of student the Mission Society brought into its fold early. She was versatile and supertalented; she could sing, dance, *and* act. She was the leader of my group when the campers broke up by age at the end of each day and performed a dance routine or skit.

Paula eventually would earn a master's degree in dance from the Juilliard School and become an Emmy-nominated dancer and actress. I've always been so proud to know her. She has perfomed and danced alongside some of the best in the business, including the late Sammy Davis, Jr., Gregory Hines, and Gene Kelly. But she could light up a stage all by herself, as she did at the Academy Awards in 1969 when she danced a solo to "Chitty Chitty Bang Bang," which had been nominated for "Best Original Song." One of her many memorable television roles was that of a lesbian confronting homophobia in *The Women of Brewster Place*, produced in 1989 by Oprah Winfrey.

Soon it was time to say good-bye to Paula and my Minisink friends. The New York couple who had sponsored my camp scholarship came to meet me at the end of the third week. They watched a final production of a play the campers performed and presented me with a silver lapel pin. I thanked them for their generosity, but at fifteen, I'm sure I couldn't adequately express what a balm Camp Minisink had been for my bruised psyche. I hope they knew.

At the end of the second two-week session, the Mission Society sponsored a social for all of the students who had been at camp that summer. I got to see friends who had not returned after the first two weeks. This time we were not in camp clothes, but dressed up. And we got to display on the dance floor all the new moves we had bragged about and occasionally demonstrated on those sweaty days in the woods.

I left Camp Minisink knowing that I had made some lifelong friends.

There was just one more stop for me before I returned to Little Rock. My eight Little Rock comrades and I had been invited to Washington, D.C., to attend the Elks convention. The nation's capital reminded me of a southern city. After those wonderful weeks in New York, a city that was a true melting pot, Washington felt more like being back in Little Rock. In the stores, on the streets, in the hotel, we were segregated. People of different races lived separately. This was shocking to me. I hadn't expected it in the nation's capital.

We were guests on a local television station's version of *American Bandstand* and got to meet a singer we all adored. He was quite handsome and charming. But as we were headed back to the hotel in a cab one afternoon, some of us witnessed an odd and somewhat startling sight: police chasing the frazzled-looking entertainer and another man out of a local park. The summer had seasoned me a bit, so what may have appeared puzzling to the more naive seemed obvious to me then. I felt worldly as I explained quietly to those sitting next to me that it appeared our idol must have gotten caught in some kind of romantic rendezvous—this at a time when no one talked openly about sex, let alone same-sex relationships.

The next day, the nine of us were scheduled to be in a parade—a long, big one with a specially designed float just for us. We arrived late, missed the departure of the float, and had to drive a short distance to catch up to it. The float featured individual desks with each of our names, and it was so high that we had to be hoisted onto it. The next thing I remember is crowds of people waving to us. We smiled big for the cameras and waved back.

Melba and Minnie especially loved the parade. I hated it. I felt embarrassed—embarrassed that we were such spectacles, embarrassed that we had arrived late, embarrassed by the largesse of it all. I wasn't ungrateful, though. I knew the Elks meant well by honoring us in a big way. At a banquet later that night, the group's leaders even presented each of us with a $1,000 scholarship. It was a truly generous gift that helped to relieve our worries about how we would pay for college, and I was thrilled to get it. But I guess after a month of fun as just another teenager at camp, I wasn't eager to return to the spotlight associated with Central High School.

Our group had been late for the parade because beforehand we had met with Thurgood Marshall for a photo session, which ran longer than expected. Six of us posed for pictures with him on the steps of the U.S. Supreme Court. In one iconic snapshot, Mrs. Bates is on one side of him and I am on the other. My comrades are sitting on descending steps—Gloria, Jeff, and Melba on one side; Minnie and Elizabeth on the other. Of all the stars I met that summer, Mr. Marshall was still my favorite. He was my personal hero, and every time I saw him, I just felt honored to be in his presence.

The time in Washington marked the end of summer break, which had felt like a little slice of heaven. Now it was time to head back to Little Rock and Central. All the way home, I was filled with dread. I knew what awaited me there.

I was returning to hell.

CHAPTER 8

Just a Matter of Time

My junior year at Central hadn't even started yet when the legal fight over integration began anew. The school board, persuaded that its initial efforts to integrate Central had been a dismal failure, returned to court over the summer to seek permission to change course. While the nine of us were being hailed as heroes throughout the country, the board began its push to return us to the all-black Horace Mann and delay integration until January 1961. There were new threats of violence, the board told the court, and the citizens of Little Rock needed more time to adjust to the inevitability of integration.

By then, the heroic Judge Davies had returned to North Dakota, and the case was assigned to an Arkansas-based federal judge. I wasn't in court for the hearing, but I was stunned to learn on June 21 that U.S. District Judge Harry Lemley granted the board's request for a delay. I wondered whether the clock would start ticking backward. Until that moment, the segregationists had been losing. The NAACP appealed immediately.

When the case went before the Eighth Circuit Court of Appeals in St. Louis in August, Thurgood Marshall returned with Wiley Branton to represent us. I was still away at camp, but it was a relief to hear that Marshall won the day. The appellate court reversed the Lemley ruling. The school board wasn't ready to give in, though, and appealed to the U.S. Supreme Court. When the new school year rolled around on September 2, 1958—the Tuesday after Labor Day—the city's four high schools remained closed. Once again, I was sitting at home in limbo, waiting for the nation's highest court to rule on the future of integration in Little Rock.

Ten days later, the Supreme Court spoke. It took Chief Justice Earl Warren just four minutes to read the decision ordering the Little Rock school district to proceed with integration. But Faubus was ready to counteract. He was even cockier than usual after having just won the Democratic nomination for his third term. In Arkansas, that was tantamount to reelection, and Faubus was about to become the first governor in fifty years to serve more than two terms. The power seemed to intoxicate him. By the time the Supreme Court issued its order, Faubus had already called a special session of the state legislature and pushed through six anti-integration bills, which gave him extraordinary powers over the school system. Just hours after the Supreme Court announcement, Faubus made his stunning move: He signed the anti-integration bills into law and utilized his new power to shut down all three public high schools in Little Rock. And just like that, thirty-seven hundred students, black and white, were left wondering: What now?

The news infuriated me. How dared the state's highest-ranking public official jeopardize the futures of thousands of students? How was I going to complete my junior year now? Ernie had left for Michigan State, Minnijean was back in New York, and the parents of two of my other comrades had decided already that their families would take no more. They had already walked through hell and had no intention of looking back. Terry had moved to Los Angeles in August to stay with his paternal grandmother and other relatives. His parents and younger siblings would leave Little Rock for good and join him there by the end of the year. Gloria and her mother relocated around the same time to Kansas City, while her father maintained the family home in Little Rock. That left Jefferson, Elizabeth, Thelma, Melba, and me. Mrs. Bates did her best to try to reassure us and our parents while we waited. I can still see the urgency on her face as she explained that we could take correspondence courses through the University of Arkansas. In the meantime, she promised, the NAACP would continue to fight for us.

My own feelings were mixed, just as they had been when Minnijean first left for New York. I regretted that those of us who had been through so much together at Central wouldn't be able to finish our journey together. But I was happy that my comrades were moving on to more peaceful lives. Five of the nine—Terry, Minnie, Melba, Elizabeth, and Thelma—were all seniors now. This was to be their final year at Central, but from all appearances, the battle was not even close to resolution. Faubus regularly strutted before the television cameras to justify his decision, as if upsetting the lives of so many were a perfectly reasonable thing to do. The results of a local election he called in September gave him even more confidence that white Little Rock stood with him. In that election, Little Rock voters were asked whether they wanted "complete integration" or "none at all." The ballot provided for nothing in between, so the outcome was no surprise: 70 percent of the voters chose "none at all."

Through it all, though, my family never even talked about leaving Little Rock—at least, as far as I knew. Perhaps to my parents, the idea of leaving their large, extended families and everything they had ever known was scarier than the prospect of facing another uncertain year at Central. My parents probably would have considered sending me temporarily to St. Louis, Kansas City, Chicago, or other cities where we had close relatives, but Mrs. Bates asked those of us who remained to stay in town. We might be needed in court, she said. At first, that was fine with me. While the thought of going to school in another city at times seemed enticing and adventurous, I felt a strong need to stay close to my parents and sisters. I felt guilty because I saw how much my family was struggling, and I knew it was because of my decision to attend Central. With Daddy having trouble earning a steady paycheck, Mother had gotten a job working for the city. I wanted to do my part, so I took on the responsibility of caring for Tina, who was three years old.

Families like mine weren't the only ones suddenly scrambling after the school closings to figure out what to do. The school board also had to act quickly to keep teachers from abandoning the system en masse. To quell the teachers' fears, the board agreed to continue paying them. Then, when an uproar rose from the community over the prospect of a year without football, the board (with the support of the governor) made provisions for the season to continue. So even though thousands of families were scurrying to find academic alternatives for their children, teachers were reporting to empty classrooms, and the football teams practiced and played a regular schedule.

The most galling development of all, though, occurred just five days after Faubus closed the high schools. The governor had the nerve to announce on television that the Little Rock Private School Corporation, a group of segregationists, would be allowed to lease the public schools. I was appalled. Did Faubus really think he could get away with allowing white parents to rent the public schools just for their children? Did he really believe he was slick enough to undermine a U.S. Supreme Court order in this way? Fortunately, the NAACP, supported by the Department of Justice, quickly secured an injunction and bulldozed the plan—at least, part of it. The corporation remained intact and ultimately purchased the former University of Arkansas Graduate Center for its school. The group also managed to hire teachers from outside the city after its efforts to hire public school teachers failed. With everything in place, the segregationists opened their whites-only

Me at about eight years old, around the time I took my first life-changing trip to New York City. *(Photo by M. A. Binns)*

At home with my parents (Cartelyou and Juanita Walls) when I was four years old. *(Photo by Earl Davy)*

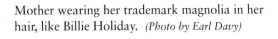

Mother wearing her trademark magnolia in her hair, like Billie Holiday. *(Photo by Earl Davy)*

Daddy, who was my rock.
(Photo by Earl Davy)

Daddy and Mother out on the town.
(Courtesy of the author)

My great-grandfather, Aaron Holloway
(Papa Holloway), the patriarch
on my mother's side of the family.
(Courtesy of the author)

Dora Holmes, Papa Holloway's longtime girlfriend, the original owner of the house that placed me in the attendance zone for Little Rock Central High School. *(Courtesy of the author)*

Med Cullins (Grandpa Cullins), my maternal grandfather, who owned a contracting business and taught my father the brick masonry trade. *(Courtesy of the author)*

Porter Walls, Sr. (Big Daddy), my paternal grandfather, who owned a café/pool hall and lots of inherited land. *(Photo by Earl Davy)*

Alfredo Andrade (Uncle Freddie), who made sure I experienced the New York of my dreams during my first trip there in the summer of 1951. *(Courtesy of the author)*

Me, Camille (on my right) with Aunt Juanita and Renata to my left. *(Courtesy of the author)*

M. E. Cullins Beard, my great-aunt, with whom I stayed in Chicago during the summer of 1959. *(Courtesy of the author)*

Mother and me at the kitchen counter during my first year at Central. *(Photo by Earl Davy)*

Little Rock Central High School, which the National Institute of Architects called "America's Most Beautiful School" when it was built in 1927. *(Courtesy of the author)*

Me, Gloria Ray, Jane Hill (standing behind Gloria), and Ernest Green as we face the National Guard on September 4, 1957, on our first attempt to enter Central; Jane never returned to Central after that day. *(Will Counts Collection: Indiana University Archives)*

THE WHITE HOUSE
WASHINGTON

October 4, 1957

<u>PERSONAL</u>

Dear Mrs. Walls:

I deeply appreciate your September thirtieth telegram, signed also by other parents. The supreme law of our land has been clearly defined by the Supreme Court. To support and defend the Constitution of the United States is my solemn oath as your President -- a pledge which imposes upon me the responsibility to see that the laws of our country are faithfully executed. I shall continue to discharge that responsibility in the interest of all Americans today, as well as to preserve our free institutions of government for the sake of Americans yet unborn.

I believe that America's heart goes out to you and your children in your present ordeal. In the course of our country's progress toward equality of opportunity, you have shown dignity and courage in circumstances which would daunt citizens of lesser faith.

With best wishes to you,

Sincerely,

Dwight D Eisenhower

Mrs. Juanita Walls
1500 Valentine Street
Little Rock
Arkansas

<u>PERSONAL</u>

Letters from President Eisenhower, expressing his support, were hand-delivered by a federal agent to all nine of our mothers shortly after he sent the 101st Airborne Division to escort us into Central High School. This is the letter President Eisenhower wrote to my mother. *(Courtesy of the author)*

Here I am on the ferry (right) passing the Statue of Liberty during our trip to New York in the summer of 1958. *(© Mildred Grossman Collection: University of Maryland Baltimore County)*

Me, Elizabeth, Melba, and Minnijean at Coney Island during our trip to New York in the summer of 1958. *(© Mildred Grossman Collection: University of Maryland Baltimore County)*

The Little Rock Nine meeting with New York City mayor Robert F. Wagner at City Hall. *(© Mildred Grossman Collection: University of Maryland Baltimore County)*

The Little Rock Nine and New York governor William Harriman after an AFL-CIO Hotel Employees Union awards ceremony. *(© Mildred Grossman Collection: University of Maryland Baltimore County)*

The nine of us and our escorts dining at the famous Lindy's restaurant in New York. *(© Mildred Grossman Collection: University of Maryland Baltimore County)*

NAACP attorney Thurgood Marshall with me, Minnijean, and Elizabeth, on his left, and Daisy Bates, Gloria, Jefferson, and Melba, on his right, on the steps of the U.S. Supreme Court. *(AP Images)*

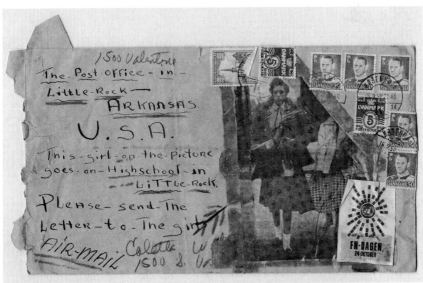

This letter from Denmark made it to me, even though the writer only put a photo of me from a newspaper clipping and a brief note on the envelope. *(Courtesy of the author)*

The Little Rock Nine with our parents at a Christmas party in our honor, sponsored by Delta Sigma Theta Sorority, Inc., in December 1957. *(Photograph by Earl Davy)*

Daddy and investigators surveying the damage from the bombing of my family's home in February 1960. *(Courtesy of the author)*

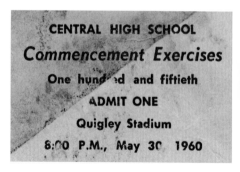

I had six of these prized admission tickets for my closest family members to attend my graduation from Central. *(Courtesy of the author)*

CENTRAL HIGH SCHOOL

Commencement Exercises

One hund'ed and fiftieth

ADMIT ONE

Quigley Stadium

8:00 P.M., May 30 1960

Central High School

Little Rock   Arkansas

Carlotta Walls

has satisfactorily completed the course of study prescribed by the Board of Education for the High School Department and is entitled to this

Diploma

July 8, 1960
Date of Award

Terrell E. Powell
Superintendent

Jess W. Matthews
Principal

Everett Tucker, Jr.
President

Ted Lamb
Secretary

(Courtesy of the author)

The most relieved member of Central's graduating class of 1960. *(Courtesy of the author)*

DAISY BATES HOUSE
HAS BEEN DESIGNATED A
NATIONAL HISTORIC LANDMARK
THIS SITE POSSESSES NATIONAL SIGNIFICANCE
IN COMMEMORATING THE HISTORY OF THE
UNITED STATES OF AMERICA
2001
NATIONAL PARK SERVICE
UNITED STATES DEPARTMENT OF THE INTERIOR

The home of L.C. and Daisy Bates, where the nine of us met practically every day that first year, eventually became a national historical site. *(Courtesy of the author)*

President Bill Clinton opening the door
to Central for me during a symbolic
moment in 1997 at the fortieth
anniversary of the Little Rock Nine.
(Courtesy Getty Images)

The nine of us with President Bill
Clinton at the fortieth anniversary of
the Little Rock Nine in 1997. *(Courtesy
of the White House)*

Hillary Clinton presents
Mother an award (with
Melba in the background)
during a ceremony at the
fortieth anniversary—the
first time our parents were
officially recognized for their
role. *(Courtesy of the White
House)*

"HARD **WORK, DETERMINATION,**
PERSISTENCE, **AND FAITH** IN GOD WERE
LESSONS **LEARNED** FROM MY PARENTS,
CARTE**LYOU & JUANITA** WALLS. I WAS
ONLY **DOING WHAT WAS** RIGHT."

CARLOTTA WALLS LANIER

The plaque next to the bronze depiction of me in the "Testament" memorial that stands on the north end of the Arkansas State Capitol in Little Rock. *(Courtesy of the author)*

The "Testament" memorial features life-size bronze statutes of each of the Little Rock Nine. *(Courtesy of the author)*

Me standing next to my bronze image. *(Courtesy of the author)*

On August 31, 2005, the United States Post Office dedicated a 37-cent postage stamp recognizing the Little Rock Nine as part of its "To Form a More Perfect Union" collection. *(Courtesy of the author)*

1957 Little Rock Nine   37 USA

obverse   reverse

President Clinton awarded the Little Rock Nine a Congressional Gold Medal in November 1999. *(Courtesy of the author)*

My family (from left: Alan Terry, Shana Terry, Russel Terry, Whitney LaNier, Brooke LaNier, Juanita Walls, me, Ira LaNier, Tina Walls, Loujuana Terry, Jevin Terry holding Cartel Terry, and Kim Terry) with President Clinton in a replica of his White House office at his presidential library in Little Rock. *(Courtesy of the Clinton Presidential Center)*

Ernie (far left), Terrence (far right), and me with then-Senator Barack Obama at a Congressional Black Caucus event in 2007. *(Courtesy of Altria Client Services)*

With my husband, Ira LaNier, at the Rainbow Room in New York City. *(Courtesy of the author)*

My children, Brooke and Whitney.
(Courtesy of the author)

My sisters, Loujuana, Tina (sitting), my daughter, Brooke (center), and me at an Inaugural Ball celebrating the election of President Barack Obama. *(Courtesy of the author)*

school in late October and eventually enrolled about 900 students. However, by the beginning of 1959, at least 675 students were not enrolled in school or correspondence courses anywhere, according to a magazine article that Superintendent Blossom later wrote. Those students just dropped out of school and settled for low-paying jobs. I'm sure Faubus lost no sleep worrying about them because the majority of them—those hit hardest and hurt the most by his foolish acts—were black.

Even though my parents were struggling financially, they were determined to keep me on schedule academically, so they scraped up the extra money to pay for the correspondence courses and rent the textbooks. So, too, did the families of Jefferson, Elizabeth, Thelma, and Melba, who also took the courses. The Dunbar Community Center arranged for students in the community who wanted to do our schoolwork together to meet there every day and get help from retired teachers and volunteers from the local library. Every day, Mother dropped Tina and me off at the center, as though we were going to school. For half a day, I did my correspondence work. My first two courses were U.S. History II and English II, and the assignments came in white folders from the Division of General Education at the University of Arkansas in Fayetteville. Each folder contained a form letter that provided basic information, such as the name and address of my instructor. Twenty-four assignments were enclosed in each packet, but I was instructed to complete no more than four per week. I quickly found that those four assignments didn't amount to nearly enough work to keep my mind occupied. Once, I was scolded for returning too many lessons at one time. Several times, I received a bright yellow slip of paper notifying me that because of increased enrollment in the courses, I was being assigned a new teacher. The note assured me that the change would not affect my progress in the course or my grade. That happened so frequently that it was hard to keep up with who—if anyone—was seriously evaluating my work. Except for the occasional correction of a misspelled word or a brief question asking for additional information, the teacher rarely made notes on my papers. Most times, the only indication that anyone had even looked at my assignment was a grade at the top of the page, usually an A. After I had completed the required two dozen assignments, an examination was mailed to me, and my grade was based on my proficiency on the test. I've kept my papers from that time, and they remind me to this day how empty those days felt. I do, however, look back fondly on the fun. On a typical day, about ten to fifteen students showed up, and it was good to be engaged with other teenagers. I missed learning, but I didn't miss the stress or isolation I'd experienced the first year at Central. At the center, most of us were done with our serious work by lunchtime, and we whiled away the afternoons at the card table. I'd hold Tina on my lap as we played bid whist, checkers, dominoes, and Scrabble. We teenagers talked a lot of noise and often spelled words we thought the little one shouldn't hear. But Tina, ever a quick study, not only picked up a lifelong affection and talent for cards and board games, she also quickly became a master speller. You could just see that phonetic wheel twirling in her brain as she tried to figure out what she was not supposed to hear. It became almost a game to her to outsmart the big kids and then blurt out our disguised words.

Despite the fun, I knew I was supposed to be in school, and I couldn't help worrying about my future, about how much my chances of getting into a good college would be hurt by these long months out of school. But there were worries far beyond me. Elsewhere in Little Rock, the city's economy was suffering. Not only was Little Rock's population declining, but no new industry was moving in. From the fall of 1957 until the start of 1959, not a single new company decided to move to the Little Rock industrial area. Even those companies with previous plans to open plants in Little Rock canceled those arrangements once the 101st Airborne

Division set up shop in the city. The city was bleeding, and others were starting to feel the pain.

Much of white Little Rock blamed Mrs. Bates and our parents for the crisis. Faubus encouraged those sentiments with his rhetoric: "If Daisy Bates would find an honest job and go to work, and if the U.S. Supreme Court would keep its cotton-picking hands off the Little Rock School Board's affairs, we could open the Little Rock schools," he declared.

A group calling itself the Save Our Schools Committee also perpetuated the notion that our parents and Mrs. Bates were at fault. In mid-September 1958, the group began running a series of newspaper ads, encouraging black ministers and other black community leaders to "appeal to Mrs. Bates and seven parents to give us time to accept this change in a Christian manner." It never ceased to amaze me how often the bigots tried to hide their fear and hatred behind the banner of Christianity.

Toward the end of the year, I started to see stories on television and in the newspapers about another group of white women calling themselves the Women's Emergency Committee to Open Our Schools (WEC). Led by Adolphine Terry, Vivion Brewer, and Velma Powell (the wife of one of Central's vice principals), they tried to become a voice of reason among whites in the community. The group's policy statement reflected the balance the women were hoping to strike: "We stand neither for integration nor for segregation, but for education," the statement read.

The group outlined a fourfold purpose: to get the free public high schools reopened, to get students back in their classes, to retain the staff of good teachers, and to regain full accreditation by the North Central Association. Behind the scenes, the committee also became a political force. When the existing school board resigned in mid-November 1958, the committee was largely responsible for recruiting moderates to run for the six vacant positions. That set up a race pitting the moderates against segregationist candidates who supported the governor's position. As fate would have it, the election resulted in a split board: three moderates and three segregationists. One of the new board's first major actions was to fire Superintendent Blossom "without cause and without prejudice" in December 1958.

When teachers returned again to empty classrooms the following January, rumors began circulating that the board was planning a "purge" of teachers. Faubus said publicly that he thought Central's principal, Jess Matthews, and the two vice principals, Mrs. Huckaby and Mr. Powell, should be fired. Mr. Powell had angered segregationists when he participated as a guest panelist at a session sponsored by his wife and the Women's Emergency Committee. Rumor had it that Mr. Powell was at the top of the list of those to go, but he instead quit and took another job in California.

As I watched much of this unfold in the newspapers and on television, I changed my mind about staying in Little Rock. I was tired of the politics. I just wanted to be in school, even if it meant moving to another city for a while. Besides, by the beginning of the year, I had completed all of the correspondence courses I could take in one semester, and I was seriously bored. I heard that Mrs. Bates had sent out an appeal asking NAACP supporters in other cities to take in black Little Rock students interested in relocating to finish their high school education. One such offer came from a white couple in Santa Rosa, California, who were dedicated to racial justice and wanted to become a surrogate family to a displaced black student. Mrs. Bates arranged for Melba to move to the West Coast to live with the couple and their four children. I also began hearing about Horace Mann students who were being placed in other homes throughout the country. I wondered why Mrs. Bates kept passing me up for such opportunities. One day, I was bold enough to ask. Mrs. Bates reiterated that she wanted me to stay close, in case I was needed in court. Perhaps she could tell from my facial expression that I wasn't too happy with that response because she soon had a change of heart. In late March 1959, she called to tell my parents that Dr. Nathan Christopher, an NAACP board member in Cleveland, had invited a Little Rock student to stay with his family and finish high school there. This time, Mrs. Bates was extending the invitation to me. Mother and Daddy discussed it and agreed that the time may have come for me to go away to school, but they let me decide whether I wanted to go to Cleveland. Of course, the decision for me was easy. The offer couldn't have come at a better time, and by the beginning of April, I was off to Cleveland for a new adventure.

I liked the Christophers immediately. They were a sophisticated couple who appeared to be in their early sixties. Nathan Christopher was a prominent black dentist, very mild-mannered and easygoing. I soon learned that one of his favorite pastimes was fishing in Canada. His wife, Edith, was the more outgoing of the two—a tall, authoritative woman who owned a couple of businesses and often fronted the capital to help young black business owners open their flower shops, beauty salons, and corner stores. She traveled in powerful political circles and easily held her own among the men who sat with her on a dozen or so boards and commissions. She was a big woman who wore bottle-thick glasses that only slightly improved her vision, which had been practically destroyed by cataracts. Because of her poor eyesight, she was no longer supposed to drive. I helped drive her around, cook occasionally, and perform light chores. The couple had both a maid and a cook, so my chores didn't amount to much more than I already did at home.

This kind of arrangement was fairly common among black families of means who were deeply committed to giving back to the community. I'd seen it close up in my own family because my great-uncle John Cullins (the older brother of Grandpa Cullins) and his wife took in students from Philander Smith. Uncle John's own children were grown, so he provided the college students free housing, food, and tuition assistance in exchange for their helping out around the house. I was the eleventh student the Christophers had welcomed into their home over the years. After raising their daughter and son into adulthood, the couple had committed their lives to nurturing the dreams of other black children, particularly those from families of lesser means who could benefit from the stability and guidance of two accomplished and well-connected professionals. Their home was an elegant flat about twenty-five hundred square feet on the second floor of a three-story, six-unit brick complex they owned. The building sat on East Boulevard in an upper-middle-class, mostly white neighborhood, across from a nice park. I slept in a room that had been built as the "maid quarters," just off the kitchen in the back of the apartment. It was comfortable, though nothing fancy. But the rest of the home was exquisitely decorated. Mrs. Christopher changed the furniture, particularly in the living and dining areas, every two years. She would call in movers to haul out the pieces she no longer wanted, and with little or no notice, a moving van loaded with her expensive furnishings would show up at her daughter's place on the other side of the city to unload. I remember her daughter sort of rolling her eyes one day as she told me about a delivery her mother recently had sent.

Because of where the Christophers lived, I was able to enroll in East High, an integrated but predominantly white high school in the neighborhood. It was one of the best schools in the city, and fortunately for me, none of my peers knew my story. There, I was just another student, going to class, trying to keep up with my schoolwork. After the year I'd experienced at Central, it felt good to go to school without being noticed. The other students were friendly enough, but I didn't develop any lasting relationships, in part because I had little time to get together with my peers outside of school. Most of my evenings were spent behind the wheel of

Mrs. Christopher's huge navy blue Lincoln, shuttling her from one meeting to another. But I rather enjoyed hanging out in the background of her life and watching quietly as this strong, smart black woman negotiated, gave orders, and made things happen. In some ways, she was the female version of my grandfathers, tough and resourceful. In her, I saw possibilities for myself.

Back then, I always liked spending time with older people like Mrs. Christopher because I believed they could teach me something. I sometimes learned by just watching how they handled themselves. I also enjoyed listening to their stories. Plus, I was very comfortable around them. So when Mother sent a letter containing the telephone number of my great-aunt Maude, I seized the opportunity. Maude Warren, then sixty-six, was the only one of Papa Holloway's siblings who had stayed in touch with him. Like my great-grandfather, she had taken a different road from that of the rest of her brothers and sisters by claiming her "colored" roots. I called her right away and asked if I could visit. To my surprise, I learned that she lived just blocks from the Christophers, close enough for me to walk.

The next afternoon, I walked the several blocks to her house. As soon as Aunt Maude stepped to the door, I saw the Holloway resemblance. She was tall and thin, with tan skin, narrow features, and long, once jet black hair mingled with gray. We greeted each other cordially, but no hugs (the Holloways aren't given to demonstrative displays of affection). I followed her to the living room, where we sat and talked between long moments of silence. Like Papa Holloway, Aunt Maude didn't talk much, and she held her past close to the vest. She asked about our family—Uncle Teet and a couple of Papa Holloway's other children whom she knew by name. She had met only the few relatives who stopped by while traveling through Cleveland. She had never traveled to Little Rock, not even for Papa Holloway's funeral the year before. After a

while, I asked if she knew any of her other brothers and sisters—
the ones passing for white. At first, she didn't answer. I had a
chance to ask again later, thinking that maybe she didn't hear me.

"No," she replied softly, "I don't know where the others are."

I didn't push. A few moments later, Aunt Maude introduced me
to her son, Ollie, when he walked into the room. He was as quiet
as a ghost, with a shock of prematurely gray hair. Family members
told me that he lived with his mother because he had been unable
to steady his life after serving in World War II. After about an hour
with Aunt Maude, it was time for me to leave. I thanked her for allowing me to visit and headed back to my temporary home. Along
the way, I thought about Papa Holloway, how much I missed him
and how happy it would have made him to know that I had visited
his sister.

I returned for another short visit with Aunt Maude, but my
time in Cleveland ran out sooner than I had expected. I had been
living with the Christophers just one month when Mrs. Christopher called me into her room for a chat. She had never summoned
me like this before, so I figured the matter must be serious. As I
walked to her room, I quickly reviewed the past few days in my
head, wondering if I had forgotten to take care of something she
had requested or whether I might have done something she did not
like. Nothing came to mind.

When I walked into the bedroom, Mrs. Christopher was sitting
on the edge of her bed. She wore a smile that told me she wasn't
upset with me, but the mood was less than happy. I took a seat in
the Queen Anne–style wingback chair across from her and braced
myself as she began to speak. She and her husband really liked me,
she said, but I wasn't exactly the kind of student she had requested. I clearly wasn't deprived or lacking in social grace and
skills, she said. I had been blessed with good, solid parents, grandparents, aunts, and uncles who were perfectly capable of providing
whatever guidance I needed henceforth. She said she believed there

were other students who might benefit more from her and her husband's help. She was very warm, almost apologetic. She didn't ask me to leave, but I figured that would be best. I knew how important it was to her to feel that she was making a difference by providing an opportunity that a young person might not otherwise have. I didn't want to stand in the way of that. Mrs. Christopher had some other ideas for me, though. She didn't think I should return to Little Rock or Central. I was smart and mature enough to skip the rest of high school and start college as early as the coming summer, she said. She sat on the board of Ferris State College in Big Rapids, Michigan, and she assured me that I could get in.

I wasn't so sure. My gut told me that I wasn't quite ready for college. After an entire year out of school, I believed I needed more math and science to have a chance at success in college. But I told Mrs. Christopher that I would discuss it with my parents and think about it.

Mother and Daddy were flattered that a woman of Mrs. Christopher's stature thought I was ready for college, but they, too, had some concerns. We didn't rush into a decision. I applied to Ferris State, and we kept our options open. During our frequent conversations and letters over the next several weeks, Mother and Daddy kept me abreast of the political changes taking place in Little Rock. A recall election in May resulted in a new school board with a majority of moderates who proclaimed that Central would reopen in the fall. One of the moderates was a man named Rhett Tucker, whose son I'd get to know many years later. The votes of the city's black residents and affluent, well-educated white residents had made the difference, my parents said. By mid-May, I received word that I had been accepted to Ferris State, but I decided not to go. My parents and I agreed that I should return to Little Rock to get my high school diploma because I needed to hone the academic skills required for college. But for me, there was an even greater need. I had been through too much over the past nearly two years—so had my family—for me to just walk away empty-handed. I needed my high school diploma, and I needed to earn it from Central. That accomplishment, I believed, was the least I could achieve now. Anything short of that would have felt like failure to me.

The problem was, even with the correspondence courses and my two months at East High, I was still short of the credits that would be needed to complete the eleventh grade at Central. I needed to attend summer school. My parents arranged for me to spend the summer with relatives in Chicago and attend summer school there. In early June, I packed my bags, thanked the well-meaning Christophers for their generosity and kindness, and boarded a train bound for the Windy City.

Waiting for me there were my great-aunt M.E. Cullins Beard and her husband, Elmer. I called her Aunt M.E. (I never knew what the initials represented; she said they didn't stand for anything). She was the youngest sister of Grandpa Cullins (my maternal grandfather), and she reminded me so much of Mother. Aunt M.E. had no children of her own, but of all her nieces, she clearly favored Mother. She even called Mother her "pride and joy." The two of them resembled each other so closely, they could easily have been mistaken for mother and daughter. Mother had picked up some of our aunt's ways, too, particularly her keen sense of fashion. Aunt M.E. was an avid reader of *Vogue* magazine and always looked as though she had stepped right off its pages. She wasn't just a fashion plate, though. She had attended Philander Smith, taught school, and worked as a secretary at one of the insurance companies located in the historic Mosaic Templar building on West 9th Street in Little Rock. She had moved to Chicago from St. Louis after meeting and marrying Elmer Beard, her third husband. They lived in the 7900 block of S. Indiana Street on the South Side, a typical Chicago suburb with neatly-trimmed trees and well-kept lawns and families headed by hardworking professional and blue-collar mothers and fathers. The next-door neighbor was a dentist. Many of the neighbors were former black southerners who had headed north, following kin who'd been part of the so-called Great Migration of the early twentieth century. They had come to break free of the stranglehold that Jim Crow had on the places of their birth. They had come in search of the opportunities touted by the *Chicago Defender,* one of the most widely read black newspapers throughout the South. They had come in search of jobs in Chicago's steel mills, meatpacking houses, and railroads and the opportunity to learn, eat, and travel as freely as any white man or woman. They had come with nothing but their sheer will and ingenuity—a kind of industriousness that, I might add, was not always appreciated by their citified black brethren, who complained behind closed doors about the ruin the country folk were bringing to the neighborhood. An article that ran during the summer in the *Chicago Defender* poked fun at the black southerners, who were said to pull old bedsprings stripped of their coverings onto their yards, dig holes in the ground for their coal, barbecue on the wire springs, and litter their lawns with chicken bones. A line from the story became a running joke between Uncle Elmer and me. Purposely written in dialect, it said something like ". . . and a n- don't care where he tho' he bone."

I was too young to understand the danger of stereotypes or the irony that white folks often painted all black folks with the same broad brush. At the time, the line just seemed plain funny, and Uncle Elmer and I would look knowingly at each other, mouth those words, and crack up if we spotted the least bit of evidence of its truth.

I soon had to share the time I spent with Uncle Elmer and Aunt M.E. with my cousin Delores Warren, who came from Little Rock to join me. The women in the family thought I'd need someone my age to keep me company. But having company was too often nerve-racking. Delores, then fifteen, wasn't in summer school, and she watched television all day until I got home. She had a sassy mouth and talked back to Aunt M.E. She also used to sneak to the bowling alley in the evenings to see her boyfriend, John Smith, who was a few years older and already in college. John was from Little Rock but had come to Chicago that summer with his friend Al Bell—the same Al Bell who would go on to become the head honcho at Stax Records. Years later, Stax would compete with the legendary Motown for the soul of black music. Al and John were as close as brothers. Al had lived with John's family in Little Rock throughout high school and college and his tenure as a popular young deejay at KOKY, the first local station to cater to black listeners. Al had come to Chicago to be close to his girlfriend, Mavis Staples of the famous Staple Singers, and John tagged along so that he could spend time with Delores.

Aunt M.E. thought the lovebirds were far too serious for their age, particularly her fifteen-year-old niece. Before John arrived in Chicago, his letters to Delores had come addressed to "Mrs. John Smith." The two indeed became husband and wife several years later, and Al brought John into Stax as a high-powered executive. But in the summer of 1959, John was just a college boy with uncertain motives in my aunt's eyes, and she didn't want him at her house. I became the excuse for Delores to get to the bowling alley to see John. I'd never bowled before in Little Rock, but it became one of my favorite new pastimes. I was thrilled for the chance to get out of the house, especially when the sparks were flying between Delores and Aunt M.E. Delores was the type who pushed the envelope, and I often got caught in that awkward spot in the middle when my aunt said to her: "Why aren't you more like Carlotta?"

I have to admit, I was more than a bit happy when Delores received a train ticket back to Little Rock from her mother, my Little Aunt Loualice (my great-aunt is Big Loualice, thanks to the confusing family tradition of passing along first names). At least, with Delores gone, I didn't have to hear my elders comparing my cousin to me. I sometimes felt tremendous pressure to live up to everyone's expectations—my family members, Mrs. Bates, the NAACP. I wanted never to disappoint any of them. Most times, that wasn't difficult. My nature leaned toward following the rules and doing the right thing. But that summer, I was a sixteen-year-old music lover in a real music town with temptations at practically every corner of the stretch I walked to and from school. I attended summer school at Hirsch High, about a mile from my aunt and uncle's home. My classes began at eight a.m. and ended at noon, just about the time that my route along 79th Street began to sizzle. I mean, it was sizzling, literally, hot as heck outside. But the music scene was just as hot. In those days, the record stores blasted the latest music through huge speakers that filled the walkways with the soulful sounds of rhythm and blues, rock and roll, and jazz. Everywhere I walked, it seemed I heard Brook Benton's smooth baritone flowing through the speakers, heating up the already hot outdoors with his hit "It's Just a Matter of Time," which was topping the R&B charts that summer.

That's probably what first drew me into the record shop, but once I realized the place was air-conditioned, it gave me another excuse to stop there every day on the way home. I'd wander around the store, listening to Lloyd Price tell the story of the barroom gambler who lost all his money and then settled the score with his "forty-four" in the chart-topping "Stagger Lee." Or that acrobatic voice of Jackie Wilson would be crooning "Lonely Teardrops." Fats Domino would start pleading in "I Want to Walk You Home," or jazz great Ahmad Jamal would take me to heaven gliding up and down the piano in his sensational "Poinciana"—I love that number to this day. I'd linger in that record store, listening, losing track of time, sorting through the LPs of some of my favorite artists: Little Richard, the Platters, Elvis, and the original "queen of soul," Dinah Washington.

One day, while walking from school, I noticed a sign that Dinah would be appearing at a popular South Side club called the Roberts Show Lounge. I had to be there. All of a sudden, it didn't matter that I was just sixteen or that I'd probably have to scheme to get there. This felt like the chance of a lifetime, and I intended to take full advantage. It helped that I had made some pretty cool family friends who were older than me but a generation younger than Aunt M.E. and Uncle Elmer. One of them was my cousin Doris, who was from Little Rock but had recently moved to Chicago to teach after marrying Lowell Zollar, who was working in a biology lab there. Doris and Lowell, who eventually became a doctor, helped to show me a grand time in Chicago. So did Uncle Elmer's children from a prior marriage, Sue and Elmer, Jr., and their spouses. I grew particularly close to Sue, who was a teacher, and her husband, George Love, who worked in an Exxon plant. They had moved in with Aunt M.E. and Uncle Elmer for a month during my time there, while waiting to move into their own house in another area of the South Side that was just starting to open to black residents. Sue and George were lenient with me and helped to bridge the generational gap between me and their parents. When I saw the Dinah Washington sign, I knew I could rely on Sue and George to cover for me.

There was no cover at the door, and I just slid in with the crowd. I always acted older, and my height made me look older, too, so I didn't stand out. I didn't drink or draw attention to myself. I just sat in that grand lounge, which had hundreds of seats around a huge stage. A big crystal ball hanging in the middle of the room mesmerized me as much as the queen herself. As those crystals glittered and bounced off the ceiling, Dinah belted with ever so perfect timing and precision:

> What a diff'rence a day made
> Twenty-four little hours . . .

Talk about Hollywood—Dinah took me there that night.

It wasn't the last time Sue and George helped me witness what would become legendary Chicago music history. Later that summer when I saw billboards advertising the first ever Playboy Jazz Festival, I gave Sue the $3.70 or so I'd saved by walking, instead of riding the bus to school, to buy my ticket. The event was being sponsored by Hugh Hefner and his then five-year-old *Playboy* magazine, so I'm sure I had no business there. But even as a teenager, I'd become something of a jazz aficionado. My parents were jazz lovers. They traveled with other couples to St. Louis for a spring musical revue, called the *Y Circus,* which featured a number of jazz artists. Mother and Daddy would bring home the music of Duke Ellington, Count Basie, Billie Holiday, Sarah Vaughan, Joe Williams, Pearl Bailey, Eartha Kitt, Ella Fitzgerald, Earl "Fatha" Hines, all the popular jazz artists of the day. One of them was always riffing in the background of our lives at home. So how was I supposed to resist when I saw on the billboard that practically all of my favorite jazz artists would be at the Playboy Jazz Festival August 7–9 in Chicago Stadium?

Sue and George again helped cover for me and told me how to take the bus to the west side for one of the best days of my life. When I got to the stadium, I struck up a conversation with a police officer and palmed him my ticket in the nosebleed section, and he let me slip onto the floor for an unbelievable view. I could hardly believe my luck as I stood there, soaking up the best music I'd ever heard in my life: Count Basie, Joe Williams, and a group that I had seen the summer before in New York, Lambert, Hendricks & Ross. Joe was the featured singer for Basie, and the trio came out as a backup on a couple of numbers. Now, that was real music. Near the end of the show, out comes a guy with his hat cocked a certain way, singing "Angel Eyes" just like Ol' Blue Eyes himself. He brought down the house. Everybody thought the man was Frank Sinatra. As it turned out, he was an imitator, a heck of a good one, though. Anyway, the show was a real thrill. It made my summer.

As the summer wound down, my parents told me that the federal courts ruled the high school closings had been illegal. The high schools in Little Rock could reopen. Suddenly, there was no more time to lose, and school officials were rushing to start the new school year early. The opening of the 1959–1960 session—my senior year—was set to begin August 12, three weeks earlier than the traditional school opening after Labor Day. Unfortunately, summer school wouldn't end until the third week in August, and I would miss the grand reopening of Central.

I stayed in close touch with my parents and Mrs. Bates, who told me that Gloria would remain in Kansas City to finish her senior year. By then, Minnie and Terrence had graduated from the high schools they had attended in other cities, Melba was preparing to take courses at San Francisco State University, and Elizabeth and Thelma had completed their senior year mostly through correspondence courses. Of the original Little Rock Nine, just two were left to return to Central: Jefferson and I.

I was quite surprised to learn that even after two years of racial unrest over school integration in Little Rock, sixty black students had applied to go to white high schools when they reopened. School officials accepted only eight—three at the formerly all-white Hall High School and five at Central. The five students to go to Central included Sybil Jordan, Frank Henderson, Sandra Johnson, Jefferson, and I.

If anyone had any illusions that things would be different in the upcoming school year or that the segregationists had finally given up their fight, those thoughts surely must have evaporated on the first day of school. I was finishing up summer school in Chicago on the morning of August 12 when back home in Little Rock, a caravan of segregationists from all over the state and elsewhere in the South descended on the Arkansas State Capitol grounds to hear

Faubus make a speech. Family members told me how the governor fired up the crowd with his anti-integration rhetoric and how the streets filled afterward with an angry mob headed for Central. I could just imagine them singing their own resistance anthem, as they had two years before:

> In Arkansas, in the state of cotton
> Federal courts are good and rotten
> Look away, look away, look away, Dixie Land.

But a new police chief was in charge—Eugene G. Smith. I remembered Chief Smith from the 1957 school year because, as assistant chief then, he was the one who had ordered his officers to get us out of Central the day the mob took control. Smith, who was considered a moderate, apparently had determined there would be no repeat of that day this time around. According to news reports, he had both the police and fire departments on alert. He used a megaphone to order the crowd to disperse, but the protesters paid him no mind. His officers even had to use nightsticks to defend themselves against the crowd. When the crowd got more unruly, Smith ordered firemen to open their hoses, unleashing a torrent of water streaming onto the crowd at half blast. When Eugene "Bull" O'Connor would apply that same controversial tactic years later on civil rights marchers in Birmingham, many of whom were children, he ordered the hoses turned to full blast, powerful enough to strip bark from trees. Before the Little Rock officers were able to restore calm, about two dozen troublemakers were arrested. Smith's actions that day would linger in the minds of segregationists, who bumped him even higher on their list of most hated public enemies. Such hatred would raise suspicions evermore in Little Rock's black community in the days ahead, when Smith's career as a law enforcement officer would come to an astonishing and mysterious end.

About an hour after the mob quieted, Jeff walked up the steps of Central to begin his senior year. He was accompanied by one who knew better than anyone else what it was like to stand alone in the midst of a hateful mob: our comrade Elizabeth Eckford. Elizabeth had finished her high school coursework through correspondence courses, but she knew I was still out of town and did not want Jeff to face the mob alone. That decision was nothing short of brave and heroic. It touches me still.

Finally, summer school was over, and it was time for me to leave Chicago. Aunt M.E. and Uncle Elmer bought me an airline ticket so that I could make it back to Little Rock in a hurry. They even upgraded the ticket so that I could get a meal on the plane. I was excited to be headed home to see my family after five long months away.

But even more, I looked forward to returning to Central. There was something I needed to finish.

CHAPTER 9

First-Semester Senior

When I made it home from Chicago, a letter from the new superintendent of schools, Terrell E. Powell, awaited me:

> Welcome to Little Rock Public Schools for the 1959–60
> school year. We are anticipating a fine year in every way. An
> identification card is enclosed for your use. Please sign it and
> have it with you at all times since you will be asked to present it for entrance to your high school.

School ID cards were practically unheard of in the 1950s South, as was the notion that anyone might try to enter a school with evil intent. But the segregationist mobs had forced school officials to change their way of thinking. On the morning of August 24, 1959, twelve days after school opened, I clutched my new ID card and headed to Central to start my senior year. When I arrived, I was surprised to find that the streets were quiet. The segregationists, who had returned to the sidewalks with their signs and chants for opening day, were long gone by the time I arrived. I could feel the tension just roll off my shoulders. I felt normal again, like just another student showing up for school. There were no glaring eyes on me—at least none that I noticed. And there were no sideline taunts. I savored the feeling. As I climbed the front steps, the air was unusually quiet and peaceful. Even in the halls, my white peers seemed almost resigned to my presence. They weren't particularly friendly, but at least I wasn't harassed at every turn. The long year off had left us all weary of the politics, I suppose. And we were just relieved to be back in school. Maybe, I hoped, we would find a way to coexist this year.

Like many students, I entered the school year with some academic shortcomings. I was nervous about taking the second half of courses, such as algebra and Spanish, after a long year away from those subjects. I also began chemistry with some trepidation because I had not taken Algebra II, which wasn't offered through correspondence classes. But the greatest source of my fear about chemistry was the teacher, whom I'd heard did not want any black students in his class. I'd learn soon enough that those fears were warranted. He was a young guy fresh out of college, and he tried hard to buddy with the roughnecks. I constantly had to watch my back in his class because the troublemakers felt comfortable enough with the teacher to pull their old tricks—glue in my chair, spitballs, flying ink. The teacher just turned the other way. I considered myself in survival mode and just lay low, kept my nose in the books, kept my mouth shut, and managed to get the grades I deserved in the class, mostly B's. But Jefferson, who had the same teacher at a different time, struggled mightily with him. Jeff was a whiz in math and science, and when an answer or explanation didn't seem quite right to him, he questioned the teacher. The teacher seemed to bristle at even the notion that a black kid had the audacity to question him, and Jeff's grades suffered for it.

My other courses included speech, physical education, and English. Once again, I was the lone black student in all of my classes. That made for some long and lonely days. While a few white acquaintances now felt comfortable enough to smile at me, exchange a few words in the halls or lockers, or partner with me in class, I missed having friends to share the school day. I missed the laughter and fun I remembered from my days at Dunbar. I missed feeling like a real part of my school. During my first year at Central, I had been so focused on survival that I hadn't spent much time thinking about all that I was missing. But this was my senior year, when I should have been looking forward to the sentimental milestones, like getting asked to the prom and filling a memory book with personal notes and photos to immortalize those special days. Instead, I was just ready for the year to end.

My two best friends, Bunny and Peggy, were both away at school. I was accustomed to seeing Bunny just on holidays and in the summer because she had attended Palmer Memorial Institute, a college preparatory school in Sedalia, North Carolina, near Greensboro, since the beginning of high school. The school, now a historic site, was an early training ground for the children of many upper-echelon black men and women. Most of all, I missed Peggy, who was in college at Arkansas State in Pine Bluff about thirty miles away. When I started at Central, Peggy transferred to Mann and was the one who kept me up to date on what was going on with our black peers. I sometimes had attended school dances at Mann with her. With Peggy gone, so was my main link to Mann and any semblance of a normal high school social life. Because black students still were not allowed to participate in extracurricular activities at Central, I had no student government events, basketball practices, football games, or pep rallies to attend after school. But I occasionally went out on dates with a guy who was a year or two older and attended Arkansas State. I think Mother and Daddy felt sorry for me because they sometimes drove me to Pine Bluff for Arkansas State's football and basketball games. My parents and I usually stayed overnight with my friend Jeannette Mazique and her family. Her father and Daddy were friends and fellow builders who had helped to construct the dorms at Arkansas State. Her parents owned a student lounge on campus called the Lion's Den, a popular hangout for the college kids, especially on weekends after the games. I had the most fun of my senior year in the Lion's Den.

Other community groups also offered their support for the five black students at Central by inviting us to their social events. One such group, a prominent community of Quakers, called American Friends, contacted Mrs. Bates to invite us to a play. It was a bitterly cold afternoon when a young white man, probably in his mid-twenties, showed up at my door to pick me up for the event. Grandpa Cullins happened to stop by at the same moment. He took one look at the young man standing there, shivering in the freezing cold without a coat or hat, and chuckled.

"He sure is one dumb sonofabitch," Grandpa muttered, loud enough for all to hear.

I was so embarrassed. But that's how Grandpa Cullins was. He didn't care what color you were. He said what was on his mind. The young man took it in good humor, which helped to lighten the moment. As the two of us left my house that evening, I didn't think about the big risk we were taking just riding together. I'm pretty sure Mother and Daddy must have been frightened. They knew that the mere sight of a young white man and black girl together could enrage the segregationists. But my parents choked back their fear and bravely let me go.

What social life I had usually centered on those occasional events. Most days, I just went to school and spent the evenings doing homework. I even lost interest in talking on the telephone. The hateful prank calls still came with such regularity that the telephone had become associated with that kind of negativity in my mind, and I had little desire even to go near it. Driving without an adult in the car was also out of the question. I'd been driving since I was twelve or thirteen, which was pretty common for young teens in the South. I had a driver's license, but that didn't matter much to Mother and Daddy because they weren't taking any chances. A driver's license couldn't protect me from the segregationists. The bad guys probably knew our car, my parents figured, and anything could happen. I didn't complain. It all would be over soon, I told myself. I just had to get through the next several months of school.

Most days, the five of us black students rode together to and from school. Our parents organized a carpool with one of them or a trusted relative assigned on a rotating basis to pick us up at our homes each morning and drop us off there each afternoon. With the legal case behind us and the protests by segregationists more sporadic, there was little need for the five of us to meet every day at the home of Mr. and Mrs. Bates. We students already knew one another through family and community connections, but we got to bond as friends during those short rides in the car and the lunch periods when two or three of us sat together. Frank Henderson's father was a Presbyterian minister whose flexible schedule allowed him to be one of our more regular drivers. Reverend Henderson would drop off his wife at Stephens Elementary, where she was a fifth-grade teacher, and then swing by my house to pick me up. His son, Frank, was a tall, big guy, built like an athlete, but he played no sports and was very studious. He had a gentle personality, was very friendly and well mannered. Like Frank, Sybil Jordan was superstudious. She was the brainy type who read voraciously, which gave her a maturity and worldliness beyond her years. She was deliberate in her speech and didn't use any of the slang of our day. In some ways, Sandra Johnson was her opposite, the effervescent one, always bubbly and upbeat. There was a naïveté about her; she seemed surprised by the mistreatment from our white peers. But she often found a way to laugh about it. Sandra was a distant cousin of mine, and our fathers were fellow contractors who traveled together to Los Angeles to find work when the segregationists tried to punish them by shutting them out of jobs.

Jefferson and I tried as best we could to help the three newcomers navigate Central, but I don't think there was any way to prepare them realistically for what they would face. The atmosphere inside the school had improved somewhat, but the harassment continued. Many of the teachers seemed to take a more active role in reporting the troublemakers, who were then forced to do their dirty work less openly. Again, most of the students just treated us as though we were invisible. I'm sure that was as tough for the new black students as it was for me the first year. But after the drama of my sophomore year, just being left alone was good enough for me. Still, I knew better than to get too comfortable. I might enjoy a few peaceful days, and then out of the blue something frightening would happen—a threatening note left in one of our lockers, name-calling in the halls, or an attack on one of the boys—to remind me that I was still unwelcome at Central. Then came Labor Day weekend.

I was sound asleep the night of September 7 when the red, city-owned station wagon used by Fire Chief Gann Nalley exploded and burst into flames in the driveway of his home. Thirty-three minutes later, firefighters were still battling the blaze at their leader's home when a second explosion blew out the glass front of an office building eight miles away. The building housed Little Rock mayor Werner C. Knoop's construction firm. Then, five minutes after that, a third explosion and fire heavily damaged the ground-floor administrative office of the school board. The blast was so powerful that it also blew out windows in a nearby monastery and shook fourteen nuns from their sleep. For forty minutes, the series of explosions and fires ripped through Little Rock and painted the dark night a fiery orange. Sirens and police cars wailed, crisscrossing downtown. As investigators combed through the smoke and ashes, they determined that arsonists had thrown fused sticks of dynamite into all three targets. All three had been empty, and no one was injured.

I slept through it all. But when I read the newspapers the next day, I immediately suspected the segregationists. I watched from a distance as official Little Rock responded with disgust. Their city was under attack, and someone would have to pay. The bombings dominated the news for days. The Chamber of Commerce met quickly and called for a reward fund to help flush out the bombers. Donations poured in—coins, dollar bills, and personal checks that in just a few days amounted to more than $20,000.

Police Chief Smith, a no-nonsense, law-and-order kind of guy, summoned all of his men to work the case, which became known as "the Labor Day bombings." Officers were posted at the homes of shaken city officials and school board members. Chief Smith also turned to the Little Rock office of the FBI for help. Tips flowed freely into the police department. The nuns who had been awakened by the bombings in their convent near the school board office were able to provide a detailed description of the suspects' car. Two days later, Chief Smith arrested two men: E. A. Lauderdale, Sr., the forty-eight-year-old owner of a lumber and roofing supply company, who had twice run unsuccessfully for the city manager board and was known around town as the leader of the segregationist Capital Citizens Council; and J. D. Sims, a thirty-five-year-old truck driver. Both men were charged with bombing a public building.

The next day brought the arrests and charges against three more men: John Taylor Coggins, a thirty-nine-year-old auto salesman; Jesse Raymond Perry, a twenty-four-year-old truck driver; and Samuel Graydon Beavers, a forty-nine-year-old carpenter who worked at the state mental hospital. Bail was set at $50,000 for all five suspects. Basking in the success of his round-the-clock police work, Chief Smith announced that the bombers had planned a fourth attack of an office building occupied by the Prudential Insurance Company. Heavy traffic downtown apparently scared the bombers away.

Sims quickly pleaded guilty for his role, after admitting to an *Arkansas Gazette* reporter that he had placed three sticks of dynamite under Nalley's car and thrown ten sticks into the school board office. He received a five-year sentence and agreed to testify against Perry and Lauderdale, the alleged mastermind. At Lauderdale's trial nearly three months later, prosecutors called the bombings a "diabolical scheme." But the suspect's attorney tried a not so subtle appeal to the all-white jury: "This man has the sympathy of the state of Arkansas and the sunny South," the attorney said, gesturing to his client. "Don't let New York or Chicago or *Time* magazine tell you what to do in this case."

The jury, which included nine men and three women, deliberated just one hour and twenty-five minutes before convicting Lauderdale. He was sentenced to three years in prison, two years fewer than the coconspirator who had cooperated with police and testified against him. Coggins and Perry also received three-year sentences. Beavers's trial was postponed for a year because of his poor health, but he was later convicted and received a similar sentence.

I have to admit that I paid scant attention to the details of the case at the time. Chalk it up to my youth—I turned seventeen the December after the bombings. But I just didn't feel personally threatened. I knew that by the time the bombers targeted city officials, they already had gone after Mr. and Mrs. Bates many times with burning crosses, rocks, bombs, and even bullets. I didn't realize, though, that Mrs. Bates felt so threatened she sent telegrams to the Justice Department and the White House, pleading for federal protection. But no such help was forthcoming. She and Mr. Bates ultimately relied on the security provided by dedicated neighbors and friends, who stood watch with their own shotguns and pistols outside the couple's home. Somehow, though, I just didn't make the leap in my mind that these bombings of city targets signaled a sense of desperation among the segregationists and that perhaps any one of the five of us black students or our family members could be next. I was just eager to put Central, the segregationists, the bombings, and all they represented behind me—so eager that I spent more time thinking about the future than the ugliness swirling around me. My graduation from Central was just months away, and all I could think about was where I would go to college.

Many of my friends at Mann were planning to attend historically black universities, including Talladega, Fisk, Tennessee State, and Tuskegee Institute. While I've always had much respect for those great institutions, I wanted to explore all of my options. I had endured Central mainly because I wanted to have a broad range of choices for my future. It didn't make sense to me now to limit myself. I knew that I wanted to go to school out of state, and I began collecting brochures and other information to research various colleges. Ernie's aunt Mrs. Gravely, a counselor at Dunbar, was advising me. It never even crossed my mind to use the college placement office at Central, and even though I was an honor student, no one in the office there sought me out, either. When Ernie came home for Christmas, he suggested I apply to Michigan State. I was lukewarm on the idea at first, but I trusted Ernie, who was now a sophomore there and a big fan of the school. So I applied. Several other colleges also caught my eye, including Brandeis in Massachusetts, Grinnell in Iowa, and the brand-new University of California at Santa Barbara. I applied to all of them, too. Mother kept pushing for me to apply to Vassar or Wellesley. Both schools had a fine reputation, but Mother also relished the idea of having a daughter at an elite private all-girls school. I just didn't think that kind of environment was for me. A coed school with people from all walks of life was more to my liking. Eventually, my heart settled in a big way on Antioch College in Yellow Springs, Ohio. The school had a work-study program that allowed students to take classes one quarter and work in the field of study for college credit the next. The program seemed so visionary. It would give me a chance to take classes in the medical field and explore whether I really wanted to become a doctor. Such real-world connections could also become a stepping-stone for future job opportunities. I was sold and couldn't wait to hear back. I still recall the moment I pulled the letter from the admissions office out of my mailbox and ran inside to open it. My heart thumped with such excitement and anticipation as I ripped open the envelope and scanned the letter for the answer I'd been waiting to hear. But just as quickly, all of that excitement was reduced to a huge lump in my throat as I read that admissions officials were recommending I take a year off. The letter said the university was aware of the stressful years I'd endured at Central and thought that before settling into the seriousness of college study, I needed to rest. Then the letter said something like "We will hold a place for you for the 1961–62 school year." I was devastated. I didn't want to wait another year to pursue my dreams. Leaving Little Rock to go to college was the one thing that had kept me motivated and hopeful. I couldn't even entertain the thought of waiting. I've never been a patient person. I felt that all of my dreams were starting to slip away. I felt rejected. I folded the letter, put it away, and walked around for weeks in silent shock.

Little did I know that life was about to get a whole lot worse.

CHAPTER 10

An Explosive Night

When I made it to my bedroom the night of February 9, 1960, it was raining mud. At least that's how it appeared to me when I heard heavy wind and rain slapping against the house. I looked up at the window and saw thick droplets of rain mixed with red dirt sliding down the windowpanes.

It was about nine-thirty, my favorite time of the night. I savored those moments of solitude just before bedtime when I got to unwind, listen to the radio, and think. The house was quiet. Daddy hadn't come in yet from his nighttime job at Big Daddy's place. Loujuana and Tina, then eleven and four, were asleep in their room a few steps up the hall, and Mother was in her and Daddy's room near the front door.

I clicked on the clock radio resting on the nightstand. The AM dial was already tuned to one of my favorite stations, WLAC, which broadcast nightly from Nashville. It was one of a few white stations that brought the soulful sounds of black rock and roll, rhythm and blues, and jazz artists—the Platters, Little Richard, Fats Domino, and Etta James—to places they'd never been before, the homes and lives of my white peers throughout the nation. It tickled me when I imagined that maybe some of my white classmates at Central were listening secretly, too. I particularly enjoyed a program called *Randy's Record Highlights,* which aired shortly after ten o'clock.

As I changed into my pajamas, my mind felt at ease. I'd made it to the home stretch at Central, I thought. For weeks, things had been calm, no protesters or major incidents, and graduation was less than four months away. I'd finally stopped sulking after the rejection from Antioch and decided on a college. My decision-making process had been quite simple: I accepted the first school that wrote to me with good news after the big letdown—Michigan State. Michigan State wanted me right then, and I was eager to be wanted. After such disappointment, I had been in no mood to wait to hear from my second and third choices. By the time the acceptance letters came from Brandeis and the University of California, I had already settled on going to Michigan. I was even starting to get excited. I liked the idea of getting lost among the thousands of students on campus. I'd get to come and go as I pleased, and no one would even notice. Finally, I would have a normal life. Dances. Concerts. Football games. Maybe even a boyfriend. I'd missed out on so much at Central. I could hardly wait to end this chapter of my life and start anew. But for the moment, it was bedtime. I clicked off the light in my room, crawled into bed with my thoughts, and let Etta and Fats serenade me to sleep.

No sooner had I closed my eyes, it seemed, than I was shaken by a thunderous boom. The house shook, and I could hear glass crashing to the floor in the front of the house. I sat up quickly with my hands gripping the sides of my bed, as if to steady the room. For a moment, I felt frozen in place. My eyes, wide with fear, darted around the pitch-black room. What *was* that? Was I dreaming? The explosion had come from the front.

Then, oh, my God—my little sisters! Mother! I had to find them. I leapt out of bed. As soon as my bare feet landed on the cold floor, I took off running through my bedroom. My first stop was the den, just outside my bedroom door. It was eerily dark and still. I turned toward the hall and ran up to the front of the house.

I was halfway up the hall when I saw Loujuana and Tina standing in their nightgowns with Mother in her bedroom door at the other end of the hall. When I reached them, Mother and the girls looked dazed and bewildered but unhurt. We stared at one another, too shaken to even speak. Little Tina's eyes moved quickly from Mother to me, searching our faces for clues. A haze of smoke floated through the darkness from the living room to the hallway, where we stood. The smoke hurt my eyes, and an unfamiliar scent filled the air. It smelled as if something had blown up in a chemistry lab.

Inside, I was trembling. I felt helpless and horrified. And I needed Daddy. He would tell me everything would be okay and make me feel safe. But he must have been working late—it was eleven, and he hadn't yet made it home. I suddenly felt a painful sense of responsibility, as though I needed to step up and somehow make the situation right. But I didn't know how. I could feel real panic rising in my throat. I had the odd thought that the stoic Carlotta, the one who always felt her hard work and smarts would make everything okay, who had believed that anything was possible if she stood firm and stayed strong, was now at a total loss.

The sound of my mother's voice quelled my panic. She was calm and restrained, but I heard helplessness, too. "Call your daddy," she said.

Relieved to be doing something, I quickly headed back down the hall to the kitchen and dialed the numbers to Big Daddy's place as fast as my jittery fingers could move. Trying not to sound frantic, I asked for Daddy and told him to come home right away, that something bad had happened. He slammed down the phone and must have dashed right out. It didn't occur to me to call the police, but by the time I hung up the telephone, officers were knocking on our front door. Mother talked to them, and I stepped inside the living room with my sisters to scan the scene.

The blinds hung askew, partially ripped down by the blast. Mother had made nice white linen drapes and matching sheers for all of the windows in the living room—the picture window overlooking the front yard and the two more traditional windows that sat on each side of a large gas fireplace on the side wall. The drapes now looked dingy in the smoky room. They flapped wildly as the cold air and rain whipped through the two windows framing the fireplace. The windows had been shattered, and tiny shards of glass covered the floor. The sight made me unspeakably sad. Mother had worked so hard to get this room just right.

My gut was telling me that this was no accident. Someone had deliberately tried to tear my home apart. My eyes roved the room as if I were an investigator. Something had clearly exploded, but there wasn't a visible hole anywhere. Through the smoke, I could see that the rest of the room, thank God, had remained intact. It didn't take long to connect the dots. Mr. and Mrs. Bates had had crosses burned in their yard and a brick thrown through their window when tensions over Central were at their hottest. And though I'd paid only scant attention to the Labor Day bombings, it all seemed relevant to me now. Could the segregationists have come after me in my home, just when it seemed my battle was almost over?

The two officers set out with their flashlights around the perimeter of our house, and Mother closed the door again to wait for Daddy. Tina stepped toward Mother, unaware of the glass that lay between them. But Mother's sharp voice stopped her in her tracks.

"Get back," she said. "Put on some shoes."

The three of us girls rushed back to our rooms and pulled on our shoes and bathrobes. By the time we made it back to the living room, Daddy was home. It had taken him less than ten minutes, but the waiting had felt like an eternity to me. The instant I saw him, I felt calmer. As I looked at him standing there in his black coat and matching hat, with his arm around Mother's tiny waist, I knew he was about to take charge and get to the bottom of this. He clearly looked worried and wanted to know: Were we okay? He kneeled down to pick up Tina. Moments later, he disappeared outside with the police. Mr. Fox from across the street came inside to talk to Mother. I kept an eye on Tina and Loujuana, who wandered around the living room, dodging the glass on their tiptoes. Mr. Fox and Mother huddled nearby. As usual, my ears perked up. Mr. Fox tried to whisper, but I caught wind of a word that sent a chill down my spine. I could hardly believe my ears: Did he just say "dynamite"? That was it. That was the strange smell.

Then I knew for sure: The segregationists had bombed my home. They'd resorted to dynamite to run me away from Central. They would stop at nothing, even murder, to keep me out. My knees felt weak as that terrifying reality sank in: My family and I could have been killed.

I suddenly needed fresh air. More than that, I felt compelled to see the damage for myself. At least then I'd know for sure what they had done. For me, knowing was a comfort. I could handle what I knew. It was not knowing that made me feel vulnerable and afraid.

Despite Daddy's instructions for us to stay inside, I felt pulled to the front door. I walked outside, grabbed the wrought-iron railing, and leapt two steps to the ground. I was startled to see that practically everyone from the neighborhood had gathered in their nightclothes under umbrellas and plastic rain caps in the Rice family's yard across the street.

"Are you okay?" a voice yelled out.

I immediately regretted my decision to leave the house. I wanted nothing more than to disappear. Maybe it was naive to think that I could go outside and watch what was going on like anyone else, but that's what I wanted—what I always wanted— just to blend in. Even in that first year at Central, when the television cameras rolled constantly, I'd managed to stay mostly in the background and let Ernie, Melba, and Minnie do all the talking. Now, I was the object of everyone's attention. And it horrified me to think that all of my neighbors were standing out in the cold rain because of me.

I was chilled by yet another new reality: My decision to go to Central and to stay no matter what had brought violence, not only to my home, but to my neighbors, to the people who'd watched out for me since I was a toddler. Any one of them could have been hurt by the explosion. My stomach churned with guilt and anger.

Still, I kept walking to the 15th Street side of the house, the same side where the windows had blown out. Just a few steps later, I stopped dead in my tracks. There, at the base of the chimney, I could see where the dynamite had landed. A gaping hole, about two feet in diameter, was a testament to the power of the blast. Bricks were strewn all about. All I could do was stand there, feeling myself become soaked with the heavy rain. What if the dynamite had gone through the window and landed in the living room instead of hitting the ground? Would my house still be standing? Would my family have survived? Would I?

Finally, I turned and walked slowly back through the door. For the rest of the night, I was numb—and that seemed to be how we all dealt with the shock. Mother sent Loujuana down the street to spend the night at Uncle Teet's house. Tina dozed on the sofa in the den. Mother and I stayed indoors, listening quietly to the loud banging from outdoors as Daddy and Mr. Fox boarded up the windows. First, we sat in the kitchen at the counter, each of us staring past the other into space. I felt more vulnerable than ever before. I wasn't normally the type that spent much time thinking about "what if," but I couldn't stop the thoughts flashing through my mind nonstop. My family and I were at the mercy of whoever had done this. Everything—our newly remodeled home, all the things that Mother and Daddy had worked so hard to attain, even our lives—could be taken away in a second with one more explosion. And maybe next time, it would be more "successful."

After a while, Mother went to check on Tina in the den, and I followed. Neither of us said a word for what seemed like hours. My heart was loaded with such guilt. What could I do or say that would either comfort or explain? Just breathing was all I could manage. As I looked at Tina, lying there so peacefully, part of me yearned to trade places, to be too young and innocent to understand the hate that bred this kind of terror.

I snapped out of it when Mother turned to me and said that I should go back to bed. I could feel myself resist. How could she possibly expect me to fall asleep, as though this were any other night and our home had not been bombed? But I knew better than to question her, so I did as I was told.

Sleep doesn't come on command, though. My brain was so crowded with thoughts that I felt dizzy. This was my home, the safest place in the world, until now. How could I possibly sleep? How could I ever feel completely safe again here? How could I ever feel safe again anywhere? It was one thing for the segregationists to spit and shake their fists at me from the sidewalks of the school when I expected it. There, I still felt some control. I could refuse to let their words wound me. I could remind myself what I'd been taught at home: that those who hate are just ignorant and that I must never, ever stoop to their level. But it was an entirely different matter to be caught off guard in the middle of the night in the place where I'd known only love, peace, and protection. Were the segregationists just trying to scare me and my family— or were they really trying to kill me?

Since all their other antics hadn't worked, the segregationists had stepped it up a notch. They'd stop at nothing to keep me from walking across that stage on graduation night at Central. But even as those thoughts rolled into my mind, I could feel myself harden with determination, as I had a thousand times in my most frightened moments in the last three years. All I wanted was to go to school. What could possibly be the harm in that? These people didn't know me. I wouldn't quit. They couldn't make me. I'd come too far. They couldn't chase me away from my home, and I wouldn't run away from Central like a scared dog. Their plan had backfired: I felt more strongly than ever that I had as much right to be there as any white high school student who lived in the neighborhood. I *would* stay. I *would* graduate. And I *would* walk across that stage. Or I would die trying. The clarity of that thought calmed me down, and I finally, somehow, drifted off to sleep.

The next morning, I got out of bed around six o'clock, like every other school morning, and quietly got dressed. Mother and Daddy were in the kitchen—who knows if they'd even been to sleep—when I walked in.

"Are you sure you want to do this?" Mother asked.

"Yes," I responded simply. "I'm sure."

Daddy knew me. He took one look at the determination in my face, and he knew there was no use trying to keep me at home. He shrugged as if to say, "If that's what she wants to do . . ."

It was exactly what I wanted to do, and I hoped that my parents were proud of me for refusing to stay at home.

Before leaving for school, I went to see Tina, who was awake in the den. Standing in her nightgown in front of the television, she pointed excitedly at the screen.

"That's our house!" she exclaimed.

Sure enough, the bombing had made the national news, and images of our house were flashing across the television screen on NBC's *Today* show. Mother rushed in, scooped up Tina, and turned off the television. From that day forward, my parents never said a word to me about the bombing. It was as if clicking the TV off could erase every memory of that horrible night. I knew that in my parents' minds, the bombing was grown-folks' business, not the kind of thing that should be on the mind of a child. As always, they believed they were protecting me, deflecting from me the side of life that I was not ready—or they were not ready for me—to handle. Soon enough, they figured, life would reveal its own ugly truths. I didn't question their authority, so I didn't bring it up, either. By now, I had my ways of finding out things. I knew that somehow I would find out what had happened and why.

While Mother drove me to school, I wondered if my white classmates and teachers had heard about the bombing. I wondered whether they even cared. I guess part of me yearned for some sign that at least some of them really did care. But the not so subtle glares, whispers, and finger-pointing of the students milling around their lockers inside suddenly made me feel like an object of ridicule. Not one of them—not even the few acquaintances I'd made or the teachers who taught me every day—uttered a word to me the whole morning. I felt more isolated than ever. As I sat through class after class with them, I couldn't help wondering: Weren't they even a little curious about the silent Negro girl sitting beside them in class, the one whose house had been bombed? Was it too much to expect a few kind words, a sympathetic smile, a friendly gesture? Even after all I'd been through at Central, I still expected at least that much. I had thought that things were getting better. I had hoped for some sign of their humanity, some sign that they saw mine. I had hoped that maybe some of them would think that the bombing had taken matters too far, that they would think about my family and the tragedy that could have been. I had hoped that maybe now in my most vulnerable moment they would finally see *me*, Carlotta, the human being with a heart like theirs, a heart that was hurting. But more than ever, their silence cut me to the core.

Back home that afternoon, Loujuana was again making her

doll clothes and having her pretend tea parties. Tina was running around, as bubbly and unsuspecting as any four-year-old. And Mother was back in the kitchen, busy as usual. I wasn't surprised. It was the Walls way. The Cullins way, too: Don't look back or linger in pain. Pull yourself up. Dust yourself off. Straighten your shoulders. Lift up your head. And walk tall, no matter what. Of course, no one ever said any of this out loud. No one had to. I'd seen it all my life in the way my parents, grandparents, aunts, and uncles had always lived. And now it was my turn to show that I'd learned their lessons well.

But being stalwart didn't mean that I wasn't curious. I always wanted to know what was going on in even the most peaceful of times, and since I couldn't count on the adults to keep me informed, I had developed the art of listening. I rarely missed a thing that was going on in my home. I also devoured the newspapers, particularly the *Arkansas Gazette,* the more progressive of the two local papers. Often, it was my only source of information. In the coming days, I saw my life unfold through the headlines.

The day after the bombing, the banner headline of the *Gazette* read: BLAST RIPS HOME OF NEGRO PUPIL AT CENTRAL HIGH. Two smaller headlines even mentioned me by name: "Carlotta Walls, Family Unhurt by Explosion" and "Carlotta, One of Original 9 at Central." Two days later, I read in the same paper that this was the first time in U.S. history that a student had been the target of a bombing. From all appearances, the police were trying to find the culprit.

I was somewhat reassured by the *Arkansas Democrat* headline that read: 24 DETECTIVES, FBI, OTHER OFFICERS OPEN ALL-OUT PROBE OF BLAST AT NEGRO'S HOME. There was no question in my mind that the violence directed at me was linked to the Labor Day bombings. Some of the bombers were still out on bail. But if others had made the connection, they did not say so publicly.

Both newspapers ran photos of the damage. The *Gazette*

showed Police Chief Smith examining the bricks blown to pieces at the base of the chimney, while the *Democrat* ran a close-up of the damaged chimney and a police officer stopping a car in front of my house. According to the papers, police determined that two sticks of dynamite had been placed or thrown under a front window of my home.

"It sounded like a cannon," my neighbor Mrs. Davis told the *Gazette.*

The newspaper also reported that the force of the blast had broken windows in the house across the street and that police said calls reporting the explosion came from points more than two miles away. Unidentified neighbors told the paper they had seen two unfamiliar automobiles drive by the house just before and after the explosion—a crucial detail that seemed to go nowhere. All the detectives in town were assigned to check out leads or to stand guard at Central and Hall High, the all-white school in the more affluent section of town. Lights inside and around all of the high schools were kept burning through the night for the rest of the week. It was as if everyone were waiting for something else to happen. I anxiously followed the developments in the newspapers.

In the *Democrat,* known as the pro-segregationist newspaper, local white leaders were speaking out. W. F. Rector, president of the Little Rock Chamber of Commerce, sounded full of outrage, but not over the violence directed at me and my family. He was concerned that the turmoil had cost the city some big business prospects.

"This is a minor incident and we have been kicked in the teeth again," he said.

Mrs. Bates fired back the next day in the *Gazette:* "It's too bad that Mr. Rector, who holds an important position in the community, would call a vicious, cowardly act of this kind a minor incident. People around the world are today judging American democracy by what is happening in Little Rock."

I appreciated Mrs. Bates even more every time I read a comment like that. Over the last three years, she'd stood in front of countless microphones, and when she opened her mouth, the fiery truth came out. She seemed so comfortable in the limelight. I often suspected that part of her relished the attention and the lights of the cameras. But I have never doubted her sincerity or her conviction.

I know Mrs. Bates was as dumbfounded as I was just two days after the bombing to read in the newspaper the wild implication by Amis Guthridge, chief attorney for the white Citizens Council. He suggested that Negroes might have been behind the bombing in some way.

"I'm not saying who did it," he added, trying to cover his tracks. "The avenue is wide open. You just can't tell what's in back of it."

The suggestion was so absurd that I couldn't even muster the energy to get angry. It seemed so outrageous that it didn't occur to me to be afraid. But his ridiculous claim stayed in the back of my mind.

I remained confident, though, that Police Chief Smith would be fair. It had taken him just three days to arrest the Labor Day bombing suspects. He must have felt tremendous pressure to pull off the same speedy investigation this time around. Despite suffering from the flu, he'd apparently left his sickbed to head a round-the-clock investigation. But it took three days for the Little Rock Chamber of Commerce to meet and agree to offer a reward to help flush out the bomber. This time, the group could muster only $2,500, one-tenth of the reward offered in the Labor Day bombings. When I read this, I felt both infuriated and hurt.

Maybe the Chamber's coffers were low after putting up such a hefty reward just a few months earlier. Or more likely, I thought, when the time came to ante up, the city's business leaders just didn't care as much this time around. The limited reward seemed to send a message that the bombing of our home was somehow less important. This despite the fact that, unlike the empty vehicle and buildings blown up during the Labor Day bombings, my home had living, breathing human beings inside.

My breakfast sat on the counter untouched that morning. And the door slammed a little harder when I left the house.

Thank God for the letters and telegrams that began arriving almost daily from around the world right after the bombing. They were, in part, what kept me going. Out-of-town family and long-lost friends sent heartwarming messages of encouragement. White strangers wrote touching letters expressing their shame. Even a well-known charismatic religious leader known as Father Divine, who claimed to be God, sent a note urging me to keep my head up. A few of the letters were written in a foreign language, and some even arrived with small amounts of cash or checks. But they all had one thing in common: They broke the silence. They let me know that this nightmare was not just mine and my family's alone, that people of goodwill around the world were watching and listening, that they were horrified by such evil, and that they cared.

Nine days after the bombing, as I'd feared, the other shoe did drop.

It was well after dark on February 18 when my father got home. He was still working nights at Big Daddy's pool hall to help make ends meet because his construction work had become so erratic. The house was quiet except for my parents' voices, coming from near the front door. I was in the kitchen, but my ears were alert for any news that I could pick up.

"They want me to go downtown to the police station," Daddy said. I couldn't see him, but I heard the door open and close again behind him. I wondered: Where was Daddy going? And who were "they"? Nothing in his voice had sounded alarming, so maybe the police had asked him to come downtown to answer more questions about the bombing. There was nothing to do but go to bed.

When I woke up for school the next morning, Daddy wasn't there, and my mother was pacing back and forth in the kitchen. Her face looked more worried than I'd ever seen, so I knew right away that it wasn't simply that Daddy had left early for work. Mother tried to go about our morning routine, but I wasn't fooled. The front-page headlines helped to explain my mother's mood:

2 NEGROES HELD FOR WALLS BLAST.

POLICE GIVE NO MOTIVE FOR ACCUSED.

My eyes sped across the newspaper page and then froze when I saw a familiar name: Herbert Odell Monts. Police were accusing Herbert, my childhood playmate—the same Herbert who'd been a faithful player on our neighborhood softball team—of bombing my family's home. Another acquaintance, Maceo Antonio Binns, Jr., also had been accused. I could hardly believe what I was reading. This simply made no sense.

Maceo, then thirty-one, was a regular at my grandfather's place, so my father knew him well. Our families were loosely connected in other ways, as black families often were in small communities. Maceo's sister and my family attended the same church, and his nephew McClain Birch was my friend. Herbert was seventeen, just like me, and we'd been buddies practically our entire lives. We were born on the same day, just fifteen minutes apart, and grew up one block from each other. I could almost pitch a stone from my front yard to his. We had played softball and marbles, ridden our bikes, and walked the streets of our neighborhood together more times than I could count.

Every day since the bombing had brought me to a new level of disbelief. Now, I was in shock.

According to the newspaper, Herbert and Maceo had been brought in five days after the bombing for questioning by local police and FBI agents. At that point they'd had no leads in the case, so they'd supposedly intensified their efforts, working late into the night. Chief Smith announced the arrests at one-fifteen that morning. He'd charged Herbert and Maceo under a statute that made it illegal to "willfully or maliciously destroy or injure property by means of an explosive," which carried a maximum penalty of up to five years in jail. The paper said it was the same felony charge that had been filed in the Labor Day bombings.

Once again, my breakfast went to waste. By the time I finished the article, my stomach was in knots and I was full of questions. What in the world did these arrests have to do with my father? He wouldn't have pointed the finger at Herbert or Maceo. Why was Daddy still away, and why hadn't we heard from him?

But as worried as I was, I told myself I could not overreact. With Daddy gone, I had to hold myself together for Mother and my little sisters. So I did what I always did on school mornings: got dressed and went to school.

I never even thought about not going. It was the only way I knew to fight back. In my mind, segregationists were behind all of it—the bombing and the arrests of Herbert and Maceo. If I stayed home even a day, those responsible might think they were winning. So my presence at school said to the enemy, better than any words ever could: You have not whipped me, whittled me down, or scared me enough to make me quit.

At times during the day, the anger and fear inside me felt like a fist in the pit of my stomach, but I refused to cry or even look afraid. I tried to appear nonchalant and intensely focused on my studies. I knew that if I failed, white teachers who doubted the intelligence of black children would feel justified. I was determined to show them that, given the resources and opportunity, black children could perform as well as, if not better, than others.

An old report card from that time shows that I earned all A's and B's the first semester of my senior year. Some of my teachers still ignored me and clearly did not want me at Central, but I found that the grades they gave me were mostly fair. After the bombing, my grades tumbled to mostly C's and a few B's. I had never made C's before in my life. So the events clearly took their toll, despite my determination.

The day at school felt surreal. Once again, none of my classmates or teachers said anything about the arrests. I was so distracted that it hardly mattered this time. All I could think about was getting back home to check on my father. When I finally returned to the house after school, Daddy still was not there. And Mother was still pacing. I had to do something. It didn't matter that I knew my efforts would get me nowhere. I knew now that Daddy was with the police, and I knew that they cared nothing about black families when they carted off our loved ones. No one was going to contact us with an update. I flipped through the local telephone directory, found the number to police headquarters, and dialed it. Calmly, I identified myself and asked to speak to my father.

"He can't come to the phone," replied the voice on the other end.

"When is he coming home?" I asked, trying not to sound like a scared child.

There was no answer.

With each passing minute, the anxiety in our home rose like a quiet flood. Word about my father spread quickly, and relatives and friends from all over the country began calling, wanting to know the latest. Every time the phone rang, my mother, sisters, and I all jumped.

Finally, Big Daddy came in with some news. He was well connected for a black man of that era, and he knew someone who had gotten "inside" information. FBI agents were involved, and they were asking my father lots of questions. Of course, we worried that they were doing more than just asking questions. After all, this was the South, where a black man taken from his home in the middle of the night by whites—even the police, even the FBI— could face unthinkable horror.

As I lay in the darkness of my room that night, my mind zoomed in on Daddy. Was he okay? Were police hurting him? I shook the bad thoughts out of my head. Daddy *would* come home. He had to. He knew how much we—I—needed him. Memories flooded my head: How he came home from work in the evenings and stopped outside to spend a few moments with me and my friends. How he'd turn the jump rope, tap the volleyball across the yard, pitch a few softballs to us, or find some other way to join in our fun. How I always slept better whenever he was in the house. He'd come in, bone-tired from working day and night, and I didn't even have to see his face to feel his presence. I'd hear the door open and close behind him, wait for the silent pause as he took off his straw hat, and then listen again for the light tap of his shoes across the hardwood floors that we had put down together. In those moments, my world suddenly felt safe again.

As the hours slowly ticked away on this long night, I couldn't close my eyes. I kept waiting for the familiar: the sound of his shoes, his voice, his laugh, something that said everything would be right again.

Instead, the next morning, I was greeted with the newspaper headline: "Police Quiz Walls in Bombing: Probe Goes On in Secrecy." In the distorted minds of white law enforcement officials, my father had something to do with the bombing! It was unfathomable to me that anyone could suspect that my father would be involved with attacking his own house while the love of his life and their three daughters slept inside.

Those next forty-eight hours dragged, and Mother and I seemed to sleepwalk through them. A haze of shock and fear hung over us as we tried to go about our daily routines. At least two days had passed since Daddy was taken away, and I still hadn't heard a word. Mother wasn't the type to cry in front of the children, but all of a sudden, I noticed that she began to take "a rest" during the day. She would disappear for maybe an hour behind the closed door of her bedroom, but when she eventually emerged, she looked even wearier than before her brief retreat. My grandparents, aunts, uncles, and the Foxes were a constant presence in our house. Mrs. Fox would sit with Mother on the bar stools in the kitchen, while Mr. Fox sat with me and my sisters in front of the television in the den. Of course, no one discussed Daddy's absence, but you could almost touch the tension.

Dusk was setting in one evening as I stepped onto the front porch to breathe some fresh air. When I looked toward the street, I noticed the distant shadow of a tall man walking slowly down the hill toward our home. His walk was unmistakable.

"Daddy!" I cried, dashing off the porch and down the road.

I threw my arms around him and held on tightly, wanting not to let him go ever again. My eyes scanned him up and down. He was wearing the same khaki pants he'd had on the night he left for work. His dark overcoat was slung across his arm. He was all in one piece, but something was wrong. Daddy wouldn't look at me. He kept staring straight ahead and didn't say a word.

I looked up at his face and found tears sliding down his cheeks. It was the first and last time I saw my father cry. Suddenly unable to speak, I just stood there. I felt as though I'd been submerged in ice water, cold and hardly able to breathe. My family was suffering profoundly because of me. And my determination to graduate from Central could have cost me my father. For the rest of the way home, Daddy and I walked side by side in silence.

Once again, I didn't dare ask questions. But, as always, I was paying attention and overheard things. Later, I heard Daddy telling Mother that the police had beaten him and tried to make him sign a confession, admitting that he and Maceo had planted the bomb to get the insurance money from the policy on the house. So this was what it was all about—the insurance money! In the narrow minds of the police, Daddy was just a desperate Negro willing to blow up his own home and possibly even kill his family to get his hands on some money. My heart raced and I could hardly breathe as I heard Daddy tell Mother how the police officers kept shouting at him:

"Do you know Maceo Binns?"

"Do you know Herbert Monts?"

Hours had turned into days as the officers kept taking him back and forth from a jail cell to an interrogation room. In his words, they were determined to make this figment of the FBI's imagination a reality—and they wouldn't give up. But they didn't know Cartelyou Walls. He wouldn't give up, either. And he refused to budge from the truth.

I stopped listening, went to my room, and wept quietly as I imagined Daddy's face, strong and determined, even while the officers beat him.

Within an hour of Daddy's arrival home, family, friends, and neighbors began stopping by to visit him: our minister, Reverend O. W. Gibson, Mr. Fox, and several others. Daddy wasn't in the mood for company, so our family friends were politely turned away at the door—all but Mrs. Bates. Daddy chatted with her awhile, and she insisted that he tell his story to Christopher Mercer, an attorney who was one of her advisers. We knew Mr. Mercer from our neighborhood, and the next day, Daddy left home to visit him. I never heard a word about what happened during that visit. But days later, I learned that indeed the police had suspected Daddy of concocting the bombing to get insurance money or as a ploy to raise money from people "up north" and that he'd paid Maceo and Herbert to pull it off.

In the days afterward, Daddy's spirit seemed bruised. He was quiet and somber. And for what seemed like the longest time, we didn't hear his contagious laughter.

CHAPTER 11

Scapegoats

My father was never charged in the bombing, but the ordeal was just beginning for Herbert and Maceo. Prosecutor Frank J. Holt sought a $50,000 bond for both of them, but a judge set it at $15,000—the same amount that had been set for the Labor Day bombers.

"It sounds as if somebody's trying to railroad somebody," Mrs. Bates told the *Gazette* in a February 20 story, gauging the reaction of community leaders to the arraignment of Herbert and Maceo. "I can't understand why they would charge these two fellows. I don't know what evidence they have, but it sounds ridiculous to me."

Amis Guthridge, the white Citizens Council attorney, seemed to gloat over news of the arrests. He was quoted at length, taking credit for getting Chief Smith to stop pursuing white segregationists as suspects and look inside the black community. Guthridge even suggested that he might apply for the reward since he'd been first to hint that blacks might be involved. And of course, Governor Faubus chimed in, suggesting he knew more than he did. He said the bombing incident "looked peculiar from the beginning" and that he had questioned how such a thing could have benefited the segregationists.

The same day, the *Gazette* editorial praised the work of the police: "Once again the department has proven itself to be one of Little Rock's finest municipal assets." The newspaper mentioned the absence of a motive but seemed to accept that the police had solved the case. In the same editorial, the newspaper declared that by all indications, "segregation extremists, like those convicted in the Labor Day explosions, had no hand in this case."

But the lack of a motive seemed to hang in the air. The next day, the *Gazette* again raised two questions:

"Is that all of it, the two Negro suspects now in custody? If they did it, why?"

I never even pondered the questions because I never—not for a moment—believed that Herbert and Maceo bombed my family's home. Even though prosecutors had not charged my father, they didn't back down from their claim that he was the mastermind. In fact, the entire case against Herbert and Maceo seemed built on the notion that my father had recruited the two of them as part of a grand moneymaking scheme. But I knew my father far too well to give credence to that ridiculous theory.

Prosecutor Holt assured readers he had a "good case." My gut told me that was not possible. But all I could do was hope that under the leadership of Chief Smith, who had always seemed fair and decent, the truth would come out somehow. I suspected the segregationists had bombed my home to send another message before my graduation from Central. I wondered if police had thoroughly investigated a neighbor's report of seeing unfamiliar cars in the neighborhood just before and after the bombing. It had been a detailed description of the getaway car in the Labor Day bombings that helped police track down those suspects. But as Herbert and Maceo sat in jail, I felt helpless and guilty at the same time. Two innocent men could go to jail because of me, because I had been so determined to stay at Central.

Within a month of the arrests, things would take another startling turn. I awakened one March morning to this shocking front-page headline:

POLICE CHIEF KILLS WIFE, TAKES OWN LIFE AT HOME.

I gasped when I picked up the newspaper. I just could not believe that Chief Smith, then forty-seven years old, was capable of the kind of brutality described in the story. According to the newspaper, Smith had shot his wife in the chest while both were seated at the kitchen table on March 18, 1960. As she fell backward, he shot her in the abdomen twice more. Then he shot himself in the left temple.

The story said that Smith had been expected at a meeting at the police station the next day, March 19. When he failed to show up, another police officer called his house but got no answer. Smith's mother, who also had been trying to reach him without success, called and asked a neighbor to check on him. When the neighbor arrived, she found the couple's front door unlocked, walked toward the kitchen, and called out for Smith's wife, Mary. The television was blaring. When the neighbor reached the kitchen door, she froze. She screamed and backed out of the doorway when she saw the two bodies. Mary Smith lay across a chair, and her husband was sprawled in a pool of blood at her feet.

The bullet had gone straight through the police chief's head and lodged in the wall. Investigators estimated the couple had died twelve hours before they were found and that the shots had been fired from Smith's .357 magnum pistol. There was no suicide note, and friends speculated that "marital woes" may have caused the shootings.

On the morning they died, the Smiths had traveled together to Searcy, Arkansas, to attend a court appearance for their son, who had been arrested for burglary and was pleading guilty. At work later that day, Smith's colleagues at the police department reported that he had been in good spirits. At the time of his death, Smith

faced lawsuits totaling $450,000, mostly those filed by white seg-
regationists still angry because of the actions he had taken to quell
the violence on the first day of school in August 1959, while I was
finishing summer school in Chicago.

Mrs. Bates said that when she heard the news, she vomited and
immediately had to be put to bed.

"This must be a nightmare, it must be—but soon I'll awaken,"
she wrote in her memoir. "Smith is dead. . . . Maybe we'll be next."

She didn't believe the death of the couple was a murder-suicide.
She suspected both had been murdered. Of course, no one will ever
know for sure what happened in the Smith home that day. But to
this day, I believe it is likely that the police chief and his wife were
murdered.

As the lawsuits against him indicated, Smith was loathed by
white supremacists, who saw him as much too sympathetic to
those of us involved in the integration of Central. Smith had been
the assistant chief when my eight comrades and I entered Central
High School in fall 1957. The following November, when Police
Chief Marvin Potts retired, Smith was named acting chief. He was
one of three men who took the civil service test on January 13,
1958, for the top position, but the segregationists fought his pro-
motion. Then, after an unexplained delay of nearly two weeks,
Smith was named chief on January 30. The wrath of segregationists toward him only grew in August 1959 when he ordered firefighters to use water hoses to disperse the protesters.

Now, Smith was gone, his good name besmirched.

The mainstream media seemed satisfied that both cases had
been solved—the death of the Smiths and the bombing of my family's home. After the arrests of Herbert and Maceo, the link the
media had made regularly between the bombing of my home and
the integration of Central High School disappeared from the headlines.

But Herbert's mother, Juanita Monts, wanted my family to

know the truth about her son. She sent a message to Mother via Mrs. Fox that she wanted to talk. Then, one spring afternoon, when Mother answered a light knock at our front door, she found Juanita Monts standing there. Mother invited her inside. The two women stepped into our living room and sat on the sofa. I lingered in the hallway just outside the room.

Mrs. Monts's voice sounded tired and sad. I felt tremendous sorrow for her. She had eight other children, six more boys and two girls, all younger than Herbert. I could only imagine how worried she must have been about her oldest child, who was in jail awaiting trial. Her husband, Hutella Monts, worked nights at Bell Telephone, and Mrs. Monts mostly stayed home with the children. They were a close-knit, upstanding family. Mrs. Monts eventually would return to college and become a full-time teacher. She had come from a family of educators, including several sisters and brothers who held postgraduate degrees.

Mrs. Monts spoke softly as she told Mother how terrible she felt about the bombing of our home. But she assured Mother that Herbert had nothing to do with it. It was important to her that we know that, she said. I've always thought that was such an honorable thing for her to do: to care enough about what my family thought of her son to tell Mother face-to-face that he was innocent.

"I know," Mother said softly.

We all knew. Herbert and Maceo were just convenient scapegoats of a system that was eager to put to bed an irksome case. I will never forget the image that day of the two Juanitas sitting there, both hurting, both bound by the fates of their two children.

On May 15, the *Gazette* ran a news story previewing Herbert's jury trial to be held in circuit court the next day. Mother had been subpoenaed by the prosecution to testify. As usual, I got details about the trial from the newspaper and the bits I could pick up from conversation around the house afterward.

About fifty spectators crowded into the courtroom for the first day. To no one's surprise, the chosen jurors were all white. Prosecutor Holt indicated in his opening statement that he would seek a maximum sentence of five years in the state penitentiary and a $500 fine. Herbert was represented by Harold Flowers, who was a well-known civil rights attorney from Pine Bluff. A few years earlier, he had defended a group of black men accused of murdering a white man. Flowers's clients faced the death penalty, but two of them had been acquitted. Another received a reduced sentence. The outcome of that trial angered the white establishment in Little Rock and likely cast an even darker cloud over Herbert's trial before it even got started. Flowers sought to have the case dismissed on the grounds that Holt had violated the Constitution with a decision to file charges without a grand jury indictment. Flowers also asked the presiding judge, William J. Kirby, to transfer Herbert's case to juvenile court. But both requests went nowhere.

Over two days, the prosecution called seven witnesses, mostly detectives and FBI agents, who reported that Herbert had confessed. That was the first I'd heard of the alleged confession, but I suspected it was coerced. I remembered that the same law enforcement authorities had beaten my father and tried to force him to confess. But Daddy was a grown man, a military war veteran who had seen the world and wouldn't be broken by the brute force and mental pressure of white law enforcement authorities. Herbert was just seventeen, on the precipice of manhood, and as grown up as he liked to act, I was sure he had been outmatched.

According to prosecutor's version of events, Herbert tried to light a match, but the head of the match broke off. Then Maceo lit the fuse while Herbert ran home, drank a cup of coffee, and went to bed. Officers testified that Herbert told them that when he heard the explosion, he got dressed again and went out to see the damage.

The prosecutor also called my mother to the stand. Mother testified that she had been in bed about forty-five minutes and was asleep when the explosion occurred. When she was asked about the Monts family, she replied: "We're good neighbors."

Mother also testified that the money from the insurance company had been just sufficient to cover the cost of the repairs, nothing more. The prosecution even tried to use Herbert's intelligence against him by calling his science teacher to the stand to testify that Herbert was a good student, smart enough to build a homemade bomb. Before resting his case, Prosecutor Holt also called Marion Davis, who said he had been hanging out with Herbert at my grandfather's place and that the two of them had left walking home together. Marion testified that they made it to his home first and that Herbert continued walking alone. Then Holt delivered what I'm sure he considered his "smoking gun." One of our neighbors, Earzie Cunningham, whom I did not know, testified that he had seen Herbert running from the direction of my home at the time of the bombing.

When it was Flowers's turn to put on a defense, he called a single witness, our neighbor Reverend O. W. Gibson, pastor of our family's church, White Memorial Methodist. Reverend Gibson testified that he visited Monts in jail February 19 and noticed that one side of his face was swollen. But Holt called a rebuttal witness, an FBI agent. The agent testified that Reverend Gibson had filed an official complaint on March 2, saying that Herbert had told him he had been kneed and struck across the face by officers who interrogated him. The FBI agent, of course, denied that Herbert had been beaten.

Flowers, as well-meaning as he was, did not call a single witness to challenge the timing of the prosecutor's account—how long it might have taken, for example, for Herbert to run up the block from my home to his house, drink a cup of coffee, and get into bed. Nor did he challenge whether it was even feasible for all of this to occur while a fuse was burning down. He called no one to point out the glaring lack of fingerprints or any other physical evidence linking Herbert to the crime. Most important, he did not challenge the prosecution's sole "evidence"—Herbert's alleged confession. We would learn later when Maceo went to trial that such a challenge might have made all the difference for Herbert.

The white jurors took just thirty-eight minutes to deliver their verdict: Guilty.

Herbert was sentenced to the maximum five years in prison.

The outcome did not surprise me. By then, I'd lost all hope that justice would prevail. But I hurt deeply for Herbert, his family, his compromised future, his deferred dreams. There was nothing I could do to help, and thinking about him hurt too much. So I pushed Herbert's case to the back corners of my mind and heart, with all of the other injustices I'd endured and witnessed in Little Rock. It was the only way I knew to survive.

Nearly fifty years would pass before I would allow myself to go back to all of that hurt. Then I'd learn the full story of how my friend had landed in the hands of the Little Rock police and what really happened to him.

But on that day in May 1960, as the judge pronounced Herbert's jail sentence, I could see only as far as my graduation from Central. It was just two weeks away, and all I wanted was to get that diploma in my hand and get out of Little Rock—for good.

CHAPTER 12

Graduation and Good-bye

When spring rolled around, the last thing on my mind was the prom. I heard the white girls in my classes excitedly discussing their dresses and dates. But I still wasn't allowed to participate in extracurricular activities at school, so attending the prom at Central was not even an option. By then, I didn't have even an ounce of energy to worry about it, so I blocked such thoughts from my mind. I was tired. Plus, the bombing had altered my perspective about the things in life that really mattered. The prom just wasn't important. I was counting down to graduation, and anything else seemed like a distraction.

My parents saw things differently, though. From their vantage point in life, they could see much farther down the road than I, and what they saw made them sad. They saw a daughter who someday would have nothing but horrid high school memories, a daughter who would have missed out on some sentimental milestones of growing up, like the prom. They set out to change what little they could. They already had taken me downtown to a local jeweler to choose a class ring. By prom time, I was wearing the one I'd selected—a small, more feminine version in traditional yellow gold, with the school's name encircling a mother-of-pearl center. Then Mother and Daddy started dropping hints about the prom at Horace Mann. I should find out when it would be held, they hinted. I could invite that nice college boy who had taken me out a few times. They even promised to buy me a new dress.

I agreed. True to her word, Mother took me shopping at some of our favorite stores, and we found a cute baby blue nylon dress with layers of lace from the waist to the floor. Underneath, I wore a crinoline slip with lots of netting that gave my dress the traditional southern belle flair. Arthur "Nick" Winstead, the college guy, was my date. He picked me up, and we spent a few hours at the prom, dancing and mingling with some of my old friends. It was a nice evening, and I'm glad I had the experience. But I can't say I truly felt like a part of the festivities. While I knew many of the students there through community connections and Dunbar, I didn't go to school with them anymore. I didn't feel a connection to their school, and I didn't feel particularly sentimental. Afterward, I went back to sleepwalking through the days and counting down the time left at Central.

As graduation drew nearer, school officials gave each graduate six tickets for family members to attend. I was excited just to hold the tickets. They were a tangible sign that this was really happening. I would graduate from Central High School. But with such a large extended family, I had to decide how to distribute the tickets. Mother, Daddy, Loujuana, and Tina would be there without question. It didn't take long for me to decide to give the remaining two tickets to the patriarch on each side of my family—Big Daddy and Grandpa Cullins. They had provided a fortress for my family during the heaviest battles at Central, and I wanted them there to celebrate our victory. My graduation was indeed a victory for all of us.

But as excited as I was, I couldn't shake the feeling of uneasiness. The attack on my home had left me feeling vulnerable. I believed the real bomber was still out there, and I couldn't help wondering whether my graduation might provide the perfect opportunity to strike again. The segregationists had been suspiciously quiet all spring, but I knew better than to believe they had just conceded defeat. School officials apparently felt confident, though, that the level of security required for Ernie's graduation was not necessary this time around. The entire Little Rock police force had been called to duty for the 1958 ceremony, but security would be much more low-key this time. I didn't worry about the details. I was determined to walk across that stage and get my diploma no matter what. Nothing could stop me now.

My anticipation only heightened when I began receiving cards and letters of congratulations from extended family, friends, and even strangers. On May 24, this kind note arrived from my maternal grandmother, Erma, who still lived in St. Louis:

"I am so glad for you to get it over with. I hope you will not have to go through with this anymore during your school times."

I also heard from Grace Lorch, the compassionate white woman who had helped get Elizabeth safely to the bus on that first day when she had been separated from the rest of us and surrounded by the white mob. The Lorches, who lived across the street from Mr. and Mrs. Bates, had been branded Communists and harassed mercilessly over the years for sympathizing with us. I hadn't heard from or seen them in a long while.

"Very exciting news is coming from all over the South these days," Mrs. Lorch wrote, "but you and the other children in Little Rock were pioneers."

Many of those who wrote called me a trailblazer and thanked me for my courage. Their letters reminded me how much strength I had drawn from them over the years, those distant friends and family, as well as strangers, who took the time to let me know that they were with me in spirit. Their words had fueled my own spirit, especially when it felt as if all of white Little Rock stood against my comrades and me.

The last days of May rolled by, and finally, it was May 30, 1960. I was getting dressed for my graduation ceremony that afternoon when the telephone rang. It was Mother's brother-in-law, Uncle J.W., calling her with some disappointing news. He had stopped by Grandpa Cullins's house and found him in no shape to attend the graduation. Grandpa was drunk—so drunk that he had passed out in the middle of the floor. Mother gave a deep sigh. She would not allow his ticket to go to waste. She dialed her aunt Henrietta, Grandpa's oldest sister and the matriarch of the Cullins family, and explained what happened. Without hesitation, Aunt Henrietta stepped up to represent the Cullins side of the family.

I wasn't surprised that Grandpa had chosen such a momentous occasion to overindulge, and at the time, I tried to pretend that it didn't matter. But I was really hurt. I wanted him to attend my graduation. It was my way of thanking him for all he had done to help make that day possible. I wanted him to see that I had been listening all those years when he talked about the importance of taking advantage of opportunities, even when it was clear that he hadn't always done so himself. I wanted to look at him and see that he was proud of me for choosing Central and sticking it out. He'd never said it. That just wasn't his way. His presence would have said enough.

My family joined the crowd in Quigley Stadium that Monday night without Grandpa. When Jefferson and I marched into the packed stadium with the 423 graduates in the Class of 1960, there wasn't even a chance that I would spot my six relatives in the crowd. But just knowing they were there filled me with pride. I wanted to walk tall for them. As I sat through the ceremony, I thought about those tough early days at Central—the sneering white mobs, the hallway battles, the exhausting days and sleepless nights. I thought about the bombing, Herbert and Maceo, and I wondered what would become of them. I thought about Michigan State. How eager I was to start anew, to leave behind Little Rock and every sorrowful memory I had accumulated there.

I snapped out of my daze when I heard Jefferson's name and

watched him take his dignified walk across the stage. We had been true comrades from the beginning, and here we were together at the end of this leg of our journey. I was proud of him. And then . . .

Carlotta Walls . . .

Relief washed over me like a cooling rain when I heard my name. It was all over: the isolation, the harassment, the death threats, the terror. I'd come a mighty long way to get to this day. I pushed back my shoulders and held my head high as I walked across the stage. I thought about my comrades—Melba, Minnie, Terry, Gloria, Elizabeth, and Thelma—who had started this journey with me three years earlier but never got to take this victorious walk. I was walking for them, too. We had risked it all and made it through.

I thought about Rosa Parks, that gracious woman whose courage I had tried to emulate on my toughest days at Central. I thought about Emmett Till, the teenager whose battered body had shown me the raw evil of the Jim Crow South. I was no longer the naive fourteen-year-old girl who had been shocked by the hatred and fear of my white classmates and their parents. Central had forced me to grow up, to learn some adult lessons about courage, perseverance, and justice. I was ready for whatever lay ahead.

The air in the stadium was quiet as I accepted the makeshift diploma and shook Principal Matthews's hand. But I imagined my family cheering, the way they had done so many times in my life. I must have floated to my seat.

Afterward, I found Mother and Daddy and the rest of my group, and they all greeted me with hugs. The other graduates and their families seemed too excited even to notice me, and for a final, brief moment things felt normal. I needed to return my cap and gown and pick up my report card, so Big Daddy and I had agreed to meet at 14th and Jones streets, where he would be waiting with the box for my items. I cut across the field and walked down 14th toward our meeting spot. The street was pitch black and eerily quiet because most of the crowds were exiting the stadium on the opposite end, closer to where the festivities had taken place. Halfway down the road, it occurred to me that Big Daddy and I were in a potentially dangerous situation. It was a risk we would not have even dared to take at another time, but we'd gotten caught up in the excitement of graduation and in planning a meeting spot to avoid the crowds. Fortunately, we made it to the corner where the robes were being collected. I handed over my robe and mortarboard, accepted my report card and diploma, and with that, my days at Central High School came to an end.

Later that night, Jefferson and I celebrated with our friends and families at a graduation party held in our honor at a hall on 9th Street. I couldn't remember the last time I'd felt so free. We danced all night long to the rock-and-roll and R&B sounds that over the years had added soul to our suffering. A new Jackie Wilson song was a big hit with the crowd that night. Mr. Excitement was singing to a woman, but the irony of some of the lyrics struck me as a kind of farewell ode to Central High:

> You better stop, yeah, doggin' me around.
> If you don't stop, yeah, I'm gonna put you down . . .

For all the celebration, Jefferson and I still had one more thing to complete before we were truly done with Central High School. The previous year of correspondence courses and summer school had left both of us short one unit required to graduate. The closing of the high schools in the 1958–59 school year had cost us all so much. But school officials had decided to let us participate in the graduation ceremony and make up the missing unit over the summer. Elizabeth and Thelma, who had finished all their other required courses, needed to make up a single unit, too. All of us arranged to attend Beaumont High School in St. Louis. The principal at Central wrote a letter of recommendation for Jefferson and me to the Beaumont principal. I found it somewhat amusing, because in it he described us both as "desirable students," a sentiment he had managed to suppress our entire time at Central.

The morning after my graduation, my parents and sisters drove me to the train station downtown, and I took the first train out of Little Rock. There were no long, sad good-byes. I hugged my sisters and parents, who reminded me that they would see me at the end of summer. I had been anticipating this moment all year. As my train rolled out of Little Rock, I knew that was the end of my time there. I'd never return to live. I had little desire to return even for a visit. My mind was fastened on the future. There was no time for looking back.

I was bound for St. Louis, where Elizabeth, Thelma, and I stayed with Frankie Muse Freeman, a civil rights attorney who served as legal counsel to the NAACP. Ms. Freeman was a dynamic woman who, like Mrs. Bates, was treading in deep waters that had been the sole domain of men. Just two years out of Howard University's law school in 1949, Ms. Freeman had become part of the NAACP team that filed a lawsuit against the St. Louis Board of Education. Since "separate but equal" was the law at the time, the suit was aimed at forcing the board to add an airplane mechanics program at the black technical high school, like one that existed at the white technical high school. She and the NAACP won the case, and the school board responded by killing the program. Five years later, Ms. Freeman was the lead attorney in the NAACP lawsuit that ended racial discrimination in public housing. She eventually would become the first woman appointed to the U.S. Commission on Civil Rights when President Lyndon Johnson selected her for the post in 1964. Later, she also became national president of Delta Sigma Theta Sorority, Inc., the professional women's organization that had thrown the Christmas party for us nine shell-shocked teenagers in 1957.

I loved Mrs. Freeman. I was excited for the opportunity again to live with and be influenced by a strong, professional black woman. She and her husband, Shelby, had a daughter, also named Shelby, who was a student at Washington University. The couple lived on Grand Boulevard, walking distance from Beaumont High School. Their house was right next door to Koontz Funeral Home.

Within a week of my arrival in St. Louis, my parents mentioned during a conversation that Maceo Binns was on trial for bombing our home. I followed the case as closely as I could in the black press. Maceo was represented by attorney Will W. Shepherd, who immediately subpoenaed Governor Faubus to answer questions about some public comments he had made in the press about the case. Governor Faubus had told the *Gazette* that he had some inside information that police had been told that Maceo and "another Negro" were paid $50 to bomb the house. Governor Faubus even went a step further and opined that the bombing was a ruse to raise money for integration causes. Shepherd argued that the remarks prejudiced potential jurors and made it impossible for his client to receive a fair trial. The governor didn't even bother to show up in court on June 7, the first day of the trial, to answer the subpoena. He claimed that as chief executive, he was not bound by such court orders.

The case proceeded with the selection of an all-white jury. All three black residents in the jury pool were dismissed. One was let go because he was a member of the NAACP, another because he knew Shepherd, and no reason was given for the dismissal of the third person. The law permits prosecutors and defense attorneys to dismiss a certain number of jurors without explaining why. But there was no question in my mind that the juror was eliminated because of his race.

Prosecutor Frank Holt, the same one who had argued the case against Herbert, called ten witnesses before resting his case. Mother was called to testify and was questioned about my father's absence from our home at the time of the bombing. As was the case in Herbert's trial, our neighbor Earzie Cunningham testified about seeing Maceo in the neighborhood near my house at the time of the bombing. Marion Davis, Herbert's friend, testified that Maceo had been with him at my grandfather's café and pool hall that night. The same detectives who testified at Herbert's trial were called to answer questions about the confession Maceo had signed. But Shepherd aggressively cross-examined the detectives. According to media reports, Shepherd asked if they used "pressure as hypnosis" to get Maceo to talk. One detective said that "psychology" was used but that it was not considered "coercion."

Maceo took the stand and angrily denounced the confession. He said he signed it because he wasn't permitted to get cigarettes, take a bath, talk to a lawyer, or call his family during two nonstop days of questioning. He said detectives told him that he would be released if he signed the confession and that he could just deny it later. Maceo also reported that one detective suggested that a "hosograph" should be used on him—a phony term that may have been a facetious reference to the late chief Eugene Smith's decision to open the fire hoses on recalcitrant segregationists at the start of my senior year.

Maceo grew flustered on the stand. He began talking so fast at one point that the judge had to ask him to slow down. When Maceo's temper flashed again, Prosecutor Holt asked: "Why are you getting mad?"

Maceo shot back: "Because you're trying to say I was someplace where I wasn't."

Maceo didn't stop there. He pointed his finger at Holt and exclaimed: "I don't know who did it. . . . As far as I know, you could have done it, and I'm not being facetious."

Holt called ten witnesses before resting his case. Shepherd made a motion to dismiss the case, but it was overruled by Judge William J. Kirby, the same judge who had presided at Herbert's trial. My father was called to testify for the defense. According to detectives, my father had procured the dynamite. Of course, Daddy testified that such claims were untrue and that he had nothing to do with the bombing. Maceo admitted to passing my house in his car the night of the bombing. He said he was on his way to the medical center to pick up a girlfriend and that he passed Herbert, who was on his way home from the pool hall. Additional defense witnesses backed up Maceo's claim that he was parked at the medical center, waiting for a girlfriend, at the time the bomb exploded.

Nevertheless, the all-white jury, made up of eleven men and one woman, took just thirty minutes the day after the trial began to find Maceo guilty. Like Herbert, Maceo was sentenced to the maximum five years in prison. However, Maceo remained free on bond while his case worked its way up to the state supreme court. Nine months later, on March 13, 1961, the state's high court would overturn Maceo's conviction in a 6–1 ruling that said confessions obtained after a fifty-seven-hour period of interrogation could not be introduced. Then, in an astonishing move, Judge Kirby and Prosecutor Holt decided to halt jury trials indefinitely for black defendants while the state fought a federal ruling against racial discrimination. The court had found that black defendants were too often tried by all-white juries.

Maceo's attorney, Will Shepherd, who had advocated for the moratorium, was an ongoing burr in the side of the white establishment in Little Rock. A new jury trial was set for Maceo to be held on December 7, 1961, but there is no record that the trial was ever held. As far as I know, Maceo was never retried and did not go to prison. I never saw him again after I left Little Rock. Cemetery records show that he died on January 13, 1972. He was just forty-two years old.

After Maceo's conviction was overturned, Governor Faubus was determined to upstage the state supreme court. In July 1961, the governor commuted the sentences of three of the Labor Day bombers: J. D. Sims, John Coggins, and Jess Perry. Then, two months later, he reduced the sentence of the only Labor Day bomber still in jail, E. A. Lauderdale, Sr., making him immediately eligible for parole.

By then, though, my parents had already cut their ties to Little Rock.

At the end of my summer at Beaumont High School in St. Louis, Mother and Daddy drove to pick me up, and we traveled together to East Lansing. They stayed a couple of days to help me get settled on campus at Michigan State. During those long hours on the road and in my dormitory room, Mother and Daddy gave no indication that they were contemplating a major life change. But about two weeks after they left me in Michigan, I received a shocking letter. The first thing I noticed was that the letter listed a return address in Kansas City. Their letter said simply that they had moved there with my sisters. That was it. There wasn't a word of explanation, nor were there any expressions of sentiment or regret. And to this day, there have been none.

My parents never explained how long they had been contemplating the move or why they left precisely when they did. As I've said, once Mother and Daddy made a decision to move forward, they were not prone to look back. But I know this: Little Rock was all both of them had ever known. Except for my father's tour of duty during World War II, neither of them had ever lived more than ten minutes from their fathers and the wide net of support provided by their extended family and friends. However quiet they kept their deliberations, the final decision to venture beyond that safety net must have been gut-wrenching.

Their sudden move told me what they could not: that I wasn't the only one who yearned for a fresh start.

CHAPTER 13

Finding Focus

At Michigan State, I was happy to be just a number. More than twenty-four-thousand students attended the East Lansing university, and nearly one thousand of us were black. My schoolmates barely even noticed when I walked past. After three years of being at the center of so much negative attention, I was grateful for the chance to just blend in with the crowd.

The university was a city unto itself, spread over fifty-two-hundred acres. It drew students of all races from every part of the country and the rest of the world. Being among people with such diverse backgrounds was exciting to me. I made friends easily. Few of them realized at first that I was one of the nine black students who had gone to Central High School in Little Rock. I certainly didn't volunteer any information. But when they learned I was from Little Rock and saw me hanging out with Ernie, they began asking questions. They didn't bombard me, though, and gave me the space I needed from Central. I had left my past in Little Rock.

I did, however, bring one thing with me: my desire to be a doctor. I had known since I was a little girl what I wanted to do with my life. I'd even chosen Central in part because I believed it would better prepare me for that career path. So I decided right away to declare a major in premed. For some reason, I thought I had to declare a major immediately. But after reviewing my transcript, the freshman counselor wasn't sure I was up to the task. I was missing some high-level math and science courses that I had not been able to take via correspondence or summer school in my junior year when Faubus shut down Little Rock's high schools.

"I can put you in the premed program, but you're going to have trouble," the counselor told me.

That comment sparked the part of me that couldn't stand people telling me what I could not do. I took the counselor's doubt as a challenge and insisted on being placed in the program anyway. I didn't recognize then that I was mentally exhausted. I just wasn't ready to work as hard as I would need to work to catch up academically. I was ready to have some fun.

For the first time, I had true social freedom. I could come and go as I pleased, without anyone watching over me and without fearing for my life. And there was always plenty to do. One of my frequent hangouts was the student lounge, where I enjoyed mingling with my peers practically every day. On weekends, I often joined my new friends at the fraternity parties on campus. And then there was football.

Football has always been at the center of social life at Michigan State. It quickly became the center of my social life, too. I knew more about the sport than most of the other girls in the dorm because in the South, high school football was what we did. If you didn't play, you sat in the stands and cheered on Friday nights. I wasn't allowed to go to Central's games, so I rooted for the teams from Dunbar and Horace Mann. In the South, Friday night football games were also part fashion show, so the girls always fussed over what they wore. But I quickly found that at Michigan State, it really didn't matter. I could throw on a casual skirt or slacks with a comfortable sweater and fit right in with the crowd of students cheering in the stands on Saturday afternoons. Michigan State had one of the top football teams in the Big Ten Conference and was usually a championship contender. The atmosphere was always electric.

My knowledge of sports helped me to befriend many of the players, including Herb Adderly, a star offensive back who was the first black tri-captain for the Spartans. He was dating my roommate and was drafted in 1961 by the Green Bay Packers. I also became great friends with basketball standout Horace Walker, who had graduated from Michigan State just months before I got there and had been drafted by the St. Louis Hawks. Horace was doing postgraduate work at the university, and I met him at a gathering for African American students at an apartment in Lansing. He would become my best friend, the big brother I never had, and the godfather of my children.

At Michigan State, I was experiencing the exciting college life I had envisioned, except for one thing. For the first time in my life, I was struggling academically. The question in my mind about whether I could make it in premed grew bigger. The counselor offered no encouragement. My grades at the end of the first quarter seemed to prove him right: I made a C in chemistry and even one D. I wasn't accustomed to making bad grades, and I was very frustrated with myself. My other roommates—Ann Wynder, Connie Williams, and Ina Smith—encouraged me to study harder and seek help from a student counseling center on campus. I went to the center a couple of times but didn't find it very effective. I had some thinking to do during the quarter break.

Before joining my family in Kansas City for the Christmas holidays, I went to Chicago in early December 1960 and worked a few weeks for the U.S. Postal Service. I stayed with Aunt M.E.— the aunt who had housed me while I attended summer school before my senior year. While there, I took advantage of every chance I got to venture downtown after hours to hear the jazz greats, among them saxophonist Cannonball Adderley, guitarist Kenny

Burrell, and my favorite songstress, Nancy Wilson. The Sutherland Lounge, which drew all of the big acts, was one of my regular spots. I also made frequent visits to a spot at 63rd and Cottage streets to see McCoy Tyner and John Coltrane. The jazz shows helped to lift my spirits.

When I took the train from Chicago to Kansas City, I found that my parents and sisters had settled in a wonderful, family-oriented neighborhood on Mersington Street. They had grown close to some of the neighbors, who had children the same age as my sisters. Mother was working part-time, since those icy midwestern winters often left Daddy out of work. It was good to see them so relaxed and happy. I couldn't bring myself to tell them I was struggling in school.

I returned to Michigan State for the winter and spring quarters, but I continued to have trouble as my core courses got tougher. Summer break gave me the time away that I desperately needed. I took the train to New York to spend the summer there, working for the Hotel Employees Union #6, the group that had sponsored the New York trip for the Little Rock Nine in the summer of 1958. A friend from Michigan State, Brucetta Hower, joined me, and I helped her get a job with the union, too. But Brucie's father, a well-to-do funeral-home owner, sent her enough money to live on, and she quit her job after the first week. She stayed a few extra weeks, though, to explore the city with me. Brucie and I split the rent on a small apartment on East 10th Street in Greenwich Village.

Now on my own, I wanted to rub up against the Sugar Hill I'd heard Mother rave about throughout my childhood. I wanted to touch and feel the Harlem I'd read about in stories hailing the 1920s renaissance. I wanted to set my feet in the legendary jazz clubs, like Small's Paradise, which joined Harlem's Cotton Club as one of the popular nightclubs and restaurants in the 1930s and 1940s. It was Small's Paradise where I first saw the husband-wife jazz duo Shirley Scott (on the organ) and Stanley Turrentine (on saxophone). I also spent time on 52nd Street, listening and watching the antics of Thelonious Monk (not yet realizing that he was the "wino" I'd first encountered as an eight-year-old on the playground of my aunt's apartment complex).

Harlem never slept. When I stepped into a fairly new high-rise for an after-hours party about two o'clock one morning, I got a taste of what I'd imagined Harlem was like during the great renaissance. Several artists lived there. My friends pointed out the apartment of one of my all-time favorites, Count Basie, and I lingered in the halls to be close to the sights, sounds, and smells all around. The intoxicating scent of food saturated the halls. Horns and a piano traded riffs in one apartment, and the strong, bluesy vocals of a female singer rang out from another. I learned later that those vocal cords belonged to Gloria Lynne, a rhythm and blues and jazz singer who recorded a number of hits in the 1950s and 1960s.

New York was also home that summer to another Little Rock native—Mrs. Bates, who had relocated there to work on her memoir. I saw her a couple of times while there, including once when she invited me to her apartment to meet Langston Hughes and his nephew, who was helping her with her memoir. I also got together occasionally with Ernie and Terry, who were working in New York for the summer in the garment district. We were all hoping to save money for college. When I told Ernie how much I was spending to rent the apartment in the Village, he helped arrange for me to rent a room from the mother of a friend of his, who lived in Jamaica, New York. By then, my friend Brucie was gone. The move helped me save enough money to buy a heavier winter coat and thicker sweaters than the ones I owned and to return to Michigan State with a few extra dollars.

While in New York, I visited Aunt Juanita and Uncle Freddie again and for the first time had a conversation with him about race. He wanted to know how I was doing and how I had endured all that happened to me at Central. Uncle Freddie also revealed his own astonishing story. His parents never talked to him about race, he said, and he would be an adult before he realized the significance assigned to skin color in this country. Both of his parents had immigrated to the United States and raised Uncle Freddie in a Rhode Island community full of other immigrants, mostly from Italy, Portugal, Ireland, and the Caribbean islands. As far as Uncle Freddie knew, everyone got along, and his childhood was happy. He was aware of his African heritage, but it seemed that everyone around him was a racial mixture of some kind, so skin color mattered little. He didn't have a clue about the Jim Crow South and how people of color were treated there. He accepted himself as the equal of everyone and was treated that way by those around him.

When World War II broke out, he joined the navy right after high school and left for boot camp. His father drove him to the train station. While waiting for his son to board, Mr. Andrade stood there silently with a pained expression in his eyes, Uncle Freddie recalled. It seemed as though Mr. Andrade wanted to say something to his son. Mr. Andrade stammered a bit as he tried to speak. But all he could manage to say to his son was: "Take care of yourself."

At first, Uncle Freddie said he thought his father just got caught up in the emotion of the moment—his son leaving home for the first time, headed to war. But as the train rolled south, the porter kept moving Uncle Freddie to railcars farther back. Finally, Uncle Freddie spoke up.

"I want to stay here. Why do you keep moving me?" he asked innocently.

Uncle Freddie recalled the sting of the porter's words: "You are a Negro, and Negroes aren't allowed to sit here."

Uncle Freddie was shocked and confused. He didn't know what to make of it all. He was disappointed that his parents, particularly his father, had allowed him to be caught so off guard by the dynamics of race and skin color. But the more he thought about it, Uncle Freddie said, the more he came to understand his father's pained expression at the train station. He believed his father wanted to issue a warning about what lay ahead but just didn't know what to say. Soon afterward in the navy, Uncle Freddie met my uncle J.W., the one who later introduced him to Aunt Juanita. Both worked as cooks, serving officers on the submarine. Uncle J.W., ever the smooth talker, had led the entire family to believe for many years that he was the head cook in charge of the kitchen on the submarine. As it turned out, though, Uncle Freddie was the head cook. But gracious Uncle Freddie never blew his friend's cover. He said he was always grateful to Uncle J.W., not just for introducing him to Aunt Juanita, but for helping him to maneuver his way through the racist South.

Uncle Freddie's story stayed with me long after I left New York.

Before heading back to Michigan State, though, I took a detour to Denver to visit my uncle Byron Johnson and his family. Uncle Byron was a distant relative on the Cullins side, but as family tradition and courtesy dictate the family elders are called "Uncle" or "Aunt" no matter the relation. He was always one of my favorite family members and earned the title through many stages of my life. He played professional baseball in the Negro Leagues as part of the famed Kansas City Monarchs from 1937 to 1940. That included a stint barnstorming the country alongside Satchel Paige as a member of the team's All-Star players in 1939 and 1940. Before being asked to join the Monarchs, Uncle Byron, who graduated from Wiley College, taught biology at Dunbar High School.

My earliest memory of him is when I was five years old and he was Little Rock's director of playgrounds for black neighborhoods. Mother had dropped me off to spend a few hours with him at the playground next to Stephens Elementary School near our home. A bunch of boys were shooting rocks with slingshots, and ever curious, I begged to give the slingshot a try. When the boys finally gave in, I put the rock in place and pulled the slingshot backward. I shot myself in the mouth, knocking out my front teeth. Blood gushed from my mouth as I fell to the ground. The first face I saw was Uncle Byron's. I'll never forget the look in his eyes, so kind and gentle, as he picked me up to take me to the hospital and assured me that I would be okay. He was one of the kindest, most easygoing men I've ever known.

During my first year at Central, Uncle Byron helped me with biology projects and offered constant encouragement. The next year, he and his wife, Christine, who had been childhood sweethearts, relocated to Denver with his job at the U.S. Postal Service. They invited me to spend a few days during my first summer break from college with them and their two children—Jackie, who was fourteen; and their son, Joseph Byron, then seven.

The first thing I noticed and loved about Denver was its cleanliness. The entire city just seemed to glisten, and the air was fresh. My mind seemed at ease when I spent a few moments gazing at the white-capped mountains. People were polite, and the color of my skin seemed not to matter. I enjoyed spending time with my aunt and uncle and even got a chance to meet Satchel Paige, who was driving through, headed to the West Coast with his wife. The former teammates had stayed in touch, and Mr. Paige came over to the house for dinner one night. I sat at the dinner table and hung on their every word as they regaled me with stories about barnstorming together through the United States and Canada with fellow players from the Negro Leagues. Uncle Byron had played shortstop, watching close up as Mr. Paige repeatedly struck out the league's best hitters. To highlight his showmanship, Mr. Paige would even send his outfielders to the dugout before striking out a well-known slugger. The crowds would go mad. The two men howled at the memory. As a child, I had watched Mr. Paige in awe and could hardly believe I was fortunate enough to be sitting across the table from him.

I spent less than a week in Denver, but the city stayed on my mind. I think Uncle Byron and Aunt Christine could tell that I didn't seem happy because they made what seemed to me a generous and enticing offer: If things didn't work out for me in Michigan, I was welcome to move to Denver with them, to work and go to school there.

When I returned to Michigan State for the fall quarter, I couldn't get Denver out of my head. I was disappointed in how my post-Central life was progressing. I continued to struggle in math and science and realized that maybe the counselor had been right: I wasn't prepared for the tough, premed curriculum. The lost year at Central had hurt in irreparable ways. Not only had I missed out on essential coursework, I was having trouble focusing mentally on my studies. I just couldn't find the motivation. This was unfamiliar territory for someone who always had been a stellar student. Maybe the admissions office at Antioch College had understood something that I had not a year earlier when I applied there and received the advice that had been so disappointing at the time. Maybe I should have taken some time off. But it was too late for second-guessing. I was tired of struggling and ready to let go of my dream. I changed my major to nursing. I figured I still might find some satisfaction if I stayed in the medical field. But it didn't take long for me to figure out that nursing wasn't for me. I couldn't get over the feeling that nursing seemed second best, close to the action but not really what I wanted to do. I just wasn't interested. In the winter quarter of 1962, I dropped nursing and left my major undeclared. I decided to focus just on taking my core courses. My life seemed at a serious crossroads.

Sometime during my sophomore year, Aunt Christine sent me a ski sweater—a soft green cardigan with a black-and-white strip that zipped in the front. It reminded me of Denver, the mountains, and fresh air. It also reminded me of a photo I'd seen of Marilyn Van Derbur, the Miss Colorado who became Miss America in

1958, posing in ski gear on a slope in her native state. I could enjoy skiing, I thought. I think I knew then what wouldn't become evident to my family for months. I stuck it out another quarter at Michigan State and stayed through the summer to take a few more courses and work. Mother and Daddy thought I was working at the telephone company, but I was actually a barmaid at a little place called Sonny's Lounge. It was a fun job that gave me free access to good music and interesting people. I even came up with a drink I called Mexican vodka, a mixture of mostly vodka, lime juice, and grenadine shaken with ice, which was popular enough for a local band to name a song after it.

At the end of summer, I packed everything I'd brought with me to Michigan State and got on the train headed back to Kansas City. But first, I made a quick stop in Chicago for the 1962 Chicago Charities College All-Star Game in Soldier Field. The popular preseason game matched the NFL championship team against a select team of college seniors. The team was to include Ernie Davis, the Syracuse University running back who in December 1961 had just become the first black college football player to win the Heisman Trophy. He was drafted by the Washington Redskins in the first round and immediately traded to the Cleveland Browns, where he was expected to join fellow Syracuse alum and All-American running back Jim Brown to create an offensive powerhouse. But while preparing for the All-Star Game during the summer, Davis was diagnosed with leukemia. The news shocked and saddened me. Nevertheless, I joined the crowd of sixty-five thousand spectators who watched the Green Bay Packers stomp the collegiate standouts 42–17 in the August 3 game without the star.

I got back on the train with my loaded trunk and headed to Kansas City to be with my family. The weeks passed quickly. As September rolled around, Daddy grew suspicious. He noticed that I had said nothing about returning to Michigan State and had never unpacked my trunk.

"When are you leaving to go back to Michigan?" he asked.

I hadn't figured out how to bring it up before now.

"I'm not going back," I told him.

Daddy remained cool. "Well, what are you planning to do?" he shot back.

I knew I had to have a plan. After high school, girls were expected to get married, go to college, or go to work. I'd left a scholarship behind at Michigan State. So I knew my plan had better be convincing.

"I'm going to Colorado," I responded. "Uncle Byron and Aunt Christine said that I could come to Denver, stay with them, work, and go to school if I want to. That's what I want to do."

My parents were always pretty good about letting me make my own decisions, and this time was no different. They asked a few questions about what seemed to them a sudden move, but in the end, they agreed to let me find my own way. Afterward, I called Uncle Byron and Aunt Christine to make certain the offer was still good.

"Sure," Uncle Byron said. "Come on."

In mid-September 1962, I boarded a Greyhound bus with my loaded trunk, bound for Denver and, I hoped, a fresh start. The trip took about eighteen hours with stops in practically every hamlet and rural outpost along the way. The trip was so long that I was able to finish all six-hundred-plus pages of the Leon Uris novel *Exodus*.

Once I arrived in Denver, I applied for a job with Mountain Bell, the local telephone company. I was hired and offered a position as a service representative. I had gone through the training program when some of the black workers told me excitedly that I would be the first black employee in my new job. They were thrilled for me. I, on the other hand, was worried. I couldn't go through that again. I didn't want to be the center of attention, a racial symbol, or the standard-bearer of anyone's expectations. I declined the service representative position and asked to be a cashier/teller.

I had been on the job for nearly two months when my parents and sisters came to Denver for Thanksgiving. Uncle Byron immediately began trying to woo Daddy to the city for good.

"So, what do you think?" Uncle Byron asked after showing Daddy around.

"I figured I'd be hip-deep in snow and couldn't work," Daddy responded.

But Daddy was surprised to learn that the winters in Denver were more agreeable to construction work than the icy winter months in Kansas City and agreed to return to Denver in January for work. The two of us shared the basement at Uncle Byron and Aunt Christine's home. Daddy transferred his union membership, found work right away, and was surprised to run into other brick masons from Little Rock. Soon he was hooked on Denver, too.

By the time Daddy arrived, I had enrolled in night courses at the University of Colorado for the winter/spring semester in 1963. I worked all day as a teller at the telephone company and then walked the two and a half blocks to class. But during the two-hour break between work and school, I often stopped at a lounge to listen to jazz, a beauty college to get my hair cut, or anywhere along the way to avoid arriving on campus early. I still wasn't quite focused on school.

At the end of the semester in May, I rode with Daddy to Kansas City in a rented truck to pick up Mother and the girls. A friend of Daddy's helped him load the truck with all of the family's belongings, and the two of them drove the truck back to Denver. Mother and I rotated driving the car. When we made it to Denver, my parents rented half of a duplex for a couple of months until they found a house they wanted to buy in the Park Hill neighborhood. We all moved into the new house together.

Park Hill had been an all-white, upper-middle-class neighborhood, but many white residents were beginning to move out as black families relocated there. One day, Mother answered a knock at the door and found Reverend J. Carlton Babbs, pastor of Park Hill United Methodist Church, standing there. He told Mother that he had heard we were new to the neighborhood, and he invited us to worship with his congregation. The previous home owners were among his members, and they must have told him about us. My parents thought it was such a gracious gesture that all of us attended services the following Sunday. When we got there, we saw only white families. We learned later that just one black family was among the three-thousand-member congregation and that Dr. Babbs was reaching out to the new neighbors in an effort to integrate his congregation. The church was convenient to our house, less than a ten-minute drive away. It had a radio ministry and vigorous youth programs, which enabled my younger sisters to make new friends. The members were friendly and welcoming. I especially liked that the worship services were orderly, meaningful, and short. I sometimes joke that I probably should have been Catholic or Episcopalian because after about an hour in church, I start looking at my watch. Park Hill was a good match for us all. My family soon became members, and we still worship there today.

Soon after we joined the church, a couple of my friends mentioned that they were preparing to go to D.C. for a massive civil rights rally, the March on Washington for Jobs and Freedom. A coalition of civil rights leaders had appealed to the masses to participate, but I hadn't followed the planning of the event closely and had no intention of going. I just didn't feel compelled to be part of the crowd. All of us have different roles, different ways of contributing to the common good. While I had tremendous respect for leaders like Roy Wilkins, who was among those involved in the planning, I had no burning desire to participate in a march that seemed to me then purely symbolic. But I must say that when I clicked on the television on August 28, 1963, I was moved by what I saw—hundreds of thousands of men, women, and children of every hue stretched from the Washington Monument to the Lincoln Memorial. I was particularly satisfied that the march was peaceful, given the doubt I'd heard expressed in the news in the preceding weeks from some who feared the large gathering might turn violent. There was no denying the persuasive political power of that moment.

Just three weeks later, on September 15, 1963, I was horrified when I heard on the news that four black girls had perished in a Sunday morning bombing at the 16th Street Baptist Church in Birmingham. I grieved for those girls, three of whom were fourteen years old and the other who was eleven. When I saw their pictures, I couldn't get their faces out of my head. I kept seeing them smiling, dressed in their Sunday best, unaware even what hit them when the bomb went off. I remembered that kind of terror. I could even smell the dynamite. I knew that the same fate so easily could have been mine.

That same chilling thought raced through my mind again on November 22 when President Kennedy was assassinated. Again, I was devastated. He had seemed so decent on civil rights, and I was looking forward to voting for him the following year. It was to be my first time ever voting. Now President Kennedy was gone, his life extinguished by the same kind of hatred that had been so rampant in Little Rock. I wondered how—and sometimes why—I had survived.

By the end of 1963, I had dropped all but a single class at the university. I felt overloaded, as much by the times and my state of mind as by the pressures of trying to work full-time and go to school. Two years passed quickly with little change as I continued working at Mountain Bell and taking an occasional class. I told no one about my background in Little Rock. I even kept my distance from the two local NAACP chapters, which I suspect may have

miffed some of the officers who knew my story. I couldn't understand why two chapters of the NAACP were necessary with so few
black residents in Denver. But I was too preoccupied trying to figure out my own life to ask questions. I wasn't ready to become an
envoy. I didn't want any reminders of my past. I was disappointed
in myself. I knew that I wasn't living up to my potential.

Things began to look up for me in 1965 when I came up with
a plan to finish college. I knew I would never get a degree at the
rate I was going. I needed to attend school full-time and focus
solely on my studies. The only way I could do it, I figured, was to
get a better job, work for six months, and bank all of my earnings.
I reached out to one of my aunts, who put me in touch with the
National Urban League. Whitney Young, the group's executive director, was pushing aggressively to end economic disparities between the races by encouraging corporations and the federal
government to create more jobs for black men and women. I admired how he was helping to catapult the Urban League to the
front of the civil rights movement with the NAACP and other
groups that had been more prominent before his tenure. But the
Urban League was more about jobs and opportunities and operated as a bridge to help black men and women who were prepared
to enter the corporate arena. After I visited the office of the Denver
chapter and registered for job opportunities, I got an interview at
the Rocky Flats Plant, a federal nuclear weapons production facil-
ity near Denver. I figured there would be a routine background
check of some kind, but I was stunned when Daddy came in one
evening and told me that the FBI had been in the neighborhood
asking questions about me. A neighbor had stopped by to tell him.
My heart rate sped up, and I broke out in a sweat. Suddenly I
flashed back to 1960 when FBI agents took my father away. It had
been my only experience with the agency. I wondered why the FBI
would be involved with my background check. Shortly thereafter,
I received a call from a federal agent who informed me that I

needed to make an appointment to answer some questions that involved classified information about my application for a government job. That made me even more nervous—almost nervous enough to skip the interview. But I needed the job. I also didn't want to disappoint those who had helped me get the interview. That was important to me.

When I arrived at the federal building for the interview, I met with one of the agents, who soon began peppering me with questions: Did I know this person from Michigan State? Did I join that Communist group? Had I participated in a certain rally at the university? He also asked about some of my associations in Little Rock. I felt jittery inside, but I kept my answers short and truthful.

"Not to my knowledge," I responded each time.

This was J. Edgar Hoover's FBI, but I didn't realize then just what that meant. It was clear, though, that the agency had kept a file on me. I surmised it was likely because of my role in integrating Central High School. The suspicion sent a chill up my spine. Many years later, in the mid-1970s, news broke that Hoover indeed had kept files filled with personal (and often embarrassing) information on public figures, political and civil rights leaders, particularly those with whom he disagreed. While visiting a friend and her husband in D.C. around that time, I planned to file a Freedom of Information Act request to view my file, but while there, I decided against it. Those days were behind me, I told myself. I wanted to leave them there.

Whatever is in my file must not have appeared too threatening, though, because I got the job at the Rocky Flats Plant. I stuck to my plan and worked for six months, putting away practically all of my salary. I decided to apply to Colorado State College (now called the University of Northern Colorado) in nearby Greeley because the tuition was the more reasonable of the two area universities on a quarter system, and I wouldn't lose any of my credits from Michigan State.

In addition to the money I had saved, I applied for scholarships. I wrote to Mrs. Bates to tell her that I was returning to school and that I had never received the scholarship the NAACP had promised. She responded with a check, for which I was grateful. I also applied for a federal student loan through the Denver National Bank, where I had small savings and checking accounts. But when a bank officer processed my application, she told me I needed to apply for the loan at my parents' bank.

The bank officer's dismissal infuriated me. I calmly asked to meet with the bank president. To my surprise, the president agreed to the meeting. I laid out my case. I first explained why I was applying for the loan. I told him that I was twenty-one years old and didn't find it necessary to apply through my parents, particularly since I had arrived in Denver before them and had been banking at his institution since my arrival.

The bank president said simply that he agreed with me. I got the loan. It was a small victory but an important one. I felt a spark of the old Carlotta, the determined and focused Carlotta.

Finally, I was grabbing the reins of my life.

CHAPTER 14

A Season of Loss

When I saw Grandpa Cullins at a family reunion in Kansas City at the end of summer in 1965, he didn't look well. He seemed thinner and slower than I remembered. I hadn't seen him in the six years since I'd left Little Rock, and a bit of the fire in him had gone out. For the first time, Grandpa Cullins seemed to me like an old man.

The following spring, a telephone call brought dreaded news: Grandpa Cullins had died. He hadn't been feeling well for days, family members said. Then, he went to sleep one night and never woke up. The news filled me with sorrow and regret. Grandpa had been a big presence in my life, but I wished I had not been so intimidated by him. Even with all he had taught me, I knew I could have learned so much more. But it was time to say good-bye for good. My parents, sisters, and I loaded the family car for a daylong trip and headed south to Little Rock.

It was my first trip home since my high school graduation, and I was a bit anxious. I wasn't sure how it would feel to be back. As the car rolled toward Little Rock, I couldn't help wondering: What had become of my old friends from the neighborhood? Had any of them returned to Little Rock? How was our old house holding up? Did it look the same? I was bound to pass it on the way to Uncle Teet's house. Would I remember all of the good years there or flash back to the bombing? And what about Central? How would it feel to drive by that grand old building again?

At least some of my questions would be answered minutes after my family rolled into town. We had just parked at my cousin's house and I was unpacking the car when a blue Volkswagen convertible pulled up behind me. The driver tooted his horn and called out to me.

I thought: I have the exact same car.

"This is Herbert," the driver shouted as I craned my neck to see inside the car.

It was Herbert Monts, my childhood friend. I was thrilled to see him and rushed to his car. We had often joked as children about our twinlike connection, and now, after six years without seeing or talking to each other, we'd somehow ended up with the same taste in cars. The moment felt divinely inspired. Here I was, on my first trip home in six years, and the first person I saw was the one whose treatment by the justice system had embodied the injustice that made me want never to return. I had wondered about Herbert often through the years—how he was coping with prison, whether he had gotten out, and what he was doing with his life. But remembering was just too painful, and this moment outside my cousin's house didn't seem like the right time to bring it up. Neither of us mentioned Central, the bombing, his trial, or jail. There was just too much to say. He expressed his condolences, we asked about each other's families and old friends, shared a bit of small talk, and then parted, promising to stay in touch.

I didn't get to talk to Herbert again on that trip, but I saw a number of old friends at Grandpa's funeral. It was held at the Cullins family church, Wesley Chapel, which Grandpa had helped to build. The church was filled with people who had come from all over Little Rock to pay their respects. The weather was uncharacteristically warm for April, and the ushers handed out paper fans. Tears rolled down my face as I thought about how much I would miss Grandpa. But on the ride to the cemetery in the family car, I got a good chuckle when one of my aunts commented about the nice eulogy the minister had given.

"Aunt Hannah Mae," I retorted, "the minister obviously didn't know Grandpa."

She smiled. We both knew the well-intentioned reverend had either made up the sweet story or significantly cleaned up the language he attributed to Brother Cullins.

The next day, I headed back to Denver and to school at Colorado State College. I was determined to do whatever it took this time to get my college degree without having to ask for my parents' help. They had done enough for me, and I felt I owed it to them and myself to finish. With the savings from my job at Rocky Flats, a low-interest bank loan, a $300 loan from Big Daddy, and two scholarships—from the NAACP and the United Methodist Church—I was able to cover the first two quarters without having to work. That allowed me to focus on school and get back into the groove of studying and performing well.

With school back on track, I treated myself in spring 1967 to a golf exhibition ticket for a matchup between Arnold Palmer and Art Wall at the Cherry Hills Country Club. While there, I ran into my uncle Byron and his son, Joe. At thirteen, Joe had developed into a talented all-around athlete, but he looked sick. He had complained to his father that he wasn't feeling well, and Uncle Byron was holding Joe's wrists under some cold running water to cool him down. Over the next several weeks, I called and stopped by periodically to check on Joe, but his health didn't seem to improve. I was shocked over the summer when my young cousin was diagnosed with nephritis, a potentially fatal kidney disease. Joe's health continued to slide downward, and he would pass away in November of the following year.

I had grown close to the entire family while staying with them, and it was tough watching Joe suffer at such a young age and seeing the helplessness in the eyes of my aunt and uncle. I delved into my studies to take the focus off my own pain. When I sat down with a school counselor to figure out the most direct route to graduation, I settled on a double major in social sciences and recreational administration. My major mattered little to me at that point. I just wanted to finish. After the second quarter, I had to get two part-time jobs to pay my tuition. Each morning, I drove my Volkswagen Bug fifty miles to school in Greeley, Colorado, returned to Denver in the afternoon, and went to back-to-back jobs. I was taking a full load of at least twenty hours each quarter, so I spent most of my downtime studying.

Graduation was just a month away when I turned on the television before heading out to school one morning in April 1968 and heard an astonishing news report: Dr. King had been gunned down on the balcony of a Memphis hotel. By then, I had moved to a Denver apartment within the boundaries of one of the top junior high schools in the state so that my sister Tina could attend, and she stayed with me during the week. The two of us stared, aghast, at the television screen as the announcer reported that King was dead. I didn't want to believe my ears. I felt great sadness for the country, but even more for Dr. King's wife and children, whose loss would be the greatest of all. Racial hatred was still burning wildly across America, and now it had consumed a giant.

I graduated in May from Colorado State. Mother and my two sisters attended the ceremony, but Daddy had to work, which was fine with me. I had not invited anyone else and was in no mood to celebrate. I had finally achieved my goal, but taking so long to do so seemed to strip away some of the sense of accomplishment. I was just relieved to be finished. Now I could move on, knowing at least that I had completed what I set out to do.

But the assassination of Bobby Kennedy on June 6, less than a month after my college graduation, deepened my angst. Another fighter for freedom and justice was gone. Anger seemed to be spewing from every corner of the country. The white supremacists seemed determined to silence the strongest voices for racial equality. And new, defiant black voices like the Black Panthers were emerging, finding converts in urban neighborhoods impatient with the pace of change. I had watched from a distance as my people burned down their own neighborhoods after King's death. D.C. burned. Baltimore burned. Cleveland and Chicago burned. I understood their rage. I'd even found myself at times trying to explain it to white schoolmates. But anger plus anger equals only more anger. I wondered if the country could ever find its way to true peace.

Amid all of the national chaos, I applied for a newly created position at the Metropolitan Denver YWCA as program administrator for teenagers, but I was surprised during the interview process when one of the black board members challenged me. I had moved to Lakewood, Colorado, a largely white suburb, and the board member wanted to know whether I would be able to relate to and create relevant programs for the black teenagers who lived in mostly black neighborhoods in northeast Denver. The tone of the question unnerved me. I felt as though my blackness was being challenged. It might have helped in that moment to mention that as a fourteen-year-old black girl in Little Rock, I had risked my life to go up against a once segregated school system and that I had persevered through hell to get the education the Supreme Court said I was due. Surely I understood what it was like to be a young black girl trying to navigate her way in the world. I didn't need to live in a certain neighborhood to know what it was like. But I had told no one that I was one of the Little Rock Nine, and it didn't even occur to me to mention it then. I've never wanted to use my experience in Little Rock to gain any kind of advantage. I wanted people to like me, to accept and respect me, for me, not because I had been some national symbol. So I kept my cool, explained that where I lived wouldn't be a problem, that I would be able to relate to teenagers wherever they lived, and that I would try to create programs relevant to their needs.

I got the job and went to work for a wonderful woman, Polly Bullard, the executive director, who over the years would become a friend and mentor.

The following September, I married my boyfriend of three years, Ira (Ike) LaNier. We had a small ceremony in the chapel of my church on Friday the thirteenth. I joked that if it didn't work out, we'd have something to blame. We had met for the first time at a house party on Thanksgiving night in 1962. He had just finished college and was working as a substitute teacher, and I was still at Mountain Bell at the time. He likes to tell a story about how he had scoped me out—"the tall, lanky one"—from the moment I walked in the door with a couple of my friends. He declares he had noticed me a month earlier on the public bus route we both took to work but that I had gotten away before he had a chance to make his move. Now at the party was his chance, he says, so he arranged for his roommate to play a certain slow Temptations song as he walked over and asked me to dance. Instead, his roommate decided to play a joke and dropped a James Brown hit. By then, Ike says, he had already asked me to dance and was doing his best to mask his now very public flaw: He couldn't dance a lick, at least not fast. According to him, I grew bored within a few seconds, waved him off, and preened off the dance floor as he stood there, thoroughly embarrassed, watching his friends cackle with laughter. Of course, I don't remember things that way at all. I don't even remember meeting him at the party.

When we met again in March 1965, Ike had just returned from military service after having been drafted a month after we'd met the first time. His roommate—the same guy who had played the joke on him—was having a house party and invited me and some of my friends. Ike says that when he heard I would be there, he was furious and finally agreed to just ignore me—"that woman," he calls me in the PG version of his story. But after having a couple of drinks, Ike says, he walked over, reintroduced himself, told me what I had done when we'd first met, and was preparing to give me a piece of his mind about my rude, arrogant manner when I stole his thunder. He says I told him that I didn't remember the party but that if he remembered the events of the night that way, it must have happened and that I was sorry for treating him so badly. I'm not exactly sure that's how that night went down, either. But apparently I was different from what Ike had imagined: kinder, more considerate. And we discovered we had some things in common, particularly golf.

I drove Ike home after the party. He didn't even have a car, but every time he tells this story, he complains about how I scared him half to death in my "raggedy" Volkswagen Bug. True, there was a little problem with my brakes, but as Ike recalls it, I had to turn the car off a few blocks away and coast down the road to his house. Anyhow, he invited me in with a promise to cook breakfast and put some jazz on his new stereo. His roommates and their girl-friends soon joined us. Ike says he was trying to impress me during our hours-long conversation in the wee hours of the morning when he asked if I liked golf. He had been a caddy in his hometown of Columbus, Mississippi, and he was hoping to introduce me to the sport. I told him simply that I enjoyed golf. He invited me out to play right then, about five-thirty a.m. I accepted, and by the time we drove back to my place to pick up my clubs, City Park course was preparing to open. Of course, I whipped him, even after re-fusing to tee off on the ladies' tee. He says I had purposely left out that I was a member of the East Denver golf club and had been winning tournaments. In any case, I wanted to give him a chance to finally beat me, so the two of us began playing golf together every day. We also found that we both liked other sports as well, and it apparently amazed him and his buddies that I could talk as much football as they could. Some of my friends from Michigan

State were playing with the Green Bay Packers, and I could analyze the game with the best of them—why a certain play didn't work, who was out of place, which coach had to go. I was even the first girl allowed to "infiltrate" the regular Sunday morning football gathering of Ike and his boys. Anyhow, I won Ike over.

He won me over, too. First thing, he was taller than me (a must). Then, he was a southerner with Mississippi roots. I'd always heard that a southern boy makes a good husband, one devoted to taking care of his wife and children. I realize that's a stereotype, but it's a good one that stuck in the back of my mind. Most of all, he made me laugh. He still does. Nobody can spin a story like Ike.

I don't think I ever really told him that I was one of the Little Rock Nine. He says a friend mentioned it to him—how a friend would have known, I don't know. But, growing up in Mississippi, Ike remembered watching television footage of my eight comrades and me. He said that when his friend mentioned my background, he remembered the television footage he had seen as a teenager, and it made him furious all over again. It also made him want to protect me. But I never mentioned my experience at Central, so he didn't either. More than a decade would pass before circumstances would force us to have that conversation, and by then we were parents.

Our firstborn, a son, Whitney, was born June 25, 1971. He was six months old when Polly, my supervisor at the Y, gave me the task of renovating an old house that had been left to the Y by a wealthy doctor in his will. Because the house was empty, I was able to bring Whitney with me to work while Ike was away for long spells in an executive training program for IBM, where he now worked. I outlined what needed to be done to transform the house and set up a committee of volunteers to make it happen. I was involved in every step from design to construction to decoration, and I discovered something about myself: I thoroughly enjoyed this kind of work. I began reading real estate manuals and decided to get my real estate license. About the same time, Polly retired, which left a huge void for me. I believed I had done all I could do for the Y, resigned from my job, and went to work for a woman-owned real estate company near my house.

My real estate career worked well with my family life, especially when our second child, a daughter, Brooke, was born in 1974. I found that I knew more than I realized about housing construction after having spent so much of my life around men who had made a living in the industry. I spoke their language, which surprised more than a few of the men I encountered in the then male-dominated real estate and construction industries. This was the age of Barbara Walters, who had just become the first woman co-host on the *Today* show and one of the more visible symbols that women were bursting into careers considered nontraditional.

My life was stable and happy, and then the bottom fell out.

In late February 1976, Daddy came down with what appeared to be the flu. He had been healthy for most of his life, but like many men, he didn't go to the doctor regularly. In recent months, I'd noticed that he seemed tired all the time. Once, when I stopped by my parents' home, I found him on the driveway, barely able to catch his breath after shoveling snow. Daddy was hospitalized one February day after his temperature shot up to 106 degrees. He also complained of muscle aches. But he still looked healthy, so I figured he would be back on his feet once the illness ran its course. I visited Daddy at the hospital every day. When nearly two weeks passed and he didn't seem to be getting any better, I grew worried. Then came a frightening diagnosis: Daddy had leukemia. The prognosis looked grim, but Mother tried to keep a positive attitude. Everything would turn out okay, she assured herself and me. But Daddy seemed resigned, too tired to fight.

"I won't be able to work," he said to me, still in disbelief after his doctor advised him to retire.

Daddy asked me to do him a favor and look into buying some property in Phoenix. I knew he was thinking of Mother. She had wanted the two of them to join some of their retired friends there, but he had always resisted. He wasn't ready to live the life of a retiree, he'd told her. He still wasn't. Something about his manner told me he was giving up. That hurt. Daddy had always been a fighter. We were from a long line of fighters. I would just have to fight for him. Maybe he could undergo a blood transfusion, or we could look into the experimental treatments in Houston that his doctor had mentioned.

I called Loujuana, who was living in Pennsylvania, and she came back to Denver right away. I decided at first against telling Tina, who was in her junior year at Mills College in Oakland, California. I knew she would worry, and I didn't want to pull her away from school unless it was absolutely necessary. We could beat this. I was sure of it. But despite my best efforts to protect her, Tina learned by chance from a friend that Daddy was in the hospital, and she called home. I decided to level with her. My best friend, Horace, the former pro basketball player, was living in California and helped to look after her. Tina spoke to Daddy on the telephone, and Horace bought her a plane ticket to return to Denver. But just before she arrived, Daddy slipped into a coma. As shocking as it was to see him lying there, unable to communicate, he looked as if he were just asleep. That gave us something to hang on to. He hadn't lost weight. His color looked good. We all remained confident that he would pull through.

On March 2, I spent the entire day at the hospital, mostly just sitting quietly with Daddy and chatting with other family members as they came and went. I left for the night about nine p.m., made it home, and peeked at my sleeping toddler and preschooler. I was just about to climb into bed about an hour or so later when I received a call from the hospital. Daddy had experienced unexpected complications, and doctors were not able to save him. The blood suddenly rushed through my body. I felt weak, but my mind re-belled: I'd just left Daddy; I was planning to see him again in the morning; I didn't even say good-bye; what do you mean he's gone? Suddenly, I was that heartbroken little girl again, longing for her daddy to come home.

I could have stayed curled in my bed forever. But through my tears I saw Mother, scarcely able to comprehend burying the fifty-three-year-old love of her life. My sisters were no better. And things needed to get done. Somehow I pulled myself together enough to make the arrangements. Mother wondered whether we should return to Little Rock to bury Daddy, but I knew he wouldn't want that. He had told me once that he couldn't under-stand why people carted their deceased loved ones all over the country just to return them to hometowns they had long since de-parted. We decided to bury him near us in Fort Logan National Cemetery in Denver.

A spring snow covered the ground as my family and close friends gathered at Fort Logan for the military burial. White head-stones, aligned in neat rows, marked the path where thousands of families had trod before. The Denver sun, usually present even after a snow, stayed tucked behind heavy gray clouds. Daddy would have appreciated the dignity of the service. Crisply dressed military men firing their rifles in a unified three-gun salute. A bu-gler hitting every mournful note of "Taps." And the U.S. flag folded to perfection and presented to Mother.

Time stopped there for Daddy and me. And then I faced the most difficult moment of my life: turning away and walking into the rest of my days without him.

CHAPTER 15

Finding My Voice

S oon after Daddy died, I received a letter from Elizabeth Huckaby, the former vice principal for girls at Central. She was working on a book about that tumultuous 1957–1958 school year, and
she wanted some input from my eight comrades and me. I read the
letter and put it aside. Those memories were buried deep in my
past. I didn't want to think about them. I didn't want to relive
them. I never responded to Mrs. Huckaby's letter. It had nothing to
do with her. I just couldn't.

I didn't hear any more about the project until 1981, when I
heard advertisements for the made-for-television movie *Crisis at
Central High*. The movie was based on Mrs. Huckaby's manuscript, which had not yet been published, and it was about to air
on CBS. By then, Ike's job had relocated us to Atlanta, and the
children were in school there. Just days before the movie was
scheduled to air, I talked to Ike, who agreed that we needed to have
a family meeting. Whitney was in the fourth grade then, old
enough to understand; Brooke was just six. We sat down together
as a family, and Ike and I talked to them about the Little Rock
Nine, my role, and the movie that was about to air. On the night
of the movie, we planned to watch it together, but I couldn't sit
still. I was washing and folding clothes, and I kept leaving the
room to start a new load, put away a bundle, and push down any

old emotions trying to resurface. Ike was teary-eyed. Whitney heard my name.

"Mommy, is that you?" he asked.

It was a young actress pretending to be me when I was a little girl, I explained. He was full of questions: Why did the people look so mean? Why were they saying those things to me and my friends? Was I scared?

Brooke was quieter and less curious about the movie, which suited me just fine. But I listened to Whitney and answered every one of his questions. I kept my answers short, child-appropriate, and unemotional. Whitney would be in high school, and our family would be back in Denver before we ever discussed Central High School again.

But after putting the children to bed, I thought about what I had seen on television. I thought the movie had done a good job of capturing the tension and upheaval of that awful year. It was told through Mrs. Huckaby's eyes, and she was the central character. History had catapulted her into the center of this drama, and she had a right to share her story—something so far from my mind at that time. Actor Joanne Woodward was convincing as Mrs. Huckaby, but I thought the Hollywood character was a bit too compassionate. I respected Mrs. Huckaby because she was fair, efficient, and a great manager. She kept up with us, tracked down the troublemakers who could be identified, and punished them, which drew the ire of the segregationists to her. But I never sensed from her the kind of warmth I saw in the movie. I didn't suspect that her stern, businesslike manner had anything to do with race, though; it was just her way.

In the days after the movie, I heard from a few friends, mostly those who already knew my story. They said they were amazed by what we went through and didn't believe they could have put up with that kind of treatment. But the buzz over the movie soon died down, and I again pushed Central out of my mind.

Mrs. Huckaby's book by the same name was released after the movie, but I didn't read it. Again, I wanted to stay as far away from that time in my life as possible.

Mother and I didn't discuss the movie either. She, too, was reluctant to talk about the painful parts of our past. But she maintained close ties to Little Rock. She traveled there more frequently than I, and she had a network of friends and relatives in Denver who had moved from Little Rock. They even formed a Dunbar alumni club. She looked forward to traveling each summer with members of the group to the Dunbar reunion, a huge affair held in different cities every two years. I occasionally accompanied Mother there. Sometimes I saw Mrs. Monts, Herbert's mother, by then a retired special education teacher. She always updated me on the accomplishments of her nine children: the son who had become a college professor, the one promoted to university dean, and the others excelling in their careers. But when she got to her oldest son, her face lit up as she said: "But I'm especially proud of Herbert. . . ." He had gotten married, moved to Detroit, and was working in the automotive industry, she said.

I even saw Herbert briefly in the mid-1980s when the Dunbar alumni group in Denver hosted the reunion and he and several of his brothers accompanied their mother. But I was busy helping to coordinate the festivities for the eight hundred alumni who attended, so Herbert and I didn't get to spend any time together. I knew what I needed to know: that Herbert had refused to let the trouble in Little Rock ruin his life. For years, that knowledge was enough. I didn't need to know the details of his arrest and prison time. I still believed he was innocent, and it brought me comfort to know that he was all right, that he had somehow found a way to move on.

I thought I had moved on, too. I had opened my own business as a real estate broker and was volunteering as a board member of the Colorado AIDS Project. This was the 1980s, when AIDS was a mysterious disease sweeping through the country, wiping out primarily young gay men in the prime of their lives. Hysteria over the disease was so rampant that our organization didn't even put the address of our headquarters on correspondence because we feared it might be bombed. A neighbor who was on the board recruited me, and I was eager to try to help relieve the suffering when I saw so many young people dying throughout the country. Discrimination against the gay community was widespread, and those suffering from the disease were often forced from their homes and jobs and abandoned by family members and friends. Our group ran a food pantry and provided case management and a volunteer "buddy" to those who needed companionship and help determining and balancing their health-care needs. Through my work on the board, I found a way to fight injustice. Few knew just how much my own past helped me identify with those who were hurting.

I'd soon learn, though, that burying a painful past doesn't necessarily mean you've moved beyond it. It's often still there, simmering, waiting for some unexpected moment to erupt, spewing forth every hurtful thing that you thought had gone away. That's what happened in 1987, when the Little Rock Nine gathered in Little Rock as guests of the NAACP for the thirtieth anniversary of our landmark school desegregation fight. It was an emotional reunion because it was the first time that all nine of us had come together since Central. I'd seen Ernie regularly at Michigan State and stayed in contact with him on and off afterward. I'd seen Terry, Jefferson, and Melba once or twice over the years, too. Several of us also had gotten together in New York to commemorate the twenty-fifth anniversary of the groundbreaking 1954 U.S. Supreme Court decision that had made it possible for us to attend Central High School. I was able to keep an emotional distance from the past in New York.

But keeping those memories buried would be more difficult in

Little Rock. I hadn't been back to Central since I graduated. At first, it felt good to see so much positive change. The student body president of Central—an African American male—greeted the nine of us in the classroom that had served as the chapel and a haven for us in the morning before class thirty years earlier. We also were welcomed home by the new African American mayor, Lottie Shackelford, who had been in Ernie's class at Horace Mann. But when we moved into the freshly scrubbed halls, I couldn't escape the old ghosts. The noise, the angry white faces, the slimy spit— they were right there in my face. The next thing I knew, the usually cool, calm, and collected Carlotta was outside, standing under those granite goddesses, gasping for air, unable to stop the tears from flowing. I knew then there would be no stuffing all of that hurt back inside. I had to find a way to make peace with my past.

First and most important, I reconnected with my eight comrades for good. The nine of us spent hours together, catching up on our post-Central lives—our families, careers, and future plans. We exchanged telephone numbers and addresses and promised to stay in touch—a promise I'm proud to say we've kept. There are only eight other people in this world who know exactly what happened to us at Central and how it felt. It helped to be able to pick up the telephone and call one of them on a particularly bad day. It felt good to share our evolving lives.

When I returned from Little Rock, I began getting calls from longtime friends, acquaintances, and even neighbors in Denver who had seen a report about the reunion on CNN. They all wanted to know: Why didn't you tell us?

"I've known you twenty years, and you never said a word," one friend told me.

At a neighborhood Christmas party, one of the neighbors commented: "I didn't realize we had a celebrity living among us."

They all assumed I was just being humble. There was no explaining how desperately I had needed to forget.

Several strangers looked up my number in the telephone directory and invited me to speak in their churches, communities, and schools. I didn't return calls and tried to ignore the invitations. But one history teacher was particularly persistent. She taught at Ponderosa High School in Parker, Colorado, a Denver suburb, and she kept calling. We were peers, she said. She remembered the stories about the Little Rock Nine, and this would be a way to make history come alive for her students. That sold me. I also reconsidered an interview request that I had initially turned down from a reporter at the Denver *Rocky Mountain News;* I called him back and agreed to allow him to sit in the class when I spoke. That way, I figured, I could avoid a direct interview.

I didn't have a canned speech and just talked to the students from my heart. I tried to connect to them by reminding them that I was their age when I made the decision to attend Central. One boy told me my story sounded surreal. There was no way they would not have fought back, several of them said. I talked to them about what life was like for southern blacks at that time. I told them that my eight comrades and I had been ingrained with the knowledge that we were as close as some white people would get to people of our race and that we were expected to maintain our dignity, no matter what. We just had to have faith that justice would prevail. I'd like to think I helped the students put a face on a story they had read in a book and helped them to understand the human toll. But even more, I hope I left them with the message that true heroism starts with one brave decision to do the right thing.

Afterward, I even talked to the reporter, who asked where my children had gone to school. When I told him that they had spent their first years in Jefferson County, one of the top school districts in the state, he recognized that the schools in the district were largely white. I told him that my family had moved out of the suburbs into southeast Denver and the public schools there in 1977. That was too bad, the reporter responded, because white kids needed to go to school with black kids. The reporter, who was white, said he had a child and was beginning to realize how much his child needed to be exposed to people of other races and cultures. I hope I helped him to understand that diversity is at least a two-way street. It doesn't belong just on the shoulders of African American children and their families. White families who believe in the ideals of a multiracial society have to be willing to make some tough choices and sacrifices, too.

What I didn't explain was that Ike and I had decided to move out of our neighborhood in Lakewood and back into Denver because Whitney was one of just two or three black students in his entire school. I had lived that experience, and my natural instinct was to protect my child. While he was never mistreated the way I had been, I knew how isolating such a situation could be. Our society—even a place as progressive as Denver—had not yet evolved to the point that race didn't matter, and I did not want my child to internalize that something was wrong with him because he looked different from his classmates. Ike and I also chose not to move to a largely black section of Denver, either. We wanted Whitney to grow up knowing and interacting freely with people of all races. We moved to southeast Denver, which was relatively diverse. The children in my new neighborhood—white and black— were bused to a school with a predominantly Hispanic population outside of the neighborhood for the purpose of integration. I don't like busing. As a parent, I would have preferred a neighborhood school. But busing was a means to an end, and that end—integration and diversity—was purposeful enough for me to make that personal sacrifice.

After the speaking engagement at Ponderosa High School, the invitations to speak kept coming, including one from a friend of my son. The two teenagers were at Cherry Creek High School one day when Whitney's friend read a story about the Little Rock Nine and saw a picture of me.

"Isn't this your mom?" he asked Whitney.

When Whitney told him that the photo was indeed me, the friend asked if I could come to their school to speak. Whitney rushed home with the invitation, and I, of course, agreed. I began accepting speaking engagements more frequently. I thought it gradually would become easier, but the opposite was true. The more I talked about Central and Little Rock, the more I remembered, and the tougher it got. From time to time, a new memory would come forth from some long-hidden place, and the tears would start to flow. Once during a speech, I mentioned Chief Smith, and suddenly that old headline flashed in my head: POLICE CHIEF KILLS WIFE, TAKES OWN LIFE AT HOME. I suddenly remembered how devastated and guilty I'd felt and how skeptical I had been of the official version of his death. My voice began to quiver, and I had to step outside to compose myself. The flashbacks and tears were scary to me at first, given my tendency toward restraint. But throughout the 1990s, I kept going, kept speaking.

I also tried to stay close to Big Daddy, who in 1995 turned one hundred years old. For his birthday, my sisters and I traveled to the Department of Veterans Affairs home in Seattle, where Big Daddy was living at the time. The staff had a big birthday party for him, and he seemed to be happy. His health was failing, though. Big Daddy had been suffering from dementia for years. He had been forced to close his businesses in Little Rock more than a decade earlier when he walked out one day without locking up and relatives found him lost, wandering around downtown.

By his one hundredth birthday, Big Daddy had been living in Seattle about ten years. His speech was impaired, but he wore a big smile and seemed to recognize my sisters and me. As I looked at him that day, I felt such peace. Big Daddy had reached his goal. He'd told me many times throughout my childhood that he planned to live to be at least one hundred years old. I never forgot that, and I protected him fiercely. When a serious bout with pneumonia had threatened his life at age ninety-seven, it seemed to me the hospital was considering his age and holding back treatment. I sent word to the doctors that my Big Daddy fully intended to live past one hundred and that somebody had better give him antibiotics right away. The medication worked, and Big Daddy recovered.

He survived five more years. On May 1, 1997, Big Daddy slipped away. I was in awe of him. He had lived to see 102.

The year before Big Daddy died, I got word that the city of Little Rock was planning a huge commemoration for the fortieth anniversary of the integration of Central. There was vigorous debate about the appropriateness of such a celebration, whether the city should spend such time and energy focusing on the ugliest chapter of its history. The local chapter of the NAACP even argued that the commemoration was more a public relations stunt than a meaningful effort at racial reconciliation. I disagreed. I thought it was a good idea to recognize the fortieth anniversary in such a special way. I wanted to see Little Rock acknowledge its past, as ugly as it was, but it was equally important to me that participants in the commemoration not get stuck there. I saw it as a positive step that the city wanted to showcase how much had indeed changed.

I called my eight comrades and suggested that we meet to talk. As I saw it, the time had come for us to take as much control as possible of our own legacy. We had been complaining for years about people putting money into their pockets by using our name and images to publicize events that we knew nothing about and to sell all kinds of T-shirts and trinkets. We needed to do what we could to assure that we were educating the next generation about the Little Rock Nine and the importance of education. We needed to make sure that our name was associated with good.

Eight of us were able to meet later in Las Vegas. I pitched the idea of starting the Little Rock Nine Foundation. Through the foundation, we could give back to the community as a group and continue the journey that we had started so many years ago toward academic excellence and equity.

"We're grown now, and it's time to stop complaining about people using us," I told my comrades. "Let's take control of our own name and get on the same page about what we accept and not."

We agreed that we would participate as a group in the commemoration. We also agreed to create the foundation as a means to do our part in helping to advance the principle of academic excellence. Several of us volunteered to kick off fund-raising for the foundation by donating a percentage of any speaking fees and honorariums. The group assigned me the task of taking care of the necessary business, including obtaining nonprofit status and establishing our name—Little Rock Nine—as a registered trademark.

I had just started the process of officially establishing the foundation when the fortieth anniversary rolled around. Indeed, the commemoration was as big as we had imagined. A committee had planned more than a week of receptions, lectures, honors, and appearances, which drew a host of dignitaries, including one from the nation's highest elected office—Arkansas's native son Bill Clinton, who was nearing the end of his first presidency.

Of all the wonderful events that week, the image in my head of the ceremony at the school on September 25, 1997—exactly forty years after we first marched up the front steps into Central—will stay with me forever. Thousands of people of all races, local residents as well as guests from all over the world, assembled at the school to welcome the nine of us home. They applauded and stood to their feet as we were presented. Then the nine of us ascended the steps to the front entrance of our alma mater. President Clinton and Governor Mike Huckabee were waiting there and held open the door for us—a gesture that touched all nine of us deeply. Forty years earlier, we had entered those doors under the protection of gun-toting federal troopers, against the will of the state's segregationist governor. Now, the president of the United States and a very different Arkansas governor stood at the door to usher us through. There were few dry eyes among us. This time, though, I was shedding tears of joy.

I was grateful that so much of my family had come to witness the events—my husband and children, Mother, my sisters, Aunt M.E., and others who had supported me as much as they could over the years. I also enjoyed meeting the children of my eight comrades. I wished Daddy and my grandfathers could have been there to see how much things had changed. I especially missed Daddy during a program later that evening at the Excelsior Hotel (now the Peabody), where our parents and Mrs. Bates were honored. Hillary Clinton presented plaques to them. Until that day, our mothers and fathers had never been formally recognized. Melba gave a moving speech about their role.

It was good to see Mrs. Bates during the festivities. I hadn't seen her in many years. She was in a wheelchair, but she looked well. I'd heard that she had fallen on difficult financial times and even faced the threat of losing her home after the death of Mr. Bates in 1980. That saddened and frustrated me, and I did what I could to help when Ernie rallied to try to save the home where so much of our history had taken place. It eventually was declared a National Historic Landmark maintained by the National Park Service, which allowed it to remain a private residence. When I saw her at the reception, I walked over and embraced her. She had suffered a stroke and had difficulty speaking, so we said little. But her eyes told me that she was happy to see me, too.

During the same reception, my husband told me that there was another woman in a wheelchair who was eager to see me. He led me to her, and I was surprised to see that it was Elizabeth Huckaby. We both smiled, and I extended my hand to her. She clasped it tightly. She, too, looked well, and I was glad to see her. We spent some time catching up on each other's lives.

I felt good about how well the nine of us were doing in our lives. We were raising families, giving back to the community in myriad ways, and enjoying success in our various careers. I had been in business as an independent real estate broker for the past twenty years. Coolheaded Ernie had earned a master's degree in sociology after Michigan State, had worked in the Carter administration, and was rising up the corporate ladder in the finance industry at Lehman Brothers. He was based in Washington. Melba, who seemed born for the spotlight, earned a graduate degree in journalism from Columbia University, worked as a reporter for NBC-TV and a communications consultant, and had recently authored a successful memoir about her experiences at Central. She was living in San Francisco. Gloria, the brainy one, had graduated from the Illinois Institute of Technology with a degree in math and chemistry and moved to Sweden to work as a systems analyst and technical writer for IBM. While there, she also became a patent attorney and later founded and edited her own magazine, *Computers in Industry*. She was living and working in the Netherlands. Terrence, a philosopher and professor long before he got the degrees to back it up, earned a bachelor's in sociology from California State University, a master's in social welfare from UCLA, and a doctorate in psychology from Southern Illinois University. He was living and working in Los Angeles as a college professor and clinical psychologist. Jefferson, the perpetual jokester of the group, earned a bachelor's degree in business administration from Los Angeles State College, served his country in Vietnam, and was working as a government accountant in Columbus, Ohio. Minnijean, who had become famously known for fighting back that first year at Central with the so-called chili incident, attended Southern Illinois University, earned a bachelor's degree, and moved to a farm in Ottawa, Canada, with her husband and six children. She worked as a writer and social worker and got involved in grassroots human rights groups. Thelma, quiet and fragile because of a heart condition, had earned bachelor's and master's degrees in education from Southern Illinois University. She worked twenty-seven years as a home economics teacher in St. Louis before retiring in 1994. And then there was Elizabeth, who had been the most scarred among us by the events of 1957. The image of her alone, surrounded by the shrieking mob, has endured more than any other as a testament of the courage it took to survive that year. She attended college in Tennessee and Ohio and served in the army before returning to Little Rock to work for a state welfare agency. But Elizabeth struggled mightily to find her way out of the darkness of the past. In 1996, when seven of us had appeared on *The Oprah Winfrey Show* with some former white classmates to discuss the first year of integration at Central, Elizabeth refused to join us. When we gathered again for the anniversary, it was clear to me she was still battling old ghosts.

The nine of us had agreed with *Newsweek* magazine to be interviewed for a cover story about the anniversary. But once we all got there, Elizabeth suddenly backed out. The reporter turned to me for help in changing her mind. I went to talk to her. We needed to do this for a number of reasons, I told her, but most importantly because we wanted to tell our own stories and set the historical record straight.

"Carlotta, I just don't think I can get through it," Elizabeth responded.

"I know how you feel," I told her. "But if I sit with you, will you do it?"

She agreed. Melba also offered to sit with her for the interview. In an empty banquet room at the Excelsior Hotel, Melba and I sat on each side of Elizabeth and almost had to hold her up as she recalled that terrifying moment when she found herself alone, surrounded by a threatening white mob.

Newsweek had sent one of its top photographers, and we spent about two hours with him snapping pictures of us all around the school. As it turned out, though, we were bumped off the cover of the magazine by CNN founder Ted Turner, who'd announced the week before the anniversary that he was donating $1 billion to charity. Our story ended up as a nice centerpiece.

Another enduring photo was snapped at the reunion, of Elizabeth and Hazel Bryan Massery, one of the white tormentors in that iconic photograph from 1957. Hazel had called Elizabeth in the 1960s to apologize for tormenting her that day, and photographer Will Counts—who had taken the original photograph of Elizabeth and the mob with Hazel at its center—arranged for the two women to meet at the fortieth reunion. The meeting would lead to what seemed to me an odd friendship between Elizabeth and Hazel, who together made television appearances and speeches about their newfound relationship. There was even talk of a contract between the two to do a book and movie together. While I believe in forgiveness and reconciliation, I was suspicious from the start. I wondered whether the contrition making headlines was sincere and worried that Elizabeth might get hurt. I shared my concerns with her, but initially Elizabeth—who even during our worst times at Central tried to find the good in our tormentors—was excited and believed Hazel to be sincere. But Elizabeth later told me that Hazel was growing tired of being seen as "the bad guy" as they told their story from place to place. The two women would go their separate ways. The reconciliation photo, which was made into a poster while the two were on the speaking circuit, is still sold with other Little Rock Nine memorabilia, but Elizabeth insisted that a sticker bearing a quote from her be attached to each one. The sticker says: "True reconciliation can occur when we honestly acknowledge our painful but shared past."

After the fortieth reunion, the honors kept coming. Just two years later, President Clinton awarded the nine of us the nation's highest civilian honor, the Congressional Gold Medal. But four days before we were set to travel to the nation's capital with our closest family members to accept the award, I received a call from Ernie, who had bad news: Mrs. Bates had died. We mentioned to the family members planning her funeral that we were set to receive the Congressional Gold Medal on November 9 in hopes that they would choose a different day for the funeral. They did not, forcing us to make a difficult decision. With so much federal red tape involved in the medal ceremony, I knew there was zero chance of getting it postponed. Mrs. Bates would want us to accept the award, I figured. When we were kids, she had escorted us to many such events herself, and in one case, she'd even insisted that she receive the honor, too. Ernie came up with a solution: He would fly to Little Rock the morning of the funeral and represent the nine of us by laying a wreath on the bier of Mrs. Bates's coffin as she lay in state. He would then return to Washington in time for the early afternoon medal ceremony.

Everything went as planned. When it was time to bestow the awards, President Clinton captured what many of us in the room felt:

"This is a special day for me—a happy day and a sad day, an emotional day," he said, calling Mrs. Bates "a good friend to Hillary and me." He told a story about the day he wheeled Mrs. Bates around the Civil Rights Museum in Memphis when the exhibit on Central High School was dedicated. She was greatly amused when she saw that it featured a statue of Governor Faubus on one side and her on the other, he recalled.

"And even though by then she had to get around in a wheelchair, she got a big laugh out of that," he said. "And what a laugh she had."

President Clinton shared the same story with a larger audience the following April when we all attended a memorial service for Mrs. Bates in Little Rock. The service drew an overflow crowd of local and national political and civil rights leaders, as well as local residents who remembered the woman who had dared to stand up to Jim Crow. This time, my comrades asked me to speak on behalf of the nine of us.

I recalled how Mrs. Bates had hired me as a ten-year-old "paperboy" to deliver her and her husband's *Arkansas State Press* and how she used the newspaper as an instrument of hope as well as a megaphone to protest the injustices endured by the black community. I talked about our transition from news messengers to news makers as the story of the Little Rock Nine played out around the world. I also thanked her for the role she had played in supporting the nine of us and our parents as we fought for justice in the delivery of education in this country. On a more lighthearted note, the audience laughed when I said that Thurgood Marshall, Roy Wilkins, and newsman Ted Poston discovered the hard way that you didn't want to play poker with Daisy Bates if you intended to win.

"Mrs. Bates 'walked the talk' of freedom for all, strode confidently forward, aware of the dangers she faced but determined to see the walls of segregation come tumbling down," I said. "This is the Daisy Bates that the Little Rock Nine remembers. This is the woman who put her life on the line for the cause of justice. This is the American whose vision for educational equality moved our nation forward."

As I took my seat, I thought about the irony of the moment. While we were at Central, I would have been the last one Mrs. Bates asked to speak for the group. She knew me well enough to know that I shunned the limelight. But here I stood, before an esteemed crowd, bidding a final farewell to the one who for many years had spoken for my comrades and me.

Here I stood, on my own, speaking for us all, finally confident in the voice emerging from within.

CHAPTER 16

Peace at Last

Even after years of talking to students and other groups about Central High School, I had a difficult time discussing the bombing of my family's home. Every time I mentioned how my father had been held as a suspect, I choked up. It was just as tough to talk about Herbert.

I still blamed myself for it all. But the deeper I dug into my past, the more difficult it was to avoid the questions: Why Herbert? How did he end up in the hands of Little Rock police? How long did he stay in prison? What happened to him there? How did he get out? What was his life like now?

A piece of my life had intertwined forever with Herbert's on that fateful night in February 1960. I had come to realize that to make peace with my own past, I first had to face it—all of it. That meant facing the part that was Herbert's, too. I decided to call him.

First, I called Herbert's younger brother, Dr. Lester Monts, then senior vice provost for academic affairs at the University of Michigan, to get Herbert's telephone number. Then, while in Chicago in August 2003 to take care of some business for my then 104-year-old aunt M.E., I made the call. It was good to hear Herbert's voice again. I explained to him that I had been thinking a lot about Little Rock and what happened to my family's home and told him that I wanted to talk to him. I asked if I could drive to his home in

Michigan to talk face-to-face. Herbert seemed happy to hear from me and agreed without hesitation to get together. The next day, I drove four and a half hours to Southfield, just outside Detroit, where Herbert had been living the past fifteen years.

When I arrived in town about seven p.m., I called Herbert, and he met me on the highway and led me to his home. I felt proud of him as I drove through his neighborhood, an upscale suburban community with towering old trees, meticulously manicured lawns, and expansive multistory homes. Southfield was widely known throughout Michigan as home to many of the area's prominent African American politicians and automobile industry executives. It had evolved since my time in Michigan as a jurisdiction with one of the highest per capita incomes for black men and women in the country. Herbert pointed out later that the town's first black mayor, police chief, and several council members were among his neighbors.

We were met inside by Herbert's wife of more than forty years, Dora, a manager for a major department store. A warm and friendly woman, she broke the ice right away and insisted that I stay overnight at their home, instead of in a hotel, as I had planned. The three of us sat in the family room and chatted amiably about Little Rock and family for a couple of hours, and then she headed upstairs to bed.

Herbert and I kept talking, first about work. He had just retired after working thirty-three years as an officer for the United Auto Workers union in various elected and appointed positions. In his union work, it seemed Herbert had found a noble purpose, a way to help protect the average worker from multimillion-dollar corporate giants. The job meant more than a paycheck to him, he said, because he knew better than most what it was like to be defenseless in the face of power.

Then Herbert steered our conversation to Little Rock and the night in 1960 when both our lives changed forever.

"I had nothing to do with it," he said softly, as if he needed me to hear him say it.

"I know," I answered.

I wasn't quite sure what to say next. But Herbert needed no prompting. He had been waiting all these years for the chance to tell me what happened. It seemed that he needed to talk about it as much as I needed to hear it. So, for hours that night, I just listened.

In that conversation and the many since, I've let Herbert take me back to Little Rock, 1960, starting with that stormy evening of February 9:

Our hangout back then was your grandfather's place, at the corner of 18th and Pine. In its incarnation at the time, it was a Laundromat. I was there with Charles Webb and Marion Davis, some neighborhood buddies. Maceo came by; he was my uncle's friend. It was a rainy evening, and 'long about nine or ten, Charles, Marion, and I started out for our homes. We walked up Pine, cut across an alley, and Charles went on into his home on 17th. Then, Marion and I continued up Maple to 15th, and he went into his home.

I passed your home and noticed a couple of unfamiliar, early-1950s cars on the street. I walked on to my house just up the street. Maceo passed me in his car and turned the corner in front of your house, onto Valentine. He was behind a truck, another unfamiliar vehicle in the neighborhood. We knew the cars and trucks of our neighbors, so it was easy to tell a stranger on the roads.

I got home within five to ten minutes after Marion went to his house. My dad was at work. He worked nights at Bell Telephone. I had two sisters, six brothers, and my mom at home. I ate a bite, saw there was nothing of interest on television, and went on to bed. I guess it was maybe fifteen minutes at the most.

I was about to fall off to sleep when I heard a big boom. I got

up quickly, went to my mother, and said: "Did you hear that?"
We had had a big rain—and there was a red clay residue that had
left puddles around. I looked out the window and saw a police
car parked on the corner. At the time, it never crossed my mind
to wonder how a police car could get there more quickly than I
could get out of my bed and look out the window.

People were gathering at the Rices' house. I told my mother I
was going on down there to see what had happened. The police
came over to the Rices' and told us to stand back. We all knew
that you were at Central, and we all figured that the white segregationists had come to pay a call.

The police suggested we break up the gathering and go on
back to our homes. I went on home and back to bed.

When I woke up the next morning, I went outside to see what
was going on. The police car was still there. I went down and
told the officer that I had seen several unfamiliar cars in the
neighborhood when I was walking home last night.

"We'll send somebody out to talk with you," he told me.

The police came to my house the next morning, and I remember going down to headquarters and telling my story. I went by
myself. They took my story, but it became clear to me that they
wanted something else from me. They wanted me to take a lie detector test. I didn't have anything to hide, so I agreed. They let
me go home and picked me up again the next morning. I went by
myself because I thought I'd take the lie detector test and come
on back home. But things began to change. They started asking
me the same questions again and again. It was night before I
took the lie detector test, and I passed it. I clearly heard one of
the officers say, "There's nothing there."

They got Marion to come down to the station, too. Later, I
found out that most of the people on 18th and Pine were also
questioned. Police tried to get some of them involved, but they
had substantial evidence backing their whereabouts that night.

After I volunteered to take the lie detector test, I requested an attorney. It was clear they were looking for a fall guy.

"You guys are trying to railroad me. Get me an attorney," I told them.

That's when I got charged.

During the questioning, the police were telling me that Maceo had already confessed. I found out later that they were telling Maceo that I had confessed.

Whatever I said, they would counter with: "Boy, you are lying."

Earzie Cunningham, who lived next door to the Foxes, across the street from you, told the police that he had seen me on the street by your house. Earzie was in trouble with the law, and they coerced him into putting me by your house at the time of the explosion. He lied. His mother even said he did not see anything, but the prosecutor, Frank Holt, found out about her statement. Before she could be subpoenaed to testify, Holt claimed that she had a heart condition and that medical reasons made it not feasible for her to testify. Word was she was whisked out of town, under a threat.

The police kept saying to me: "Did you register to go to Central? Didn't you go to school in Connecticut for a while? Aren't those schools integrated?"

All of these questions I could answer in the affirmative, but they kept repeating the questions as though my "yes" answers annoyed them.

I had been there all day and into the night by this time, and it was the usual treatment for blacks back then—no bathroom breaks, no food, no water. They would not let me call my parents. I kept repeating my request for a lawyer. As soon as I did, they charged me with the crime and started to beat me. The FBI agents were federal employees, but it is important to remember that in Little Rock they were also, for the most part, southern white men. They were every bit as bad as the police, just as racist as the locals. They weren't there for justice. They were on the side of the segregationists. When I asked for a lawyer, which I did repeatedly, Frank Holt came into the room, but this was after they had prepared a confession. He was the prosecuting attorney, and no help to me. In fact, he wanted me to take the fall, and it was his plan to make that happen.

I didn't see Police Chief Gene Smith until the next morning. I knew Chief Smith because I mowed the yard of one of his neighbors, and he would come over to talk with me and my friends when we were in the neighborhood. This morning, however, he made like he didn't even know me.

"I had nothing to do with the bombing," I told him.

But he was so determined. And determined to get somebody black, it seemed to me. During this marathon day with the authorities, and after I had asked for an attorney, which I kept doing, they would beat on me, three and four at a time.

They had prepared a confession. I kept asking for an attorney. I never got an attorney, but they were successful in breaking me. I signed something.

The next day I was arraigned, along with Maceo, who apparently was somewhere in the station, but in a different room. At the arraignment, Mr. Bates came down and told me I was being railroaded, that whatever was going on was just a smoke screen to throw shame onto blacks.

After I had been arraigned and bail was set, Dr. Routen, a prominent black physician, covered my bail for me. He put up his property, knowing that I wouldn't skip out. I would show. It was my own word, and I would honor Dr. Routen's trust in me.

The trial, it was a kangaroo court. Every black person in the courtroom knew it. But it was my life that was being railroaded, nobody else's. I knew I was in trouble when Judge Kirby got impatient at one point when the jury left the room. He turned to the bailiff and said aloud:

"Get that convicting jury back in here! We don't have any
more time to waste."

My attorney turned to me and said, "Oh my, you don't stand
a chance. Did you hear what the judge said?"

That was it. I was sentenced to five years, the maximum allowed for the charge.

I reported to Cummins State Farm in October 1961. It was a
working farm. The one thing you didn't want was a job harvest-
ing cotton. They ran that part like a plantation; it was legalized
slavery. But I had some connections; my uncle was able to get me
a job that wasn't a part of the farm work. Blacks were often
given the job of cooking or driving. I was a driver and would
often make trips off-site to run errands in Pine Bluff for the officials.

I wasn't doing any of the hard labor. In some ways, the place
was run by the prisoners, and back then, it was still segregated.
Some prisoners knew people in Little Rock who had ties to the
legislature. They were in, and quickly they were out. Because
Cummins wasn't that far from Little Rock, I had visitors. My
family stayed supportive.

I always believed I would be able to get out. In high school, I
used to work part-time as a waiter at the country club, and a lot
of powerful politicians and attorneys used to come in there. I
thought one of them might be able to help.

But one afternoon my daddy was downtown, and he ran into
Charles Bussey. Everybody knew him. He became mayor of Little
Rock in 1981, but back then, he was a black deputy sheriff, and
he had real good political connections. He asked about me, and
Daddy told him I was still in jail for the bombing. Everybody
knew that I didn't do it. Bussey said he would arrange a meeting
with Governor Faubus, and he did.

My parents went to see the governor. They told him I was still
in jail for a crime that I didn't commit. He promised them that he

would see to it that I was released. It's kind of ironic that the man who had caused all of this trouble in the first place ended up helping me get out. About three weeks after that, in June 1963, I got out. I got out early. I had a five-year sentence, but I served twenty months of actual jail time.

I was planning to leave Little Rock right away, but everybody I ran into was kind. They all knew I had been railroaded. They knew I was innocent. Little Rock had been my home, so I had lots of friends. It's like a small town, so I was bound to run into the people who had put me behind bars. I saw Earzie Cunningham going up Oak Street one day in our old neighborhood. He pulled his car up beside me and apologized. I said to him, "Why did you lie about me?" He told me that they pressured him, that he could have been arrested for something he had done, but he made a deal.

Not long after that, I took my car to be serviced, and I ran into Frank Holt. I went up to him and said: "You convicted me of something I didn't do."

He responded by saying, "You said you did it."

My last words to him were something along the lines of, "So, that's what you call police brutality."

Still later, one Sunday morning when I went to get a newspaper, I saw Judge Kirby.

"Why don't you come to my office? I have some things I want to discuss with you," he said.

Judge Kirby knew I was innocent, but that line about the "convicting jury" made me want to stay as far from him as I could. I didn't trust him, not one bit.

I heard that Cunningham was shot by a woman; he died in 1982. I think both Holt and Kirby are dead, too.

I ended up staying in Little Rock longer than I thought I would. A plumber who belonged to the church my family attended, First Baptist, hired me to work for him. Then, in 1963, a friend of mine introduced me to Dora. She was from Jackson, Mississippi, but she was living in Little Rock. We hit it off, and three years later, we got married. Another friend of mine had moved to Detroit and liked it. He told me job opportunities were wide open there. I had an uncle who lived there, and he promised to help me get a job in the automobile industry. I just felt like there was something better out there. So in August 1968, I packed up and moved to Detroit. I found a job at a General Motors subsidiary in Lavonia, Michigan. When I got settled a few months later, I sent for Dora and Rod, our son, who was two at the time. We've been here ever since.

I got involved in the union 'long about 1972. Vietnam veterans were returning from the war to their old jobs in the General Motors plants, and they felt like the union didn't really represent them. They were in a different mood, rebellious. They wanted change. Most of the people in office were older. Some of my friends and co-workers encouraged me to run for office, so I did. I was elected as an alternate on the committee that handled grievances, health and safety issues for the union. In the next election, I was elected a full member to the committee. I went to work for the union full-time, and I just kept rising through the ranks from there.

Although I'm retired, I still get called on from time to time to do work for the union, and every now and then, I volunteer for political campaigns. I'm a grandfather now, too. My son, Rod, is a journalist. He got a master's degree from Wayne State in Detroit and worked as an editor for NBC Online. Now, he and his wife own a public relations firm.

It's kind of funny how life works out because I used to want to go into journalism when I was in high school. I used to work for the school newspaper. My second choice was the military. But after everything that happened, I didn't really have that chance.

Things turned out all right for me, though. Yes, things turned out just fine.

There is no record of Herbert's case at the Pulaski County courthouse, where his trial was held. The attorney who represented him is deceased, and the attorney's family members were unable to find any records related to Herbert's case among his old files. It's as though he were never charged.

Herbert doesn't know what might have happened to his criminal file. For all these years, he has believed it was right there in Pulaski County, though he never had any interest in digging it up. If there was any justice in this case, I suppose that's it—that this innocent man doesn't have to live the rest of his days with a criminal record.

But, no doubt, Herbert suffered in ways that can never be measured. Dreams died. A seventeen-year-old boy entered manhood behind the bars of a maximum-security state prison and spent the first twenty months of his adult life there. And even now, among those old-timers in Little Rock who remember the bombing, Herbert's confession, and his trial, there may be a few who still wonder whether he was involved.

Somehow, though, Herbert emerged from it all strong and determined. He dreamed new dreams and built a new life—a successful and productive life of service.

For Herbert, that has been vindication enough. For me, knowing his full story has left me more convinced than ever that he is innocent. Sharing it and doing what I can to clear his name has helped to bring my soul what I have most sought: peace.

CHAPTER 17

Touching the Future

Wherever I go to talk to students, I usually encounter some who know little or nothing about the Little Rock Nine. Sometimes they're African American. Sometimes they're white, Latino, or Asian. But when they hear my story, often they get angry, like the white kid whose hand went up slowly in the back of the room after my first speech at Ponderosa High School in a Denver suburb many years ago.

"Why am I just learning this?" he asked. "Why haven't I learned this in school before now?"

I hear that often from high school and college students who feel their school systems and parents neglected to share important pieces of American history. I don't blame the children for not knowing. I blame the parents and schools. I bear some responsibility as part of a generation that I don't believe has done enough to ensure that our children and their children know and fully appreciate our collective history, particularly the hard-fought battles of the 1950s and 1960s for African Americans to gain full access to educational opportunities and civil rights.

It distresses me to see that the nation's public schools have largely become resegregated. But even more, I'm disturbed by the low regard for education in many of these schools. I didn't go to Central because I felt a strong desire to sit next to white people in class. I put my life on the line because I believed Central offered the best academic opportunities. I had hoped that the resulting interaction with people of another race would be a bonus, a great exchange of cultures and ideas. It is hurtful now when I hear that in many urban schools, where the student populations tend to be overwhelmingly black, it is not considered cool to be smart. It makes me downright angry when I hear that smart black kids often feel a need to play down their brainpower just to fit in. How did we—particularly black men and women who endured the struggle and benefited from it—allow such a cultural shift from the time when education was widely viewed in our community as the way to a better life?

Entertainer Bill Cosby was severely criticized by some black scholars and activists for comments he made in 2004 on the fiftieth anniversary of *Brown v. Board of Education* about the decline in parenting and personal responsibility in poor black communities. But I think he was on to something. Many of the problems that we see today, such as single mothers, deadbeat fathers, and extreme poverty, are not new. They are as old as people. But there was a sense in my day that the fate of black people, poor or not, was collective. Thus, our standards were defined by the best among us, not the worst. Our parents—whether Daddy was living at home or not—our grandparents, our teachers, and all of the adults in our realm of influence held us to high expectations at home, at school, and in the community. While the problems that plague the poorest among us today—rampant crime, poor education, and broken families—are indeed multidimensional, I believe strongly that better parenting and greater outreach from those of us in a position to help can go a long way toward restoring education to its vaunted place. So, too, can efforts to reconnect students to their history.

In recent years, the federal government, the state of Arkansas, and some respected artists have taken great strides to make the history of the Little Rock Nine more tangible. For the fiftieth anniversary in 2007, the National Park Service constructed a powerful new multimedia exhibit just across the street from Central High School. The high-tech building features a photo gallery with black-and-white images from 1957. Film footage from that year also runs constantly on large television screens posted throughout. Visitors can pick up telephones and hear my comrades and me sharing parts of our story. They can hear old recorded interviews of Governor Faubus and *Gazette* editor Harry Ashmore and more. Park rangers—including Minnijean's daughter, Spirit Trickey—share what happened inside the walls of Central as they guide guests on tours of the school. Some parts of the exhibit are still tough for me to see and hear, but that just speaks to its power.

Another touching monument of the nine of us stands on the north end of the Arkansas State Capitol. Life-size bronze statues capture each of us as the children we were then in a memorial simply called *Testament*. Editorial cartoonist John Deering and his wife, Kathy, spent seven years bringing his idea to fruition after getting permission from the Little Rock Nine Foundation. When it was unveiled on August 30, 2005, it was the largest bronze statue in Arkansas and the first monument honoring the civil rights movement on the grounds of a southern state capitol building. State lawmakers not only agreed to pay the bulk of the costs to finance the memorial, they also agreed to locate it on the Capitol grounds within view of the governor's office. That made me proud. I'd like to think that whenever the Arkansas governor has to sign a bill, especially education or human rights legislation, he will think twice about his actions when he glances out his window. There we are, nine bronze statues, staring back at him in a silent testament to history.

These days, I am inspired by the hope and optimism I feel in the air, motivated mostly by the successful campaign of President Barack Obama. If nothing else, the high visibility of the new First

Family—our smart and eloquent president, his equally intelligent and charming wife, both committed to their two beautiful daughters—will have a lasting, positive impact on the psyche of black people everywhere. The Obamas are bound to transform not only how black people see ourselves collectively, but how others see us. It is a proud day in America—one, I admit, I did not see coming.

I was in the crowd in Denver's Mile High Stadium that night in August 2008 when then senator Obama accepted the Democratic nomination for president. It marked the first time that an African American had headed the ticket of a major party for the nation's highest political office. The crowd of eighty-four thousand supporters—an amalgam of people, representing the country's diversity—was absolutely ecstatic.

From my spot in the crowd, I soaked up every bit of this historic moment—the faces, the cheers, the energy, the joy, the hope for this young man who looked like me. I had seen this country at its worst, and now I was able to see and touch the monumental change unfolding before me.

"I stand before you tonight because all across America something is stirring," Obama said as the crowd roared its approval.

Fireworks shot up into the clear, dark night. Confetti rained down over us all. Something was stirring indeed.

I had been late to get on the Obama bandwagon. Hillary Clinton was my candidate. I had known her personally since that evening my Little Rock comrades and I chatted the night away with her and then Governor Bill Clinton at the Arkansas Governor's Mansion in September 1987. When I made it back to Denver, I told my husband that Governor Clinton was considering a run for the White House.

"What do you think of him?" Ike asked.

"I like him. He's smart," I responded. "But the smartest one is his wife."

That's how I truly felt about her. But I also believed her to be genuine, experienced politically, a good manager, and a tough woman capable of making the difficult decisions that would be needed down the road. I had nothing against Obama; I just thought Hillary was the better, more experienced candidate. The color of a candidate's skin had never been—and would not be this time—the driving factor in how I voted. I've always voted my conscience. But Obama had tapped into something that Hillary just couldn't overcome: the overwhelming desire for change. When it became clear to me that Hillary was in trouble, I began listening to Obama with a more willing ear. I watched him on the campaign trail and in the debates and scoured the news coverage of his proposals for change. He was sounding all the right notes on the issues that mattered a great deal to me, particularly health care, the war in Iraq, and the tanking economy. He came across as supersmart and unflappable. The more I listened and learned, the more I liked him. When Hillary exited the race, I began volunteering for Obama's campaign in Denver and worked as hard for him as I had worked for her.

But as proud as I was of Obama that night in Denver when he accepted the Democratic nomination, part of me was worried. I sat in the stadium, taking in every moment because I thought that would be the highlight, the most significant political moment I would ever witness: a black man accepting his party's nomination for president of the United States. Part of me was worried that Obama just couldn't win. I'd seen too much hate, the kind that had fueled the white mobs of my youth and then took Dr. King, the Kennedys, and those four little girls who died in the church bombing in Birmingham. I'd seen, too, the more subtle (but no less destructive) racism and discrimination, the kind that flies below the radar and often makes the accuser seem paranoid, the kind that had forced my friend Horace Walker finally to give up his dream of earning a doctorate. The black man always has to do more and prove more, and more times than not, he still falls short in their eyes, Horace would say in his most frustrated moments. And this from a man who succeeded anyway, who through hard work and sheer determination rose to the ranks of vice president of two major corporations before his death in June 2001.

I'd seen a lot of good, too—genuine color-blind goodness from white men and women who had been able to look me in the eyes and see me for what I am: a woman, a child of God, no more, no less. But in spite of the incredible hope I felt stirring across the country, I couldn't answer with certainty when I wondered: Would enough white Americans really be able to pull the lever for a black man once they got in the privacy of the voting booth? Had the United States really come that far? And even if so, what new (or old) tricks would emerge to upset the will of the people? Would ballots suddenly turn up missing in key battleground states? Would the power brokers find some other way to disqualify or discredit him?

On November 4, election day, I arrived at Obama's Denver headquarters about eight-thirty a.m. I spent the next ten hours making telephone calls and running errands between headquarters and the polls. Soon after I arrived home and ate dinner, a friend called.

"I know you're going to stay up," she said excitedly.

I wasn't. I figured the election would be too close to call that night, and I was planning to go to bed. I was tired and, I admit, nervous. I would have plenty of time in the morning to wait out the results—at least, that's what I thought. But when I glanced at the television, I quickly got sucked into the election coverage. Before long, newscasters were announcing Obama victories in key states. When Ohio moved into the Obama column, my telephone rang. It was my comrade Jefferson Thomas.

"I delivered my state," he said jubilantly. "It's all over now!"

And then reporters announced Pennsylvania for Obama, too. I thought: *He could win. He could really win this!*

By nine p.m. mountain standard time, national newscasters had put Virginia—a Republican stronghold in presidential elections and a hard-fought battleground this time around—in the Obama column, too. He ultimately won my state (Colorado) as well. Things seemed to snowball after Virginia was announced. McCain conceded. President George Bush called to congratulate him. Obama supporters were gathering by the thousands in Grant Park in Chicago. Tears streamed down black faces, white faces, brown faces, cream faces. Jesse Jackson, who had been on the balcony with Dr. King when the fatal shots rang out, looked genuinely overcome with emotion. Strangers were hugging. Horns were honking. Obama signs were flapping. Black news reporters, trained to maintain a poker face, were choking up, talking about their own mothers, fathers, and grandparents.

Before I could even process it all, my phone began ringing off the hook with calls from tearful peers, my sisters, Mother.

They all asked the same question: "Can you believe it?"

And then they'd say: "I never thought I'd see this day."

Even Whitney and Brooke, who had grown up in a much different world from mine, were surprised that Obama actually pulled off a victory.

Ike and I were quiet and reflective, two children of the segregated South, perhaps still in a state of shock.

Just before ten p.m. MST, Obama took the stage with his wife and children. Even he seemed somewhat subdued and awed by the magnitude of it all.

"If there is anyone out there who still doubts that America is a place where all things are possible, who still wonders if the dream of our founders is alive in our time, who still questions the power of our democracy, tonight is your answer."

He was talking to me. The tears began welling inside. Yes, I had my answer. America had proven me wrong—or at least filled in the blank. We were indeed a country ready to move beyond its racial scars and wounds into a more hopeful future.

What a long journey it had been from Little Rock and Central to this moment.

When I climbed those steps at Central, flanked by federal troopers on that September morning more than fifty years ago, I was just a fourteen-year-old girl doing what felt right for me. In time, I would come to understand the greater good—that my eight comrades and I were helping to start a journey sure to outlast any of us. But even with that knowledge, I could not imagine a future as spectacular as this. I could not imagine that I would live to see an African American—born of a black man from Kenya and a white woman from Kansas—pick up that journey and chart it successfully all the way into the Oval Office.

As I sat before the television watching news reports about the impromptu celebrations throughout the country, my she-ro Rosa Parks came to mind. With her quiet determination, she had shown me long ago what an ordinary woman could do. But like so many of the good soldiers who had marched out front, she had to witness this victory from heaven.

I felt grateful to be alive. Now, nothing could stop the tears.

A NOTE ON SOURCES

This book reflects many years of digging into the depths of my memory, unearthing painful pieces of my history that I buried when I walked away from Central High School in May 1960. After years of prodding me to tell my story for the public record, my friend Dr. Margaret Whitt, then an English professor at the University of Denver and a civil rights scholar, started the process officially in 2006 by recording dozens of interviews of me and taping my presentations to her class. Those interviews and much of Margaret's subsequent research helped to provide the foundation for this book. She also traveled with me to Southfield, Michigan, and recorded an interview with my childhood friend Herbert Monts, whom I believe was wrongly convicted in the bombing of my family's home in February 1960. My initial conversation with Herbert after contacting him in 2003, the discussion recorded by Margaret, and later interviews of Herbert were all combined into the segment of chapter 16 that is written in Herbert's voice.

The family stories shared in the book are based mostly on my recollections and those of my family members. But some of the family history, described in the first chapter, is based on genealogical research conducted over several years by my sister Tina Walls.

The narrative on the history of Paul Laurence Dunbar, Jr. and Sr. High School was drawn from many sources, primarily the old Central High School Museum, which was located in a refurbished Magnolia gas station; the National Dunbar History Project, a traveling exhibit that resulted from a collaboration between the National Dunbar Alumni Association and the Special Collection/Archives of the Ottenheimer Library at the University of Arkansas at Little Rock; Mary S. Hoffschwelle's book, *The Rosenwald Schools of the American South*, published in 2006 by University Press of Florida; and, of course, my personal experiences and those of my family members who both attended and worked there.

I used old newspaper clippings, particularly the *Arkansas Gazette*, to jog my memory in some cases, as well as to cross-check my recollection of the court battles and the political and social upheaval swirling around me during that time. The following two memoirs and biography also were very helpful for their perspectives: *The Long Shadow of Little Rock* by Daisy Bates; *Warriors Don't Cry* by Melba Pattillo Beals; and *Faubus: The Life and Times of an American Prodigal* by Roy Reed.

Also helpful in transporting me back to my days at Central were the photographs, papers, and other files of Daisy Bates and Elizabeth Huckaby, archived in the Special Collections Division of the University of Arkansas Libraries in Fayetteville.

NOTES

Chapter 1: A Different World

5. **"In slave times"** Interviewer, Samuel S. Taylor, WPA Slave Narrative Project, Arkansas Narratives,1936–1938, vol. 2, part 3, Federal Writers' Project, United States Work Projects Administration; Manuscript Division, Library of Congress.

Chapter 2: The Playing Field

38. **"as little integration as possible"** Roy Reed, *Faubus: The Life and Times of an American Prodigal* (Fayetteville: University of Arkansas Press, 1997), 184.

Chapter 4: Wait and See

65. **Now that a federal court** Orval Faubus speech on late-night television, Little Rock, Arkansas, September 2, 1957 (Labor Day). Orval Eugene Faubus Collection, series 14, subseries 1, box 496, Special Collections, University of Arkansas Libraries, Fayetteville.

67. **"I have a constitutional duty and obligation"** Juan Williams, *Eyes on the Prize: America's Civil Rights Years 1954–1965* (New York: Viking Penguin, 1987), 100.

74. **"You addressed me several times"** Grif Stockley, *Daisy Bates:*

Civil Rights Crusader from Arkansas (Jackson: University of Mississippi Press, 2005).

80. **"The testimony and arguments this morning"** "Making a Crisis in Arkansas," *Time*, September 16, 1957, 25.

Chapter 5: D-Day

84. **"Go home, you son"** Gene Roberts and Hank Klibanoff, *The Race Beat: The Press, the Civil Rights Struggle, and the Awakening of a Nation* (New York: Alfred A. Knopf, 2007), 177.

91. **"In the final analysis"** Mayor Woodrow Mann telegram to President Eisenhower, Eisenhower Presidential Library and Museum website, "Civil Rights: The Little Rock School Integration Crisis," www.eisenhower.archives.gov/Research/Digital_Documents/Little-Rock/littlerockdocuments.html.

91. **"I want to make"** "President's Statements," *New York Times*, September 24, 1957, 18.

92. **"The immediate need"** Mann telegram to Eisenhower, "Civil Rights: The Little Rock School Integration Crisis." Eisenhower Presidential Library and Museum website.

95. **"I don't care if the president"** Daisy Bates, *The Long Shadow of Little Rock* (Fayetteville: University of Arkansas Press, 1986), 102.

96. **"You have nothing to fear"** "Quick, Hard and Decisive," *Time*, October 7, 1957, 24.

Chapter 6: The Blessing of Walls

117. Though I remembered seeing the card "One Down . . . Eight to Go" and others that appeared around campus after Minnie's expulsion, the exact wording was found on cards archived in the collection of Elizabeth Paisley Huckaby (MC 428), series 2, box 2, Special Collections, University of Arkansas Libraries, Fayetteville.

Chapter 7: Star-Studded Summer

133. **"She ultimately won a lawsuit"** Mildred Grossman Collection (PHMS 2002–23), series 1, box 1, Special Collections, Albin O.

Kuhn Library and Gallery, University of Maryland, Baltimore County.

Chapter 8: Just a Matter of Time

147. **"If Daisy Bates would find an honest job"** Bates, 155.
147. **"We stand neither for integration"** Sara Alderman Murphy, *Breaking the Silence: Little Rock's Women's Emergency Committee to Open Our Schools, 1958–1963* (Fayetteville: University of Arkansas Press, 1997).

Chapter 9: First-Semester Senior

170. **"This man has the sympathy"** "Bomber's Fate," *Time,* December 7, 1959, 24.

Chapter 11: Scapegoats

195. **"This must be a nightmare"** Bates, 182.

Chapter 12: Graduation and Good-bye

208. **"pressure as hypnosis"** "Police Testify Binns Admitted Bombing Home," *Arkansas Gazette,* June 8, 1960, 2A.
208. **"Why are you getting"** "Binns Draws 5-Year Term in Bomb Case," *Arkansas Gazette,* June 9, 1960, 1A.

ACKNOWLEDGMENTS

Carlotta Walls LaNier

This book would not have been possible without my wonderful family, friends, and supporters who have encouraged me from beginning to end and reached out to help in so many ways. First, to Mother, thank you for your quiet strength and for helping to make me who I am. You and Daddy were a great team. I've never stopped missing him, but I know he is smiling down on us all from heaven. Loujuana and Tina, I realize that my Central journey uprooted you in your formative years, but you moved on without complaint, accomplished great things, and lived your lives with grace and dignity. I feel fortunate to be your older sister, and I am proud of all of your accomplishments. To Ike, Whitney, and Brooke, thank you for your love, support, and patience over the years. You gave me the time and space I needed to finally be able to tell my story, and you've allowed me to tell it this way. My love for you is everlasting. And to the rest of my family—the aunts and uncles who helped to raise me, the many cousins who have shared my life, the in-laws who are as close as blood kin, my nephews, nieces, and great nephew, whose very existence made it necessary for me to tell this story—I carry all of you in my heart.

I also owe deep gratitude to

—Herbert Monts and the Monts family—I hope that revealing

the truth of what happened to you during those dark days in Little Rock starts a healing process.

—Karol Merten, a retired associate communication professor at the University of Denver, who never stopped telling me for twenty years that I should write a book.

—Jacquelyn Benton, a professor of Africana Studies at Metropolitan State College of Denver, whose excitement and encouragement fueled the fire early on.

—Margaret Whitt, whose persistence, contacts, and guidance finallly helped me to get this done. You will retire as "chief of posse" after the North Carolina book tour.

—Leslie Trumble, director of the Visual Media Center in the School of Art and Art History at the University of Denver, who added order to my world by putting the many photos under consideration for the book onto a single disc.

—Denise Anthony, an archivist professor in the University of Denver's School of Art and Art History, who generously helped me to preserve my tangible memories by putting together a team of students to archive the many boxes of papers, photographs, and artifacts that I've kept from Central for half a century; and her graduate students, Annie Nelson, Shannon Walker, Sarah Johnson, and Emily Tormey, who put in countless volunteer hours after class to do the work; and Mary Stansbury, the Library and Information Services program director, who graciously approved the purchase of materials for the project; I could never repay you for your dedication, hard work, and professionalism.

—Dudley Delffs, vice president and publisher of trade books for Zondervan, the first publisher I approached, who took the time to read an early draft and offer suggestions. Your encouragement helped me to recognize the potential of this book.

—Brian Kracke, a representative for Pearson Custom Publishing, whose openness and honesty about the publishing industry broadened my mind to the range of options and helped me to make the right decision.

—Kira Stevens, whose wise advice led me to the perfect literary agent.

—Linda Loewenthal, my representative at the David Black Literary Agency, who saw the potential in this project and guided me expertly through the process, starting with connecting me with Lisa Frazier Page.

—Lisa Frazier Page, the writer who found the right path to help me complete this journey. Your listening skills and research enabled you to question, probe, and grasp the meaning of my emotions and words and craft them into this finished book. I will be ever so grateful. I look forward to a long friendship.

—To Kevin Page, Sr., Enjoli, Danielle, Kevin, Jr., and Kyle, thanks for loaning me your wife and mother, even on family vacations. You have been great sports during this project.

—John Turchiano of the Hotel and Restaurant employees Local 6, whose encouragement, introductions, support, and suggestions were invaluable.

—Melody Guy, my editor at Ballantine/One World, whose passion for this project and great editing suggestions helped to make the book better. Your parents carried on the torch for the Little Rock Nine when they rose those early mornings in the late 1970s, escorted you to your bus stop and watched you set off for a twenty-five-mile journey to get the best possible education. It makes my journey seem worth it to see you—such a talented and accomplished young woman—living the legacy.

—Porscha Burke, Melody's assistant, whose sense of organization, enthusiasm, and persistence kept this project on task from start to finish. Your knowledge of the process and cheerful attitude impressed me greatly and assured me that the book was in good hands.

—The staff at the William J. Clinton Foundation, particularly Helen Robinson, whose friendship and wise guidance helped to get many areas of this book locked down; Laura Graham, whose intervention and professionalism iced the cake; and Ana Maria Coronel, whose assistance and follow-through kept things flowing smoothly.

—Johanna Miller, a historian at the University of Arkansas, whose invaluable insight, research, and willingness to help cannot be measured.

—Michael Madell, National Park Service superintendent at the Little Rock Central High School Memorial Site, whose encouragement and focus helped me through the many projects we shared.

—Laura Miller of the National Park Service, who gave me the possibilities to publish; however, I am glad I waited.

—Spirit Trickey, whose enthusiasm never waned.

—James "Skip" Rutherford, dean of the Clinton School of Public Service, who has helped whenever and wherever I needed it. Our business relationship started with a handshake in 1996, but it has developed into a lasting friendship. From Skip to dean Skip—what growth!

—Bunny & Peggy, my best buddies, who have been an integral part of my life forever.

—The Denver Chapter of the Links Inc., my sisters, who have always been there for me.

—Melba, whose willingness to share a wealth of expertise and experiences will never be forgotten (even though I did not quite follow "the program").

—My eight comrades and friends (Elizabeth, Ernie, Gloria, Jefferson, Melba, Minnijean, Terrence, and Thelma), for enduring the journey.

Lisa Frazier Page

I thank God for the generations of civil rights warriors, particularly Carlotta and her eight comrades, who with great personal sacrifice and suffering, kicked down the doors that I have walked through. It has been the honor of my life, Carlotta, to help you share your powerful, historic story. Thank you for trusting me and opening your life to me. I am grateful for the wonderful friendship that has developed. Thanks, too, Ike, Whitney, and Brooke for sharing your wife and mother with me these many months.

To my literary agent, Linda Loewenthal of the David Black Literary Agency, you have been an awesome adviser and representative. I will be forever grateful for your connecting me with Carlotta and this wonderful opportunity.

To the staff at Ballantine/One World and Random House that had a hand in producing this book, thank you for putting so much care and consideration into every step of the process. I'm especially grateful to our editor, Melody Guy, whose thoughtfulness, passion, and great ideas helped to refine the book; and Porscha Burke, who was always there with the right answers, a kind spirit, and a quiet assertiveness that kept things moving on time.

I could not have done this without the support of my husband, Kevin Page, and our children—Enjoli, Danielle, Kevin, Jr., and Kyle—who fill my days with purpose. You remind me what's really important. I love you all beyond meaure.

I am forever indebted to my parents, Clinton and Nettie Frazier, who gave me the diary where I first learned to tell stories. Your love and support have been a steady source of strength in my life. Thanks also to the rest of my family, who have always been there for me, especially my sister and brother-in-law (Melissa and Zeke Moses), my brother and sister-in-law (Clifford and Tiffani Frazier), Aunt Joyce (Joyce Richardson), Buffy (April Bruns), and all of my nieces and nephews. I have been blessed, too, with wonderful in-laws, particularly my husband's parents, Richard and Miriam Page, who have been patient and understanding (especially those times when I've had to "borrow" your office all day during family visits). I've appreciated every word of encouragement, home-cooked meal, and the moments you, Kolin, and Geraldine (my brother- and sister-in-law), or Zina (my sister-in-law) entertained the children while I worked.

To my life mentors, Ada Hannibal Green and the late Barbara Butler, thank you for seeing something worthwhile in me early on and investing your time and heart to open the world beyond Bogalusa to me through my girlhood travels with you and the Spartanette Service Club.

I am also grateful to work at *The Washington Post,* where my editors generously granted me the time away to do this important work, even as our industry was experiencing tremendous change and uncertainty. Thanks especially to my editors: Milton Coleman for your early encouragement and advice; Tom Wilkinson for your enthusiasm about the project and kind words; and Robert McCartney and Phyllis Jordan, for letting me go and welcoming me back. Thanks also to my journalism colleagues and cherished friends, who eagerly read chapter drafts, advised and encouraged me, and even babysat, most especially Wil Haygood, Karima and Dion Haynes, Cheryl Thompson, Donald Washington, Avis Thomas-Lester, Deneen Brown, Lonnae O'Neal Parker, Tracey Reeves, Tammy Collins Carter, and Keith Woods.

To my dear friend, Lavette Broussard, who fills in for my out-of-town family, I'm grateful for all you do. And to the girls (and guy) who grew up with me into adulthood—Deadra Courtney (Ann), Veronica Smith, Cassandra Price, Kelvin Preston, and Tess Snipes—I value all we've shared and learned along the way.

ABOUT THE AUTHORS

CARLOTTA WALLS LANIER attended Michigan State University and graduated from Colorado State College—now the University of Northern Colorado, on whose board of trustees she sits. After working for the YWCA, she founded her own real estate brokerage firm, LaNier and Company. A sought-after lecturer, LaNier speaks across the country, and she has received the Congressional Gold Medal and two honorary doctorate degrees. She is the mother of two children, Whitney and Brooke, and lives in Englewood, Colorado, with her husband, Ira.

LISA FRAZIER PAGE, an editor and award-winning reporter at *The Washington Post,* is co-author of the *New York Times* bestseller *The Pact: Three Young Men Make a Promise and Fulfill a Dream.* A graduate of New Orleans's Dillard University, Page holds a master's degree from Northwestern University's Medill School of Journalism. She grew up in Bogalusa, Louisiana, and lives in the Washington, D.C., area with her husband. They have four children.

ABOUT THE TYPE

This book was set in Sabon, a typeface designed by the well-known German typographer Jan Tschichold (1902–74). Sabon's design is based upon the original letter forms of Claude Garamond and was created specifically to be used for three sources: foundry type for hand composition, Linotype, and Monotype. Tschichold named his typeface for the famous Frankfurt typefounder Jacques Sabon, who died in 1580.